PARTIES
AND
PRIMARIES

Copublished with the Eagleton Institute of Politics, Rutgers University

PARTIES
AND
PRIMARIES
Nominating State Governors

Malcolm E. Jewell

American Political
Parties and Elections

general editor
Gerald M. Pomper

PRAEGER SPECIAL STUDIES • PRAEGER SCIENTIFIC

New York • Philadelphia • Eastbourne, UK
Toronto • Hong Kong • Tokyo • Sydney

Library of Congress Cataloging in Publication Data

Jewell, Malcolm Edwin, 1928-
   Parties and primaries.

   (American political parties and elections)
   Includes bibliographical references and index.
   1. Governors—United States—Nomination. 2. Primaries—
United States. I. Title. II. Series.
   JK2447.J48 1984   324.5'0973   83-24688
   ISBN 0-03-063689-2 (alk. paper)

Published in 1984 by Praeger Publishers
CBS Educational and Professional Publishing,
a Division of CBS Inc.
521 Fifth Avenue, New York, NY 10175 USA

© 1984 by Praeger Publishers

456789 052 9876545321

Printed in the United States of America
on acid-free paper

Acknowledgements

This study was supported by the National Science Foundation under Grant No. SES-8195701. NSF is not responsible for the findings, interpretations, or conclusions offered in this volume.

The data from national election surveys, particularly that of 1978, were made available by the Inter-University Consortium for Political and Social Research. The data for the American National Election Study, 1978, were originally collected by the Center for Political Studies of the Institute for Social Research, the University of Michigan, under a grant from the National Science Foundation. Neither the original collectors of the data nor the Consortium bear any responsibility for the analyses or interpretations presented here.

Anyone who works in the field of comparative state politics finds it necessary to rely on the help of colleagues who have detailed knowledge about individual states. I am indebted to a number of political scientists, particularly those who helped in the study of state endorsing conventions. During my brief visits to these states, they provided background information, contacts with political leaders, and even hospitality. I particularly want to thank Jerome Mileur, Paul L. Hain, and Craig Grau for such assistance. Jerome Mileur and John White shared the results of a survey of Massachusetts Democratic delegates, and F. Chris Garcia agreed to include in a voter survey he was conducting questions on the impact of endorsements. Elmer Cornwell, John Piczak, Everett C. Ladd, Jr., and John F. Bibby were particularly helpful in explaining developments in their states. I benefited from the information and insights of Sarah McCally Morehouse, whose research brought her to many of the endorsing conventions.

I appreciate the assistance of political party officials who agreed to be interviewed during or after the conventions, including James Roosevelt, Representative Jack Murphy, and Representative Charles Flaherty (Massachusetts Democratic party); Don Meikle (Connecticut Democratic party); Donna Micklus (Connecticut Republican party); Mike Hatch (Minnesota Democratic-Farmer-Labor party); William D. Morris (Minnesota Independent Republican party); Nick Franklin and Richard Kennedy (New Mexico Democratic party). Several newspaper reporters were helpful in analyzing the conventions, and I am particularly indebted to Tim Kiska of the Detroit *Free Press*, who made available to me the results of a voter survey in Michigan.

Much of my information on endorsing conventions comes from the questionnaires returned by more than 1,500 delegates in ten state parties. Their cooperation was indispensable to the success of the study.

The staff of the University of Kentucky Survey Research Center was very helpful in carrying out the surveys of voters in three states with a high degree of professionalism; I am particularly indebted to Kathy Cirksena, Tom Arcury, Tim Johnson, and Phillip Roeder.

Gerald M. Pomper, the editor of the *American Political Parties and Elections* series, encouraged publication of the study and provided valuable advice on the manuscript.

Obviously the many persons who provided various types of assistance to me during the course of the study are not responsible for my use or misuse of the information they provided.

Some of the material in Chapter 6 was previously published in the *American Politics Quarterly*, and material on campaign spending in Chapter 9 was published in *State Government*.

Contents

PART I: THE STATE PRIMARY

Chapter

PART II: PARTY ORGANIZATIONS AND ENDORSEMENTS

PART III: WHO VOTES IN WHAT PRIMARIES?

PART IV: WHO WINS PRIMARIES AND WHY?

PART V: CONCLUSIONS

List of Tables and Figures

TABLES

FIGURES

Part I
The State Primary

1

Introduction

The direct primary election is a distinctly U.S. institution, but there is no national primary system in this country. In reality there are fifty primary systems, one in each state, and the variations among them are much greater than any differences found in the operations of general elections in the states. This volume is an examination of the ways in which primaries operate, and how they differ, in the states.

The laws of most states require that political parties use direct primary elections to nominate candidates; a few states permit nomination by conventions — and parties occasionally use that method. Some states require voters to register in advance with a specific party to vote in its primary; others require only a public choice at the polling place; and others permit a voter to make a secret choice of the party primary.

In about one-third of the states, the political party organizations attempt to influence the outcome of primaries by endorsing candidates, sometimes informally and other times under systems authorized by the legislature. In most states there is little or no structured support by party organizations for primary candidates.

In most southern states, until recent years, the winner of the Democratic primary was assured of winning the general elections, often unopposed; consequently the Democratic primary assumed major importance and attracted more voter turnout than the general election. A runoff was held if no candidate won a majority in the first primary. In northern states there are significant differences in the proportion of voters in Democratic and Republican primaries and in the proportion of persons voting in either primary.

The laws, political practices, and voters' behavior pertaining to primaries differ among the states, but we know very little about the causes and consequences of these differences. In the last fifteen years the rapid expansion in the number of states using presidential primaries has spawned a number of books and articles on that topic, but there has been no such revival of scholarly interest in state primary elections. The classic work on state primaries was published in 1908 (Merriam 1908) and revised twenty years later (Merriam and Overacker 1928). Since that time there has been no comprehensive study of state primary elections. Few efforts have been made to use modern research techniques to examine state primaries.

This study is not intended to be a comprehensive survey of state primary elections. The goals and the scope are both less ambitious. The major goals are to describe the differences in state primary system, to explain those differences, and to explore their consequences for state political systems. It is impossible to describe and analyze in any detail all primary elections in all states over the last thirty years or so. The scope of this study is limited in several ways:

1. The study is focused almost entirely on the nomination of the governor. There are several reasons for this focus. From the standpoint of state parties, the governorship is the most important election. Because governors seek renomination fewer times, gubernatorial primaries are more often competitive than those for congressional office.

2. The time frame for most of this study is the 1982 election, in which gubernatorial candidates were nominated in 36 states. Data are presented for previous years (approximately 1950-80) on several topics, including development of party endorsements and voting turnout in primaries.

3. In order to describe the nominating process in greater detail, several chapters concentrate on a few states where preprimary conventions were held or where primary campaigns and outcomes were particularly interesting in 1982.

The purpose of this chapter is to provide some historical background and a brief description of the varied patterns of state primaries.

The next chapter summarizes theoretical questions to be addressed in the book. Part II examines the role that some political parties play in nominations through the use of endorsing conventions. Part III seeks to answer the question: who votes in primaries? Part IV describes some of the gubernatorial primary campaigns of 1982 in an effort to explain their outcomes. Part V explores the consequences of primaries for state political systems.

DEVELOPMENT OF THE DIRECT PRIMARY

"Throughout the history of the American nominating practices runs a persistent attempt to make feasible popular participation in nominations and thereby to limit or destroy the power of party oligarchies" (Key 1964, p. 371). This theme, emphasized by V. O. Key and other historians of the nominating process, is fundamental to understanding why the legislative caucus was replaced by the nominating convention and the convention gave way to the direct primary. But it was not inevitable that the attempt to give the public a role in nominations would succeed when it did or take the form of direct primaries. We must examine other historical forces to understand why primary legislation was passed in many American states early in the twentieth century.

According to V. O. Key (1956, p. 88), "The direct primary method of nomination apparently constituted at bottom an escape from one-partyism." The Civil War and Reconstruction led to a partisan realignment, with the Democratic party controlling the southern states, and the Republican party controlling most northern states. A second realignment in the 1890s further solidified one-party monopolies in the South and in the Northeast and Midwest. Even in those northern, border, and western states that were more competitive, most counties were dominated by a single party. In states and localities where most voters were loyal to a single party, and where nominations within that party were tightly controlled by a small group, the voters had little effective voice in the selection of candidates.

Although the development of the direct primary is related to one-party dominance at the state and local levels, the primary seems to have been as much a cause as an effect of one-party control. The causes and consequences of the direct primary movement differed significantly in the North and South, and therefore must be analyzed separately.

The Progressive Movement and Northern Primaries

Outside the South the campaign for direct primary elections was an important plank in the platform of the Progressive movement, and it represented a direct challenge to the conservative political leaders who dominated one or both of the parties in most states. One of the major goals of the Progressive movement was to give the people a direct voice in government and to break up those economic, social, and political institutions that inhibited popular control. Specific planks pertaining to governmental institutions included the initiative, referendum, and recall; the direct popular election of U.S. senators; nonpartisan local elections; regulation of the internal affairs of parties; adoption of the Australian ballot; and the direct primary.

The Progressives believed that other reforms would be difficult or impossible as long as party bosses and machines controlled the nominating processes and used that control to select candidates who would oppose such reforms. Moreover, they perceived the political bosses as being allied with the powerful corporate interests that were fighting social and economic reforms in the Progressive platform.

There were a variety of caucus and convention systems (sometimes called primaries) used in the states, with varying levels of participation by party activists. In order to maintain their control over this system, political bosses, when necessary, engaged in a variety of dubious practices, ranging from outright fraud and vote buying to more sophisticated manipulation of the machinery (Merriam and Overacker 1928, pp. 4-14). To curb these practices, the Progressives promoted passage of legislation regulating the internal affairs of political parties in considerable detail.

Other laws were adopted to prevent fraud in general elections. One step was the gradual adoption of registration requirements for voting. Another reform that spread rapidly across the country in the 1890s was the Australian ballot: the use of ballots printed by the government rather than those supplied by the parties. In addition to guaranteeing the secrecy of the ballot and inhibiting fraud, this reform had broader implications, one of which was described by Merriam and Overacker (1928, p. 24):

The Australian ballot law recognized the political party and gave it legal standing. Since the government was to print all ballots there must be a method of determining what names were to appear on the ballot, and under what party designation; in short, a legal definition of a party. Therefore the law provided that nominations for office might be certified by party officers to the proper legal officers, and then be printed as the officially recognized party list of candidates. . . . When the party was given a legal standing, the way was opened toward regulation of the entire nominating process.

Robert LaFollette, the Wisconsin Progressive leader who was often regarded as the founder of the compulsory direct primary made this case for the primary in 1898 (Torelle 1920, pp. 29-31):

Under our form of government the entire structure rests upon the nomination of candidates for office. This is the foundation of the representative system. If bad men control the nominations we cannot have good government. Let us start right. The life principle of representative government is that those chosen to govern shall faithfully represent the governed. . . .

With the nominations of all candidates absolutely in control of the people, under a system that gives every member of a party equal voice in making that nomination, the public official who desires re-nomination will not dare to seek it, if he has served the machine and the lobby and betrayed the public trust.

The Progressive movement was strongest in the West and some midwestern states. Progressive leaders promoted the direct primary not merely because of a theoretical belief in direct democracy, but also because the primary offered the best vehicle for wresting control over the parties − and nominations − from conservative forces. The Progressives concentrated most of their efforts on the Republican party, which was the normal majority party in most states. The Democratic party usually offered a poor alternative, both because of voter loyalties to the Republican party and because Democratic leadership was often conservative and/or ineffective. Third parties flourished briefly in some of these states, but their success was intermittent at best.

The experience of Robert LaFollette of Wisconsin is typical of the problems faced by Progressive leaders. As V. O. Key (1956, p. 93) put it, "La Follette and the voters who followed him perhaps wanted to go to heaven but they insisted on traveling under Republican auspices." LaFollette twice lost the gubernatorial nomination at the convention; in 1900 he was nominated and elected, and he finally was able to persuade the legislature in 1903 to pass a compulsory, comprehensive primary law, the first one in the nation.

The movement spread rapidly across much of the country, as states changed optional, local, or limited primary laws into statewide, mandatory ones; some states having no experience with the primary followed Wisconsin and adopted a full-scale system. By 1910, 15 states, almost entirely in the West or Midwest, had followed Wisconsin's example in enacting mandatory, statewide primaries. By 1917 the trend had become almost universal; 33 of the 37 northern states had adopted direct primary laws, with the only holdouts being Connecticut, Rhode Island, New Mexico, and Utah. Moreover, 29 of the 33 were mandatory laws covering, at least, all state offices and requiring administration by the state government (not the party). The adoption of the direct primary must have been one of the most rapidly adopted state reforms not mandated or encouraged by the federal government.

It is surprising that comprehensive primaries were adopted not only in states where the Progressive movement was strong, but, after brief delays, in most of the urban, industrial states where Progressives were weaker and where party organizations appeared to be well entrenched, states such as New York, Massachusetts, Pennsylvania, New Jersey, Ohio, and Illinois. In some of these states primary legislation may have been accepted by party organizations in an attempt to reduce voter support for third-party movements (Galderisi 1982). The direct primary did not become solidly established in some urban, industrial states, however. During the 1920s, when the mood of the country had grown more conservative, there were serious efforts made to repeal or weaken primary legislation in every one of the northeastern states, as well as in many of those in the Midwest and West. New York soon replaced the primary with a convention for statewide candidates, and Indiana took a similar step.

In several of these states where the primary remained in place, state or county political leaders developed the practice of screening potential candidates and endorsing a slate before the primary. Often the nonendorsed candidates were persuaded to withdraw (or run for lesser offices); local party organizations provided various kinds of support for those endorsees who had primary opposition. This endorsement system was particularly effective in Illinois and New Jersey, and was also practiced to some extent in Pennsylvania and Ohio. During this period the party organizations in Rhode Island and Connecticut succeeded in preventing the enactment of primary legislation. In general, the primary election system was less widely accepted and effective in the major urban states of the Northeast and Midwest than in other areas.

If the direct primary was adopted in northern states partly because of one-party dominance, an important consequence of primary systems was to frustrate efforts of the minority party to become competitive. In a two-party system the minority party is supposed to hold a monopoly on opposition, but in many northern states the primary became the arena in which challenges to the administration in power were made and conflicts between major social and economic interests were resolved. In most northern states the minority Democratic party remained ineffective, relying on traditional ethnic and religious support but unable to compete successfully for new voters.

Southern Primaries: Preserving Democratic Control

The period following Reconstruction in the South was one of turmoil and confusion. As the leaders of the Democratic party tried to reestablish their control in the states, they faced opposition from Republicans, independents, and a variety of third-party movements — forerunners of the Populists in the 1890s. Much of the support for these opposition groups came from black voters. It was estimated that in the early 1880s more than half of adult male blacks voted in gubernatorial races in nine of the eleven southern states, and blacks held some local and legislative offices. In these years the Democratic party could seldom count on more than 60 percent of the vote in state races (Kousser 1974, pp. 27-29).

Most southern Democratic parties were led by conservative interests, particularly plantation owners in the black belt counties. They were determined to eliminate black voting both as an end in itself and as a means of eroding support for opposition parties. Initially this effort took several forms: intimidating black voters to prevent their voting, bribing them to vote for conservative Democrats, or manipulating the vote count to reverse the results of their votes. But these tactics were localized and not fully effective; moreover, the Populist movement, with its appeal to black and poor white voters, became a growing challenge to the Democratic leadership. The result was a tidal wave of state legislation and constitutional amendments to prevent black (and much poor white) voting: poll taxes, literacy and understanding tests, property qualifications, registration requirements, and the Australian ballot (which handicapped the illiterate voter) (Kousser 1974, ch. 9).

The result of this legislation was a dramatic and rapid drop in the proportion of blacks who voted, and in some states a substantial drop in white voting. Consequently, the support for Republican, third-party, and independent candidates dropped sharply. The movement to disenfranchise blacks led directly to the supremacy of the white Democratic party.

The direct primary began to be used for statewide elections in the late 1870s and grew more common during the next few decades as a result of party rules and eventually state legislation. The direct primary was not a significant tool for restricting black voting for two reasons: most blacks were Republicans, and other legislative restrictions had already accomplished that goal before the primary became well established. By the early 1900s, however, most state Democratic parties had passed regulations explicitly prohibiting black participation in primaries (Kousser 1974, ch. 3).

The major purpose, and effect, of the primaries in southern states was to guarantee Democratic control of southern politics. "According to its proponents, deciding party nominations in semi-public primaries rather than in backroom caucuses would legitimate the nominees, settle intraparty differences before the general election, and greatly reduce the power of opposition voters — most often, Negroes — by confronting them with a solid Democratic party" (Kousser 1974, p. 74). Democratic unity was facilitated by the requirement that primary candidates pledge not to challenge the winner in the general election. Supporters of the primary were very explicit about its goals: "to insure the continued success of the Democratic party," to assure "the final burial of Republican or other opposition parties in North Carolina," "to secure permanent good government by the party of the White Man," to avoid "a return to the deplorable conditions when one faction of white men call upon Negroes to help defeat another faction" (Kousser 1974, p. 76).

In specific southern states, of course, adoption of a primary served the interests of a particular candidate or faction expecting to have greater success at the polls than in caucuses. But the southern primary was not the product of the Populist movement; it was not generally designed to advance the interests of a single faction (like the northern Progressive movement) but to unite the Democratic party, generally under conservative leadership, and thereby erode opposition movements and reduce the temptation to mobilize black voters.

By 1924 all 11 southern states had enacted some form of state-wide direct primary law. However, in 8 of the southern states the law made the primaries optional and/or specified that they would be conducted by the parties, or made primaries mandatory for only some statewide races. In many southern states the political parties were given a great deal of authority to establish rules for the primary, including rules of voter eligibility (Merriam and Overacker 1928, pp. 66, 93-94). This fact made it possible for state and local parties to exclude blacks from participating in the primary. Although these restrictions initially had little practical effect, during the New Deal period blacks began to shift their allegiance to the Democratic party; the white primary became an increasingly serious obstacle until it was finally outlawed by the courts in 1944. Effective judicial action was frustrated for years because of the ingenuity of some states in transferring complete authority over primaries to the parties.

The Democratic primary achieved its goals: in most southern states it became the only significant election. The Republican parties in most states made few efforts to run viable candidates for state-wide office and virtually no efforts to contest congressional and legislative races. Even when there was a contest in the general election, voter turnout was usually much lower than in the Democratic primary. The only southern states with a semblance of two-party competition were Tennessee, North Carolina, and Virginia, all states with significant numbers of mountain Republicans. Because there were so few Republican candidates, that party nominated by convention rather than in primaries.

Recent Trends in Primaries and Endorsements

In the years since World War II there have been two interrelated trends in state nominating systems: the expansion of primary elections to those states that had been holdouts, and the growing use of preprimary endorsing conventions by the parties, either informally or under state law. The last two states to adopt direct primary legislation, Rhode Island (1947) and Connecticut (1955), both incorporated strong party endorsement systems into the original primary laws. Utah and New Mexico, both of which adopted primaries in the mid-1930s, have used legal endorsement systems in recent years (New Mexico intermittently). New York extended its primary to statewide races in 1967 and provided for preprimary endorsements by the state central committee. When Indiana began to nominate statewide candidates by primary in 1976, however, it abandoned the convention entirely. Among the other states where party endorsing conventions have been developed in the last three decades — either legally or informally — are Massachusetts, North Dakota, Minnesota, and Wisconsin. (See Chapter 3 for details on these developments.)

CHARACTERISTICS OF STATE PRIMARIES TODAY

Most state laws now require political parties to nominate state-wide candidates by direct primaries, but there are several southern states that permit parties to choose between primaries and conventions, including Alabama, Arkansas, Georgia, South Carolina, and Virginia. The Republican party used conventions until recently in several southern states, and it still uses them in Virginia. Very recently the Virginia Democratic party has several times used a convention instead of a primary for statewide nominations (Sabato 1977).

In eight states there are legal provisions for party conventions to make endorsements in the primary, laws that often give candidates easier access to the ballot if they get some minimum vote at the convention. In four of these a candidate can get on the ballot by getting a required share of the convention vote or by petition: Colorado, New York, North Dakota, and Rhode Island (where the share is a majority). New Mexico offers a similar choice, but candidates must seek endorsement before petitioning. Utah conventions endorse either one or two candidates, and there is no petition alternative. Connecticut has what is called a challenge primary; a 20 percent convention vote is required to get on the primary ballot.

The Connecticut convention has so much influence that its endorsements are rarely challenged in a primary. The Delaware convention is so powerful that there have been no primary challenges to its gubernatorial selection since the statewide primary was established in 1968; from 1968 through 1976 a candidate had to get at least 35 percent in the convention to run in the primary. (The convention endorsing systems in all states are surveyed in Chapter 3.)

All states establish by law what requirements a registered voter must meet to vote in the primary. In 26 states there is a closed primary, where a person must register with a party, usually in advance of the primary; there is often a deadline several months before the primary for shifting party registration. There are 12 states, mostly southern, where no such advanced registration is required or record of party preference is kept, but the voter must make a public choice at the polls of the party primary to enter. Nine states, mostly western, have a completely open primary in which the voter may choose in secret which party primary to vote in. Two other states, Alaska and Washington, have a "blanket primary," which is like the open primary except that at one time the voter may cast votes for a Democrat for some offices and a Republican for others. Finally, Louisiana has what amounts to a nonpartisan primary, with voters and candidates of all parties participating in a single primary, and with a runoff if no one gets a majority.

There are some important differences between southern and northern states in the way the primary operates. Until the last two or three decades, the southern Democratic primary was by far the most important state election, overshadowing the general election in the intensity of competition and voter turnout. In recent years, as the Republican party has gained strength and won statewide races in every southern state, the general election has gained in importance, and in voter turnout relative to the Democratic primary. Moreover, there has been a steady increase in the frequency of contested Republican primaries, though voter turnout remains much lower than in Democratic primaries (Black and Black 1982).

Some differences remain between southern and northern primaries. Southern states (except Tennessee and including Oklahoma) provide for runoff elections, and these are frequently required in statewide races. There are variations in northern states in the normal proportion of persons voting in the Democratic and Republican primaries, but (given a contested primary) the imbalance is rarely as great as it is in southern states. In nearly half of the northern states, but in almost no southern state, we find some evidence that the party organization, or a party-related group, makes an organized effort through some endorsement system to influence the outcome of primary elections.*

QUESTIONS ABOUT PRIMARIES

When one looks at the primary systems operating in American states, their most obvious feature is variation, and the most obvious question to be answered is the reasons for this variation. A second impression is change: trends in the electoral systems that affect primaries (such as growing costs) and also experiments in individual states with the primary institution. A third impression one gets from talking to state political leaders and party activists is ambivalence about how the primary ought to operate and what role the political party should play in nominations.

This volume is an effort to understand and explain the varied patterns of state primary systems and the changes that are occurring in them. The starting point, in Chapter 2, is an exploration of theoretical issues and research findings pertinent to primaries. It will examine the ambivalent attitudes of scholars and practitioners regarding the nominating process. It will also summarize research findings from studies of party organizations and voting behavior that are pertinent to the analysis of primaries.

The chapters in Part II concern the effort of political parties to influence the outcome of primaries through endorsing conventions. Why have some parties tried to accomplish this? What explains the success or failure of such efforts? Do such efforts help to revitalize party organizations? Evidence for answering these questions is drawn largely from first-hand observation and delegate questionnaires in five states where parties held endorsing conventions in 1982.

Chapter 6 is devoted to the question: Who votes in primaries, and why do the proportions of voters vary so much among the states? From previous research, we know a lot about why persons vote, or do not vote, in general elections. The purpose here is to find

---

*Very recently the Louisiana parties have made endorsements in the nonpartisan primary, as described in Chapter 10.

reasons for voting that are unique to primaries, both personal and institutional reasons. Chapter 7 is concerned with who votes in which primary. Do the laws on open and closed primaries have an impact on voting behavior? On what basis do voters in a closed primary state choose to register as Democrats or Republicans? In an open primary state, what proportion of voters stick to one party's primary, and what proportion shift between primaries from time to time — for what reasons? How do voters who consider themselves to be independents choose a party primary? Chapters 6 and 7 are based on both aggregate voting data and surveys of voters.

Chapters 8 and 9 are focused on the question: Who wins primaries and why? Are the choices made by voters based on reasons different from those motivating general election voting? How much has voting in primaries been affected by high levels of spending and media advertising? What happens when the candidate with a long record of party service runs against an outsider, or amateur, with a large bankroll and a skillful campaign manager? Evidence for these chapters will be drawn from the 1982 primaries.

The final chapter of this volume deals with the impact of variations and changes in the primary on the political party system in the states.

2

Theoretical Questions

A search for the theoretical issues underlying the study of primaries leads us to studies of political parties, their organization and functions, and to studies of voting behavior. We are interested in the arguments that have been made about the role that party organizations and voters should play in the nominating process and the empirical questions that underlie these arguments.

THE PARTY'S ROLE IN NOMINATIONS

Most of the theoretical work that has been done on the role of parties in nominations is at least partly normative in character. We can identify four normative issues that have frequently appeared in debates over the primary system and the role of political parties in nominations:

1. The simplest, most direct argument in favor of the direct primary is the democratic one: the party's voters should have the right to nominate its candidates.

2. A fundamental argument for giving the party organization the right to nominate candidates, or at least to endorse them in a primary, is that such a function is essential to maintaining strong party organizations.

3. The principle of party responsibility, a major theme of much of the party reform literature, requires that candidates be accountable

to the party, an argument that may be used by advocates of party endorsement or direct primaries.

4. It is often argued that the purpose of the nominating process is to select the strongest candidate — the one most likely to win in the general election. This leads to the question of whether party organizations or voters are better able to select winners.

We will examine in more detail the arguments that have been made about these four issues, and then look at the empirical data — and the unanswered questions — regarding each of them.

Normative Issues

The basic theme underlying the Progressive campaign for the direct primary was simply that control over nominations must be taken away from the bosses and given to the people. Some Progressive reformers, committed to the concept of direct democracy, were seeking to dismantle or emasculate party organizations.

Other advocates of the direct primary were not trying to undermine political party organizations but to reform them. They advanced the concept of intraparty democracy as a goal. The members of the American Political Science Association committee who wrote "Toward a More Responsible Two-Party System" emphasized "the responsibility of party leaders to the party membership, as enforced in primaries, caucuses, and conventions" (APSA 1950, p. 23). They believed that members of the party should play an active role in determining both policy goals and candidates. The concept of intraparty democracy has been challenged by other political scientists. E. E. Schattschneider, though an author of the APSA report, had argued earlier (1942, p. 60) that "democracy is not be be found in the parties but between the parties." Austin Ranney, in a commentary of the APSA report (1951), emphasized the ambiguity of the concept of party membership, to which leaders should be responsible: "Will the party leaders, for example, be 'responsible' to all those persons who register as party members and vote in the closed primaries? Or will they be 'responsible' to all those persons who vote for the party ticket?" (p. 490). Earlier, Schattschneider (1942, p. 59) had suggested that it might be better if "the concept of the party membership of the partisans is abandoned altogether" and "if the party is described as a political enterprise conducted by a group of working politicians *supported* by partisan voters who approve of the party but are merely partisan (not members of a fictitious association)."

Those who argue that the party should play a major role in the nominating process often seem to assume that this will strengthen the party organization rather than making the argument explicit. They may simply assert that nominating candidates is an essential function of parties, but several more specific arguments can be made. One way to attract active workers in a party organization is to give them meaningful functions to perform, such as selecting or at least endorsing candidates. A minority party, in particular, must recruit candidates for office in order to achieve competitive status, and it is difficult to recruit candidates if the party cannot guarantee or at least facilitate their nomination. A minority party that does not play a role in recruiting or endorsing (and by definition has no patronage to dispense) may wither away.

Party responsibility was the dominant theme of the 1950 APSA committee report, as its title indicates, and it has been a recurring theme of party reformers. The concept of party responsibility to the voters means that parties should adopt platforms in which they take stands on issues and that they should be able to carry out those commitments if elected to office. In order to accomplish this, the parties must nominate candidates who are committed to the party's position on these issues. The question is how to make sure that the candidates nominated by the party are in fact committed to its policies. Supporters of endorsing conventions argue that the party activists who attend conventions are better able to evaluate candidates and choose those whose views are compatible with party principles. They assume that convention delegates can be trusted to uphold party policies and in fact often are the persons who adopt party platforms. Advocates of the direct primary argue that candidates should be held accountable to voters in the primary. There is an implicit assumption that the voters can decide which candidates are most supportive of the party's policies — or at least those policies that are salient to the voters. The APSA committee recommended both direct primaries and "formal or informal proposal of candidates by preprimary meetings of responsible party committees or party councils" (p. 72), but it did not explain specifically how either primaries or preprimary endorsements would make the parties responsible. Critics of the party responsibility model often take the pragmatic position that the party should select candidates not on the basis of their ideological purity but their ability to win elections. Such an argument can lead plausibly to quite different conclusions about nominating methods. One is that the best test of electability is the ability to win primary elections; the other is that party activists in a convention can make better judgments about which candidate, or slate of candidates, has the best chance of winning a general election.

It should be clear that there are two levels of controversy involved in these issues. One concerns goals and the other the means of achieving goals. There is disagreement about whether voters should have maximum opportunity to select candidates, or whether it is more important to build strong party organizations. There is disagreement about whether the major goal of party organizations is to develop and carry out policies or to win elections. There is also disagreement, among those who agree on goals, about whether some of these goals can be carried out better by party organizations or by voters. While empirical evidence cannot determine which goals should have priority, it can shed light on the question of how these goals can be carried out.

Empirical Evidence

The argument that candidates should be selected exclusively by primary elections because these are more democratic raises questions about the breadth of participation and the factors that affect how voters make their choices, questions that are dealt with later in the chapter. This section reviews the existing evidence on three other questions. What are the effects of primary elections, and such modifications as preprimary endorsements, on the vitality of political party organizations and the incentives for party workers to become active in the party? What evidence is there about how delegates to party conventions evaluate the policy positions of prospective candidates, and are these delegates representative of the party electorate? What effects do various types of nominating systems have on the party's ability to choose candidates who have the best chance of winning?

In recent years most of the debate over the party's role in the nominating process has been concerned with the presidential nominating process – and particularly the reforms in the Democratic convention delegate-selection process. Critics have argued that the goal of nominating the strongest candidates has been overshadowed by the obsession with representing all interests in the delegate selection process and assuring broad participation in caucuses and primaries (Ranney 1975; Kirkpatrick 1976). Similarly, most of the empirical research on nominations has concentrated on the presidential level. For example, we have learned something about the personal characteristics and viewpoints of delegates to national conventions and to state conventions that choose national delegates (McClosky, Hoffman, and O'Hara 1960; Kirkpatrick 1976; Sullivan, Pressman, Page, and Lyons 1974; Crotty 1983; Soule and Clarke 1970; Soule and McGrath 1975; Jackson, Brown, and Bositis 1982; Kweit, Kweit, and Pynn 1982). We have also learned about national primary electorates (Ranney 1968, 1972; Norrander 1982; Kritzer 1980). But we lack comparable information about those who participate in conventions and primaries that endorse or nominate state officials.

V. O. Key (1956, p.168) raised the question "whether the direct primary mode of nomination may not set in motion forces that tend to lead to the atrophy of party organizations." He tested this hypothesis with data on competition for state legislative races in several states before and after introduction of the direct primary, and in states using the convention system. In states where the primary was introduced the number of contested legislative elections declined. This suggests that local minority-party organizations, deprived of their nominating function, began to atrophy and failed to recruit legislative candidates. Key suggests that there is less evidence of atrophy in majority-party organizations, although the high level of district primary competition in parties that hold safe seats indicates the party is not attempting to influence nominations. (Key 1956, ch. 6).

Key's assumption is that when local political leaders lose their ability to nominate local candidates and participate in the nomination of state candidates, they have less incentive to recruit candidates and to maintain a strong, active organization. This is particularly damaging to a party organization that is in the minority locally; as it grows weaker, there is no mechanism for recruiting or assisting candidates, and the absence of candidates reinforces one-party domination of the area. The establishment of a primary for statewide races deprives a party organization that was outnumbered at the local level of a chance to participate in conventions at the state level, where the party might be competitive.

Key's theory is plausible, but his evidence — as he recognizes — is circumstantial and perhaps coincidental. We do not have evidence from Key, or from anyone else, that shows directly how party organizations change in reaction to introduction of the primary. The historical record (summarized in Chapter 1) suggests a different causal relationship: In those states where party organizations were strong, there was the longest delay in establishing direct primaries, and the party organizations were most likely to set up formal or informal endorsement procedures.

One way of evaluating the importance to the party organization of nominating or endorsing candidates and of recruiting them is to survey state and local leaders about the extent to which they engage in such activities, and a number of such studies have been conducted (Bowman and Boynton 1966; Tobin and Keynes 1974; Harder and Ungs 1966; Patterson and Boynton 1969; Olson 1963; Jewell and Olson 1982, pp. 100-104). Not surprisingly, there is great variation among the states, localities, and parties in the extent to which leaders recruit candidates and help them to get nominated.

The authors of a recent major study of state party organizations (Gibson, Cotter, Bibby, Huckshorn 1981) have developed a systematic and comprehensive measure of state party institutionalization. One component is the level of programmatic activity, and within the category of such activity that is candidate-oriented, the authors include preprimary endorsements. They do not find that such endorsements are substantially correlated with other measures of candidate-oriented programmatic activity.

At the heart of the debate over party responsibility is the question of how to bring about the nomination of candidates who are committed to the major policies advocated by the party. The debate on this issue, however, has failed to produce any evidence about the effects of various nominating and endorsing systems on responsibility and accountability. One obvious question is to what group of party members should candidates be accountable? If it is important to nominate candidates whose position and record on policy issues are compatible with the party's position, who should set the party position and monitor the commitment of candidates?

It seems plausible that delegates to a state convention will have more interest in issues and more familiarity with the position of candidates than most voters would have. The more important question is whether the delegates adequately represent the broad range of viewpoints and interests in the party, or whether certain particular views and groups are overrepresented. There have been several studies showing that national convention delegates, like other party activists, tend to be less moderate or centrist than rank-and-file voters who support the party (McClosky, Hoffman, and O'Hara 1960). We lack comparable data on the views of delegates to state endorsing conventions. If such delegates are also unrepresentative of the votes, would they be likely to choose candidates who are too liberal or too conservative for the voters? How likely is it that single-issue groups will elect enough delegates to conventions so that they can demand that candidates support such narrow and sometimes extreme positions?

A question can also be raised about whether those voters who participate in primary elections are typical of the larger number who vote in general elections — in terms of their viewpoints and interests. There have been studies comparing the characteristics and viewpoints of those who vote in presidential primaries with those who vote only in general elections. These results have been inconsistent, but some have shown that primary voters differ on some issues from those who identify with the party or vote for that party in the general election (Scheele 1972, ch. 4; Ranney 1968). These studies have not been replicated for state gubernatorial elections. The impact of single-issue groups in a primary election may be substantial — perhaps greater than in a general election. In states with open primaries, there is the possibility that a candidate who is out of step with the party on issues can win because of the ability to attract crossover votes.

In other words, there are characteristics of both the convention and the primary that make possible the endorsement or nomination of a candidate who does not conform to at least some definitions of the party's position on issues. Similarly either system may choose a candidate whose stand on issues is not congruent with those of the party's usual supporters in the electorate. There are two reasons for being concerned about such an outcome. It can be argued that party responsibility requires candidate accountability to the party electorate broadly defined, rather than to a smaller group of party activists or primary voters. In more pragmatic terms, it can be argued that the party's nominees cannot get elected if they do not share the views of the party electorate on major issues. It is possible to find examples of candidates whose rather extreme views helped them win endorsement or nomination but who failed to win a majority from the general electorate, but there are no systematic data available on the frequency of such developments.

One of the arguments in favor of party conventions to endorse or make nominations is that the voters in a primary are less likely to choose the most electable candidate. V. O. Key (1956, pp. 145-68) explained this may occur because the primary electorate is not representative of the party's voters in the general election. State and local elections are often held at the same time, and contests at either level may attract voters to the polls. Consequently, Democratic voters, for example, are most likely to vote in the primary if they come from a county or city where there are close Democratic primary contests, and these are likely to be local units dominated by the Democratic party. Voters in statewide Democratic primaries come disproportionately from areas of Democratic dominance and are likely to choose candidates from those areas. This will produce a ticket that is unbalanced, representing primarily one regional, ethnic, or ideological bloc within the party. Thus, as illustrated by Key, the Massachusetts Democrats are likely to nominate Irish, Catholic candidates from the Boston area. This is a particularly serious problem for a minority party in a state. Because of its minority status, it must make a particular effort to nominate candidates who can appeal to independents and members of the other party. At the same time, because it is a minority, it is unlikely to have had many close statewide primary races, and its voters get out of the habit of participating, unless there are close local primaries. Consequently, when a statewide primary does develop, the choice is made by a small group of voters representing traditional areas of party strength. The average voter lacks the sophistication and motivation to make tactical political decisions and vote for a balanced ticket.

Key provided data from several states to show the disproportionate makeup of the primary electorate, and used Massachusetts to illustrate the resulting geographic and ethnic imbalance of Democratic candidates. No comprehensive effort has been made to test Key's hypothesis empirically, although there is more recent evidence from other states of the disproportionate primary electorates (Jewell and Olson 1978, pp. 156-61; Black and Black 1982).

If primary electorates are distorted and nominate unbalanced tickets, there is no certainty that convention delegates will do better, despite the assumption that they have tactical skills, knowledge, and motivation that most primary voters lack. Conventions may overrepresent geographic areas of party strength, because the allocation of seats is often based on the party's vote in the last general election. Moreover, if delegates are highly motivated by issues and are less moderate in their views than primary or general election voters, they may choose candidates whose ideological stands will handicap them in the election. Moreover, the campaign efforts by supporters of a particular candidate or a particular policy may elect enough delegates to capture the convention, producing a majority of delegates who are not principally concerned with choosing the party's strongest slate of candidates.

State laws regulate political parties in a number of ways, some of which are pertinent to nominations. Some state laws authorize preprimary endorsing conventions; some specifically prohibit them; and other states have no legislation on the topic. No evidence has been collected to show whether legal endorsement systems, and particularly those that give the endorsee some advantage on the ballot, have a different impact from endorsements that are adopted informally by state parties. Previous studies of endorsements have been descriptive or anecdotal, and provide few clues to the question of whether or how party endorsements affect the outcome of primaries. What advantages can a party give to a candidate it endorses? Why should other candidates drop out of the race? Why should party activists work for the endorsed candidate? Is there any reason to expect voters to be familiar with the endorsement and to vote for a candidate in the primary simply, or largely, because of the endorsement? While there are a few studies that systematically assess the impact of campaign workers in general elections (Cutright and Rossi 1958; Katz and Eldersveld 1961), there are no comparable studies in primaries, and of course none on the effect of endorsements in primaries.

THE CHOICES OF VOTERS IN PRIMARIES

Those who believe that candidates should be selected by voters in a primary without any interference by party organizations are making some explicit or implicit assumptions about primary electors. One is that the primary electorate will be large in size and reasonably representative of all voters in the party. A second is that those who vote in the Democratic party, for example, will be mostly Democratic voters rather than Republicans. A third assumption (perhaps less broadly accepted) is that these voters will select candidates who generally support the major policies of the party and are capable of winning the general election. The question is whether these assumptions are based on a realistic understanding of voting behavior in primary elections.

There are essentially three choices made by voters in primary elections that we seek to understand:

1. Why do voters choose to vote in primary elections?
2. How do they determine whether to register as Democrats or Republicans in a closed primary state, and how do they choose whether to vote in the Democratic or Republican primary in an open primary state?
3. How do voters decide for whom to cast their votes in primary elections?

There is only limited evidence available from research on any of these topics. To a large extent, we must review what is known about voting behavior in general elections, determine what findings might be pertinent to primaries, and use these as the basis for research questions and hypotheses.

Studies of turnout in elections have proceeded at two levels: personal and institutional or contextual. A few national surveys of turnout in primary elections have emphasized the importance of several personal variables that are also pertinent to general elections: Age and education are the most important of these. Those who are younger and more poorly educated are less likely to vote in general elections and even less likely to vote in primaries (Scheele 1972, p. 48, ch. 3; Wolfinger and Rosenstone 1980; Ranney, 1968; Rubins, 1980). There is nothing surprising about these findings. More interesting are the data suggesting that the strength of party identification has a greater effect on voting in primaries than it has on voting in general elections (Jewell and Olson 1982, pp. 133-4). Is this because persons who lack a strong identification with a party are reluctant to register with a party? If so, the impact should be more pronounced in states with closed primaries. Or is the act of voting in a primary perceived by voters as a partisan act, something that those with little sense of party identification are reluctant to undertake? Does voting in a party's primary, like voting a straight party ticket in November, reinforce the sense of party identification?

At the institutional level, it is apparent that voting in general elections is affected by the complexity of legal requirements for registration and voting. Moreover, turnout is obviously higher in years when more important offices (such as the presidency) are at stake, in states with traditional patterns of high competition, and in individual races that are competitive (Wolfinger and Rosenstone 1980, ch. 4; Milbrath and Goel 1977, ch. 5). Presumably turnout in primaries should also be higher in states with easier registration and voting requirements and closer competition in primaries, and in specific races that are closer. There are also institutional variables applying only to primaries that should affect voting. We would expect higher turnout in the majority party — partly but not entirely because of greater competition (Key 1956, pp. 104-10). We would also expect more turnout in states with open primaries, because there is no party registration requirement to discourage voters and because they have the freedom to move into the more competitive and interesting primary.

If institutional variables have a significant effect, there should be sizable differences in voter turnout rates from state to state. These do exist and they are substantial. In the period from 1951 through 1982 gubernatorial primary turnout as a percentage of voting age population (when both primaries were contested) averaged over 40 percent in 6 northern states and under 25 percent in 12 other northern states; in southern states the average turnout in the Democratic primary as a percentage of voting age population ranged from over 40 to 14 percent. These variations cannot be fully explained by legal restrictions on registration and voting or by other variables that affect turnout in general elections. In other words, to explain why voter participation in primaries varies so much from state to state, we must examine variables that are unique to primary elections. This is the goal pursued in Chapter 6.

How does the voter determine which primary to vote in? I know of no research that deals with this question at the level of the individual voter; obviously the literature on voting behavior in general elections offers no clues. In closed primary states voters must usually make the decision several months before the primary because advance registration is required. To what extent do voters make this choice on the basis of party loyalty and their normal voting preference in general elections, and to what extent do they choose party registration for pragmatic grounds: to be able to vote in the majority party where the races are more competitive and more important? Registration records suggest that, in states where there is a shift in the party balance, party registration figures lag far behind shifts in the two-party vote, and even behind changes in party identification (Jewell and Olson 1982, pp. 38-43).

In states with open primaries, voters have the choice of sticking loyally with one party or shifting back and forth from year to year. There has been no research to determine what proportion of voters follows which course, although studies of presidential primaries occasionally report aggregate data that show a large cross-over vote in particular races. If voters do cross over frequently, what is the reason: to vote in a more competitive race, to choose a candidate who is particularly attractive, or (the least plausible choice) to vote for the candidate most likely to be beaten by a candidate in one's own party? If voters seldom shift primaries in an open primary state, what is the reason? When changes occur in the two-party balance in a state, does the minority party gain voters in its primary more rapidly in an open primary state than it does in a closed primary state? If not, why not? These are questions to be considered, with a limited amount of new data, in Chapter 7.

The range of choices that a voter has in a party's primary depends of course on the number of candidates competing. More research has been done on the causes of primary competition than on any other aspect of primaries. Thirty years ago V. O. Key (1956, p. 172) advanced the hypothesis that "The extent to which a party's nominations are contested in the primary by two or more aspirants depends in large measure on the prospects for victory for the nominee in the general election." He found this to be true in a number of states, and his findings have been confirmed for more recent periods by a number of studies covering gubernatorial, legislative, and other races (Jewell and Olson 1978, pp. 134-36; Jewell and Olson 1982, pp. 120-26; Grau 1981). These same studies also consistently show (as Key found) that competition is reduced when an incumbent is running for renomination. Because incumbents are most likely to be found in the party that is stronger in the state or district, the correlation between primary competition and the party's prospects for victory is greatest if incumbency is controlled for. There is also evidence that gubernatorial primary competition is more likely to occur in states where party conventions do not make endorsements (Jewell and Olson 1982, p. 123).

When voters make a choice in gubernatorial primaries, are they motivated differently than voters in general elections? Obviously voters in primaries cannot be guided by party identification to vote a straight ticket. Moreover, the partisan cues are missing that usually affect voters' perceptions of candidates and issues. It is possible that voters — particularly those with a strong sense of party identification — would be influenced by endorsements when these are made by party conventions. The low level of most voters' information and their suspicion of politicians, as reflected in the voting behavior literature, must make us skeptical about the direct impact of endorsements on voters — until there is clear evidence of such an impact.

In the absence of party identification or endorsements as factors, we would expect voters in primaries to be more influenced by the other variables that are important in general elections: the name identification and perception of candidates, group identifications, and issues. Largely because of the importance of name identification, incumbency should be a major asset in primaries.

In recent years, including 1982, there have been many examples of statewide primaries being won by candidates who lacked a long record of public service and party activity, but who were wealthy or had access to extensive funding, and who used these resources to hire skillful campaign managers and buy large amounts of time on television. The potential for success of such candidates is presumably greater in primaries than in general elections because party identification is not a factor.

Very little attention has been paid by political scientists to statewide primary campaigns — for governor or any other office. Most of what we know about voting behavior in primary elections comes from presidential primaries. These are quite different in a number of respects. Depending on the particular presidential race, some candidates may have much more visibility, and some much less, than major gubernatorial candidates would have. Voters in a presidential primary may be motivated to use their vote to "send a message to Washington," as George Wallace used to say. Early in the presidential primary season, it may be difficult for voters to determine which candidates have a serious chance of winning, while later in the race there is a tendency for voters to be influenced by presidential bandwagons. Despite these differences, studies of voting behavior in presidential primaries are useful in illustrating the importance of both candidate images and issues in voting decisions (Norrander 1983; Marshall 1982; Gopoian 1982).

Anyone who examines a number of gubernatorial primaries must be impressed by the range of variables and political situations that appear to have major effects on the outcome. In Part IV of this study, an effort will be made to advance some generalizations about primary outcomes without either ignoring or becoming a prisoner of the mass of detailed examples. These generalizations will be drawn largely from examining media accounts of the 1982 primaries, and exploring available voter surveys.

Part II
Party Organizations
and Endorsements

3

The Pattern of
Party Organizational Endorsements

Primary elections transfer to the voters a function traditionally reserved to the political party: the selection of candidates for office. The consequence is to deny the party an opportunity to choose candidates who have the best chance of winning and who represent the major viewpoints and interests in the party. The result may be not only to weaken the party's electoral prospects but also to erode its organizational vitality.

In some states the political parties have tried to retain some influence over the selection of candidates by establishing machinery for endorsing those who are running, or seek to run, in the primary. These efforts are designed to discourage nonendorsed candidates from running or, if that fails, to help the endorsed candidates to secure voter approval.

In a number of states the political parties have been able to get laws enacted authorizing party organizations to endorse candidates, and in some cases giving the endorsed candidate some advantage in getting on the primary ballot. In other states there is no legal authority for endorsements, but the party organization (or at least some party body) makes such endorsements. A few states have shifted back and forth between legal and informal systems of endorsement.

This chapter begins with a brief description of the various endorsement methods used in the states in recent years. The next step is to describe the reasons why party endorsements were originally adopted in those states where they are used. An examination of these states may also provide some clues as to why endorsements have not been used, or have been abandoned in other states. The most important goal of this chapter is to determine what effect party endorsements have on the primary. How often, in what states, and under what conditions, do the endorsed candidates win in primary elections?

CHARACTERISTICS OF ENDORSEMENT SYSTEMS

The most obvious distinction to be made among endorsement systems is between those mandated or authorized by law, and those adopted by party organizations without legal sanction. Because in many states primary elections are regulated in some detail by state law, it is not surprising to find examples of endorsements being authorized and regulated by law in a number of states. Table 3.1 describes legal provisions for endorsement in eight states where such laws now apply and three others that have had legal endorsements in the recent past.

State laws providing for endorsements must specify what party group will make the endorsements. In all but two of the states listed in Table 3.1 the endorsements are made by party conventions whose delegates are specifically elected for that purpose. The exceptions are New York and Rhode Island, where endorsements are made by state central committees.

In most of these states a majority vote is required to endorse, and consequently several ballots may be taken before any candidate gets a majority. In Colorado and New Mexico, however, the party conventions take only a single ballot, with the size of the vote for each candidate being a measure of party support that affects access to the ballot — as noted below.

From the viewpoint of the political party that wants to makes its endorsement machinery effective, one advantage of a legal base is that the endorsed candidate can be given a preference over others in access to the ballot. This advantage may be given to the winner of the endorsement — the candidate with the largest percentage — or to all candidates that reach a minimum percentage. Those who fail to meet the required threshold in the party convention may be denied access to the ballot, or may have to pass an additional hurdle by getting petitions signed.

Table 3.1
Legal State Party Endorsement Systems

State	Years	Ballot Provisions
Colo.	1912-	Candidates qualify for ballot by getting 20% on single ballot at convention; also by petition. Candidates appear on ballot in order of vote at convention.
Conn.	1958-	Candidates qualify for ballot only by getting 20% on ballot at convention.
R. I.	1948-	Endorsed candidate qualifies for ballot and is listed first; others qualify by petition.
Utah	1948-	Only endorsed candidates qualify for ballot. Convention must endorse two, unless one gets 70%.
N. Y.	1970-	Candidates qualify for ballot by getting 25% on any ballot at convention; others by petition.
N. D.	1968-	Endorsed candidate qualifies for ballot; others qualify by petition.
N. M.	1952, 54, 64, 66, 1978-	Candidates qualify for ballot by getting 20% on single ballot; others qualify by petition, but must first seek endorsement.
Del.	1968-76	Candidates qualify for ballot only by getting 35% on ballot at convention.
	1980-	Convention endorses a candidate, but other candidates may compete in primary.
Mass.	1934-36, 1954-70	Endorsed candidate qualifies. Any other candidates getting 20% qualify with some signatures on petition; others by petition with more signatures. Endorsee listed first on ballot.
Idaho	1966-70	Candidates getting over 20% qualify; others by petition if 10% at convention.
Neb.	1946-52	Convention may endorse one or two; these qualify for ballot; others by petition.

Source: Compiled by the author.

Table 3.1 shows that endorsed candidates have the greatest advantage in Utah and Connecticut because in those states a degree of convention support is an absolute prerequisite to getting on the primary ballot. In Utah conventions two candidates must be endorsed (but only one if the winner has 70 percent) and no one else may run in the primary. In Connecticut it is necessary to get 20 percent (on at least one ballot) in order to enter the primary. Until the law was revised in 1978, Delaware required candidates to get 35 percent of the convention vote, although in practice challenges to the convention nominee were very rare.

Candidates who win a certain percentage of the convention vote automatically get on the primary ballot in Colorado, New York, North Dakota, and New Mexico, but other candidates can qualify by getting petitions signed. (Similar provisions were used in the Massachusetts, Idaho, and Nebraska systems that are no longer in effect.) Rhode Island gives the single endorsee automatic ballot access; others must use petitions.

Obviously, in states where endorsement and petitions are alternative routes to ballot position, the advantage enjoyed by endorsees depends on how difficult and time consuming it is to get petitions signed. The petition route is used frequently in New York and New Mexico, but very rarely in Colorado. A few states require candidates to seek convention endorsement; in others a candidate can use the petition route alone.

Table 3.1 shows that there are several states where the endorsee is identified on the ballot and/or where those who win convention support are listed on the ballot in order of the number of votes won at the convention, with nonendorsed candidates listed last. It is not evident how much advantage there is to explicit recognition on the ballot, but research suggests that ballot position is a considerable advantage.

There are several states where party endorsement of candidates is not authorized by law but where one or both of the political parties has followed this practice. Informal endorsements may occur for a period of years before the practice gains legal sanction, as happened in North Dakota. On the other hand, in Massachusetts, after legal endorsements were abolished in 1973, the Republican party continued to make informal endorsements and in 1982 the Democratic party resumed the practice. In most states where informal party endorsements are made, however, there seems to have been no serious effort made to provide for legal authority.

There is great variety in the methods of endorsement used informally by state parties; Table 3.2 summarizes some of the more important differences. The endorsing body is a part of the official state party (recognized by law) in Massachusetts, Minnesota, and Illinois. In Wisconsin, because legal restrictions on the official party organizations are so rigid, most party functions are performed by unofficial party groups (Sorauf 1954); it is this group on the Republican side that makes endorsements. In California several unofficial party groups have made endorsements in recent decades; the most significant and prominent endorsing groups have been the Republican Assembly and the California Democratic Council.

In some state parties the endorsements are made by conventions meeting in public and attended by relatively large numbers of delegates. This is the case for the endorsements made in Massachusetts, North Dakota (previously), Minnesota, Wisconsin, and California. Endorsements are generally made behind the scenes by groups such as state party committees, for example, the Democratic committee in Illinois. Table 3.2 includes all the state parties that in recent years have made publicized, open endorsements, as well as those that have most consistently made unpublicized endorsements.

There are other states where the party organization, or some of its leaders, may make behind-the-scenes endorsements from time to time, but these are neither well enough publicized nor consistent enough for inclusion in Table 3.2. One example is the Illinois Republican party, which sometimes makes endorsements through its central committee or its county chairman's association. Pennsylvania and Ohio are states where the party leadership has often played some role in recruiting and endorsing statewide candidates. In New Jersey major county leaders have often become involved in endorsements for state office.

Generally in these states the convention endorses only a single candidate for each office, and a majority vote is required for endorsement. In both Minnesota parties, however, a vote of 60 percent is required to endorse. Frequently, multiple ballots are necessary to reach the required 50+ or 60 percent.

Because these are informal endorsements, without any legal sanction, the endorsed candidates have no advantage in getting on the ballot and gaining ballot position. An unusual exception occurred

Table 3.2
Informal State Party Endorsement Systems

State	Party	Years	Endorsing Body	Provisions
Mass.	R	1952, 74-	Convention of party	Endorsement by majority, multiple ballots.
Mass.	D	1982	Convention of party	Endorsement by majority, multiple ballots; 15% required to qualify for primary ballot.
N.D.	Both	before 1968	Conventions of party groups	
Minn.	D	1944-	Convention of party	Endorsement by 60% on multiple ballots.
Minn.	R	1960-	Convention of party	Endorsement by 60% on multiple ballots.
Wisc.	R	1950-	Convention of party, unofficial	Endorsement by majority on multiple ballots.
Ill.	D	1930s-	Central committee of party	Conducted in private meetings.
Calif.	R	1942-	Republican Assembly, unofficial	
Calif.	D	1954-	Convention: Calif. Democ. Council	

Source: Compiled by the author.

in the Massachusetts Democratic party in 1982, however. The state party rules for the reinstated convention specified that a vote of 15 percent on any ballot for endorsement was required to get on the primary ballot, and a state court ruled that this provision could be enforced. More details on this unusual case are provided in the next chapter.

Candidates who win endorsement of informal party conventions gain no legal advantage of ballot access or position, but they gain the same potential political advantages as candidates endorsed by party organizations acting under legal authority. One political advantage is that nonendorsed candidates may be discouraged from running in the primary. A second is that endorsement may bring a candidate campaign resources such as workers and funding. A third possible advantage is that some voters in the primary may be inclined to support the endorsed candidate. Later in this chapter the effectiveness of endorsements — both legal and informal — will be explored. The importance of these political advantages will be assessed further in the case studies in Chapters 4 and 5.

REASONS FOR ENDORSEMENT LAWS AND PRACTICES

Why do we find endorsement procedures written into law in some states, practiced informally by parties in others, and nonexistent in most states? Why have endorsements been adopted in some states, only to be abandoned after a few years' experience? What were the specific objectives of those party leaders and legislators who initiated or legalized endorsement procedures?

The answers to these questions are not simple; they are not the same in every state; they are obscure in some of the states where endorsements were adopted many years ago. Like most reforms or changes in the political system, endorsements were adopted for a variety of reasons. The persistence of endorsement procedures in a state, or a state party, may mean that the system is serving its intended purposes — but it may also persist through inertia.

An endorsement system may serve the interests of one political party, or the leadership of that party, better than it serves the other party in a state. Under these conditions, we might expect to find no legal base, but only an informal endorsement procedure in one party. However, a majority party may be able to win legislative approval of a legal endorsement system, imposed on both of the parties. We would expect to find endorsement established by law in states where either it serves the interest of the majority party or where both parties are agreed on its benefits.

We have already described (in Chapter 1) the reason why the direct primary was adopted in most of the states, particularly during the early part of the twentieth century. It was an effort to undermine the power of the entrenched leadership of political parties, particularly in states dominated by a single party. It grew out of the third party movements, notably the Populist and Progressive movements, and represented a challenge to the existing party structure. The movement for direct primary legislation was part of a larger trend toward imposing legal restrictions on the electoral process, a movement that produced the Australian ballot and requirements for voter registration.

The effect of primary legislation was not only to open up the party nominating process generally but to give those groups and interests that lacked political power a chance to win nominations if they could mobilize voters in the primary elections. In those states where legislation provided for open primaries, with no requirement of party registration, the opportunities for challenging the entrenched leadership were enhanced.

If primary legislation was a weapon used by those challenging party leadership, the endorsement process may be considered a weapon used by party leadership to maintain a share of power. It was a reaction to the institution of the primary. If the party leadership could no longer make nominations by convention, it might still be able to use the convention to endorse particular candidates who were seeking nomination in the primary. It might even succeed in making such endorsements a legal prerequisite or advantage in the primary election.

In several states the preprimary endorsement system was authorized by law as part of the initial primary legislation. In other words, the political party leadership was strong enough to demand that the endorsement system be adopted as its price for accepting the direct primary. These states are Colorado, Rhode Island, Connecticut, New York, and Delaware.

In most states, however, the endorsement process was adopted legally or developed informally after extensive experience with primary elections. Often certain features or consequences of the primary elections created problems; the endorsement system was viewed as one method of coping with those problems. In several states the open primary system in particular led to demands for endorsements. In California the cross-filing system, another product of the anti-party reform movement, inspired party endorsements. In several states primary elections produced large numbers of candidates and frequently winners who had much less than a majority vote, and endorsements were intended to deal with these specific problems.

In addition to the problems created by the primary system, there were often specific political factors that led to the creation of endorsement machinery. In several states there was a deliberate effort to strengthen the political party as an institution, sometimes in an effort to make a minority party competitive. In several states the support for endorsements came from an ideological, regional, or ethnic faction within the party that was seeking to gain a greater voice in nominations.

The best way to understand how these various forces combined to produce endorsement legislation or informal endorsement practices is to look more closely at some of the states that use or have used endorsements. The goal is to understand why endorsements were adopted and sometimes abandoned, and what was at stake in the controversies that surrounded these changes.

Endorsements Coinciding with New Primary Laws

In Colorado the endorsing convention was part of the direct primary law adopted in 1912. The campaign for a direct primary in Colorado was a result of the Progressive movement, and it was championed by a Democratic governor who was supporting a number of Progressive reforms. Opposition came from conservative interests and entrenched political leaders in both parties. When the opposition found that it could not prevent enactment of a primary law, it worked successfully to add the endorsing convention as an amendment. The endorsing convention has remained a part of the direct primary in Colorado ever since (Eyre and Martin 1967, ch. 2).

Two of the last states to adopt a direct primary law were Rhode Island (1948) and Connecticut (1955). These were states with strong party organizations that maintained a firm grip over the nominating process, and that fought a prolonged rear-guard action against adoption of a direct primary law. When they finally yielded to the pressure of reformers for primary legislation, they were able to incorporate an endorsing system in the law, thereby maintaining a substantial role for the party nominations.

A detailed study of how the Connecticut law was adopted (Lockard 1959) shows that major leaders of both parties were opposed to a primary law but believed that open opposition would be politically damaging. One faction within the Republican party favored a primary because its members believed this would provide a more favorable arena for the factional struggle. Although many political leaders had grave doubts about the compromise plan that was passed with great difficulty, it has remained in effect with very few changes and is widely accepted.

The endorsement method adopted in Connecticut, usually referred to as the "challenge primary," gave the party organization the maximum influence over the nomination. In order to challenge the candidate endorsed by the convention, any other candidate would have to win 20 percent of the convention vote and also get a significant number of signatures on petitions (although the petition requirement has since been dropped). The Rhode Island law maintained unusually strong party organizational control because endorsements were made by the state party committee rather than by an elected convention. In both states relatively few party endorsements were challenged in the first few years after adoption of the primary.

Another state in which endorsements were incorporated into the original primary law was New York, which had used the convention system for statewide nominations until its adoption of a primary law in 1967. (Primaries had been used for elections at other levels.) The law provided for preprimary endorsements by the state party committees, with any candidate who got 25 percent of the committee vote entitled to a place on the primary ballot without getting petitions signed. The convention system in New York had come under considerable criticism, largely because of machine control over the delegates.

There was no consensus among New York politicians on adopting the primary with endorsement by party committees. Governor Nelson Rockefeller preferred a direct primary without endorsements, and some politicians feared that the new system would make campaigning much more expensive. No party leader wanted to be blamed for blocking enactment of a primary law, which appeared to have broad popular and press support. The compromise was obviously an effort to maintain some party control over the nominating process.

Delaware, which was one of the last states to adopt a primary (in 1968), has continued to use the convention to make endorsements. In practice the convention system is so well entrenched in that state that the endorsee is almost never challenged in a primary — at least in a gubernatorial contest.

Illinois is an example of a state that adopted the direct primary relatively early (a series of laws in the 1908-19 period), and apparently no effort was made by the party leadership to incorporate endorsements in the law. Instead, the state party organizations adopted the practice of making informal endorsements. These have been particularly effective on the Democratic side, because of the strength of the Cook County organization. The Republican party has made endorsements intermittently.

Endorsements in Progressive States

Wisconsin was the home of Robert M. LaFollette, one of the leaders of the Progressive movement and most important advocates of the direct primary. Wisconsin was the first state, in 1903, to adopt a comprehensive direct primary law. For these reasons, Wisconsin is an interesting state in which to observe the development of party endorsements.

The endorsing technique was developed by conservative Republicans, seeking to gain control over nominations from the Progressive wing of the party. From its inception in 1906, the Republican primary became the central arena for decision-making, and the Progressive wing of the party dominated most elections for the first twenty years. In 1925 a group of conservative Republicans established an unofficial party organization and began to make endorsements. In its first few years, the group had some success in the primaries. Then in 1934 the Progressive faction left the Republican party and formed a third party. This left the conservative group in control and its endorsees won most statewide primary races over the next twenty years, although the party organization did not make endorsements in every race (Sorauf 1954; Epstein 1958, pp. 37-40).

In 1949 the Republican party organization amended its constitution to require that endorsements be made in every statewide race. The growth of the Democratic party, which became seriously competitive in the postwar period, may have been one factor that inspired the Republican organization to mandate endorsements. In 1979 the Wisconsin Republican party amended its constitution to make endorsements optional rather than mandatory; a majority of the delegates must vote to have endorsement for a race. The change occurred because the party's endorsement no longer carried the weight that it had in earlier elections. This was largely because the party had accumulated a debt from elections in the early 1970s, and was unable to provide much tangible help to the endorsee. In 1978 the gubernatorial endorsee lost the primary; the winner, who became governor, was naturally opposed to compulsory endorsements. No effort was made by any of the gubernatorial candidates in 1982 to get the party to make an endorsement.

Why did the emerging Democratic party in Wisconsin not follow the Republican example of endorsements in an effort to strengthen its competitive position? In the mid-1950s some Democratic leaders proposed such action, but it was rejected by the state convention. As Epstein (1958, p. 95) explained,

> Opposition to endorsement stems from the Democratic inheritance of the old progressive antimachine tradition associated with the first LaFollette's successful substitution of the direct primary for the "boss-ridden" Republican convention. For old LaFollette supporters, anything that resembles convention control over the nomination is antidemocratic, and it is too much for the organization even to seek to direct the voter's choice in the primary.

During the postwar years, while the Democratic party was becoming competitive in Wisconsin, a similar development was occurring in Minnesota. In 1944 the Democratic party and the Farmer-Labor party united to form the Democratic-Farmer-Labor party (DFL). The Farmer-Labor party had a strong rural base and a Progressive tradition. The Democratic party had an urban, Catholic base, and had been under conservative leadership, but during the 1940s a new generation of liberal Democrats came to the fore, and under Hubert Humphrey's leadership forged the alliance with the Farmer-Labor party (Mitau 1960, pp. 23-28).

The leaders of the new Democratic-Farmer-Labor party believed that preprimary endorsements were essential to maintain party unity, win elections, and elect candidates who would be committed to DFL principles. They believed this was particularly necessary because the DFL was in the minority and because Minnesota has an open primary system, which would permit Republicans or independents to enter the DFL primary. In the early years, there was some opposition from those who had belonged to the old Farmer-Labor party and presumably were loyal to Progressive principles (Mitau 1960, pp. 47-48).

In Minnesota it was the Republican party that was slow to adopt endorsements, despite considerable debate over the issue in the 1940s and 1950s. In 1959, however, the party amended its constitution to permit endorsements, and they have been frequently made since that time.

California is another state in which the Progressive movement had a strong impact, producing a primary system that created serious problems for the political parties. In each of the parties an endorsing organization was created in order to cope with these problems and in order to strengthen a party that was weak, in both organizational and electoral terms.

The direct primary was established in California in 1909. Although it was a closed primary, an amendment adopted in 1913 legalized the practice of cross-filing, under which a candidate could run in both primaries. A major consequence of this system was that popular or well-known candidates were often able to win the primaries of both parties, making a general election unnecessary. In fact from 1940 to 1952, one candidate won both primaries in 68 percent of all partisan contests. Because incumbents were usually better known than their opponents, they very often won both primaries; in fact more than 80 percent of those who won both primaries were incumbents (Rowe 1961, ch. 6).

The cross-filing system had a devastating effect on the political party organizations. It prevented them from having any influence over nominations. Moreover, it often prevented the party from even having a nominee in the general election, if its own candidates were beaten in the party's primary. If two Democrats were seeking the nomination to challenge an incumbent Republican, it was very likely that both would be defeated by the Republican in the Democratic primary, eliminating the possibility of a one-on-one contest between a Democrat and a Republican. Furthermore, candidates who were elected to office as a result of winning both primaries seldom had any sense of loyalty or obligation to their party; some, in fact, could not be identified clearly with either party. The cross-filing system was one reason for the great weakness of party discipline in the legislature, making it almost a nonpartisan body (Rowe 1961, ch. 6).

The first effort by a party organization in California to establish some control over nominations came on the Republican side in 1934, a time when the party had been badly shaken by the Roosevelt landslide and by losses of congressional and legislative seats. A group of Republicans established the Republican Assembly, outside the structure of the official state party. The major goal of the group was to revitalize the party, and it moved cautiously and uncertainly toward the practice of making endorsements. In 1942, for the first time, the Assembly endorsed a slate of candidates for statewide office, including Earl Warren for governor. The slate was successful in the primary, and the practice of Republican Assembly endorsements was well established (Rowe 1961, ch. 7).

The success of the Republican Assembly increased the problems faced by the Democratic party because the endorsed slate of Republicans, particularly those who were incumbents, were often able to win both primaries. Governor Warren accomplished this in 1946 and Senator William Knowland won both primaries in 1952. Eisenhower's victory in 1952 contributed to Democratic losses of congressional and legislative seats. Democratic leaders decided to follow the Republican example and establish an organization, the California Democratic Council (CDC), to make endorsements at a statewide convention (Rowe 1961, ch. 8).

The CDC made its first endorsements in 1954, and in most cases it succeeded in persuading nonendorsed candidates to stay out of the primary; partly as a consequence, the endorsed candidates were able to win the Democratic primary against cross-filing Republicans, though most lost in the general election. Four years later the CDC once again succeeded in endorsing a slate of candidates, persuading most nonendorsed candidates to drop out, and winning the primary victories for its slate; in addition most candidates endorsed for congressional and legislative seats by local CDC groups won primaries. The most significant development in 1958 was that the Democrats won most statewide races, including the governorship, and won legislative control. One of the first orders of business in 1959 was abolition of cross-filing in the primary system (Rowe 1961, ch. 8).

North Dakota was one of the states where the Progressive movement was strong, and it was one of the first states to adopt a comprehensive direct primary law, in 1907. The established party leadership reacted to the primary by moving very quickly to create informal preprimary conventions. In 1915 leaders of the Progressive movement established the Nonpartisan League, which from time to time played a major role in North Dakota politics. The League held conventions to endorse candidates for statewide office. Most of the candidates endorsed by the League ran in the Republican primary. The League generally avoided the tactic of becoming a third party. Because the Republican party was the dominant one, the party's primary became the major battleground in the state. In the 1950s the Democratic party was revitalized, and the Nonpartisan League changed its tactics and in 1956 began to endorse candidates for the Democratic primary (Omdahl 1961).

Although the practice of informal endorsements by the Nonpartisan League and by party organizations (particularly Republican ones) has existed since the early years of the direct primary. The first legal authority for party endorsements occurred in 1967. Because the practice was so well established on an informal basis, the legislation had no major effect, although it did give the endorsees the right to get on the ballot without petitions.

Idaho, like North Dakota, was a state that adopted the primary early (1909) and one in which Progressive forces sought to use the primary to win control of a major party. After the Non-Partisan League entered a slate of candidates in the 1918 Democratic primary, the legislature abolished the primary and returned to the convention system for more than a decade.

The Idaho primary was reinstituted in time for the 1932 election, but it continued to come under criticism. Because it was an open primary, and party organizations were weak and divided into factions, voters often crossed party lines to participate in primaries, and the large number of candidates often led to nominations by less than a majority vote. One source of divisiveness within the parties was a controversy over legalizing gambling. In 1959 the legislature adopted a runoff primary, to be used if no candidate got over 40 percent in the primary elections. In 1963 this plan was dropped and the legislature adopted a preprimary endorsing system in an effort to end minority nominations and strengthen the party organization. It provided for convention endorsement of more than one candidate. The experiment with endorsements ended, however, in 1971 (Eyre and Hjelm 1969).

Utah also adopted an endorsing convention as an alternative to a runoff primary; unlike Idaho, the primary was adopted relatively late (in 1937), and the runoff was a feature of the original system. The duty of the endorsing convention was to select two candidates who would compete in a primary. In a sense the convention replaced the first stage of the two-part primary. It was hoped that the new system would be cheaper and less divisive. Subsequently the Utah system has been changed to permit endorsement of a single candidate if that person gets 70 percent of the vote.

Endorsements to Balance Tickets

No state has demonstrated greater ambivalence to preprimary endorsing conventions than New Mexico. The state did not adopt the direct primary until the 1940 elections. Legislation authorizing endorsing conventions was in effect for the 1950, 1952, and 1954 elections and was then repealed. Endorsing conventions were again required in 1964 and 1966, and were again abandoned. The endorsing convention was adopted for a third time, beginning with the 1976 election, and remains in effect.

Several reasons explain support for endorsing conventions in New Mexico. Because of the sharp ethnic cleavages in the state, political leaders want to put together slates that will balance Hispanic and Anglo candidates; conventions offer the best method of accomplishing this. When the primary was first adopted, there were frequently large numbers of primary candidates, some of whom ran in order to hurt one of the leading candidates by dividing the vote within a particular ethnic community (Sittig 1962, ch. 2; Holmes 1967, ch. 8).

The effort in the mid-1970s to revive the endorsing convention was also partly motivated by large numbers of candidates in the Democratic primary. There were nine Democrats running for lieutenant governor in 1970, with the winner getting only 21 percent of the vote; 25 ran for the Senate in 1972, with the winner getting 30 percent; and 6 candidates ran for the Democratic nomination for governor in 1954, with the winner getting only 31 percent. Moreover, a judicial decision in 1972 had invalidated the filing fee, thus removing one device that tended to limit the number of candidates (Hain and Garcia 1981, pp. 231-33).

Support for the endorsing convention has also come from specific candidates, particularly Democrats, who wanted to avoid a primary contest. The supporters of Joseph Montoya, for example, worked for restoration of the endorsing conventions in time for both the 1964 and 1976 elections, years in which he was running for the U.S. Senate. Just as the endorsing system serves the interests of some politicians, it hurts those who have less strength within the party organization than they do at the polls. In the mid-1950s the supporters of Senator Dennis Chavez, for example, favored repeal of the endorsing convention. Despite Chavez's success at the polls, his faction was unable to control the state Democratic party organization. The fact that the endorsing system was twice repealed suggests that such short-term political factors have often played a big part in legislative decisions about endorsement (Key 1956, pp. 125-26).

Massachusetts offers one of the more interesting examples of conflicts among partisan and ethnic groups concerning the principle of endorsement. Both parties in Massachusetts face the problem of balancing their tickets to accommodate various regions and their ethnic constituencies. In the absence of slating by an endorsing convention, a primary election is likely to produce a purely Yankee Republican ticket and a Democratic ticket dominated by Boston Irish.

The Republican party in Massachusetts has shown greater interest in adopting the endorsing convention to produce balanced tickets, perhaps because the party's minority status forces it to make efforts to broaden its base. Moreover, during periods when the endorsing convention has been used, the Republican party has been much more successful in rallying behind the endorsees; Democratic conventions have often been only the first stage of a bitter battle for the nomination.

Within the Democratic party, support for the endorsing convention has usually come from members in the western part of the state and from non-Irish ethnic groups, notably the Italians.

Massachusetts first adopted a legal endorsing convention system in 1932, under the leadership of Democratic Governor Joseph Ely, who came from western Massachusetts. It applied to the 1934 and 1936 elections. The 1934 convention, controlled by Governor Ely, denied endorsement to James Michael Curley, but Curley mobilized his Boston Irish support to win the primary and the election. In 1937 the legislature decided to abolish the endorsing convention (Key 1956, pp. 123-24).

In 1951 an effort to revive the endorsing convention in Massachusetts was made by a bipartisan coalition. Litt (1965, pp. 105-6) describes the reasons behind this move:

> The Republican leadership, although it had a heritage of party discipline, could not clear the way for non-Yankee candidates in the Republican primary. Therefore, in order to construct a slate that took into account the preferences of other ethnic groups with significant leverage in the general election, they sought a forum in which the Yankee political leadership could bypass the normal ethnic prejudices of their Yankee followers. Jewish, Irish, Italian, and other Republican minority groups provided the main support for the change to a preprimary convention. The small-town, Yankee Republicans from western Massachusetts who led the opposition preferred the battlegrounds of the primary because that was where they occupied the major fortresses. Similarly, the Italo-American Democrats, and the other ethnic groups chafing under the long party regime of the Irish, saw the preprimary convention as a better place to push their political ambitions.

The Republican majority in the 1951 legislature, with some votes from Italian Democrats, passed an endorsing convention law, but it was vetoed by Democratic Governor Paul Dever. The Republicans then held an informal endorsing convention in 1952, which chose a balanced slate that won the primary with little opposition. The strategy led to the election of a Republican governor, and this made possible adoption of legislation authorizing endorsing conventions (Key 1956, pp. 122-23).

For twenty years the Republican party used the convention effectively to unite behind a balanced slate of candidates. The Democratic conventions on the other hand, failed to produce unity; the endorsees were usually challenged and sometimes beaten in the primary. In 1973 the Democratic legislative majority overrode the arguments of Republicans and a few Democrats, and overrode the veto of a Republican governor, to repeal the endorsing convention.

The Republican party has continued to hold informal endorsing conventions. Within the Democratic party there was sentiment among many liberals and members from the western region to revive the endorsing convention. When a party charter was adopted, these groups succeeded in getting a preprimary convention established, and it went into effect in 1982. Efforts by supporters of a convention to get the legislature to give it legal authority were unsuccessful, however. The dispute over the Democratic convention is described in more detail in the next chapter.

Summarizing the Reasons for Endorsements

It is much easier to explain why legal or informal endorsing conventions have been used in specific states than it is to make broad generalizations about their use. It is generally true that some form of legal or informal endorsement is found in most of the urban-industrial states in the Northeast and Midwest. On the one hand, strong party organizations in some states have been able to establish endorsing conventions as an integral part of the direct primary system. On the other hand, in states where the Progressive movement and the primary system (often an open primary) threatened to erode the political party system, party organizations have reacted by making informal endorsements or gaining legal authority for endorsements. In several states minority parties seeking to become competitive have used the endorsing technique as a way of gaining the necessary unity and putting together a slate that will have broad voter support. In most states a full understanding of the reasons for adoption of endorsing conventions requires some knowledge about factional and/or ethnic conflicts.

This list of reasons for adoption of endorsing systems fails to explain why endorsements have not been used in the remaining two-thirds of the states. In the southern and border states we would not expect to find preprimary endorsements because the dominant Democratic parties do not have strong enough organizations; moreover, until recently, the threat from the Republican party has not been great enough to force such a step on the Democratic party. In some southern states, where the law permitted it, the Republican party until recently used conventions rather than primaries to make nominations. The Republican party in Virginia still uses only a convention, and in recent years the Democratic party in that state has used a convention to make the final nomination (Sabato 1977).

Outside the southern and border regions, there are about 20 states that have not made any use of endorsing conventions, at least in the last three decades, and it is impossible to generalize about why this has not happened. In those states where one party has generally predominated, there would presumably be less interest in endorsements. But over the last three decades there has been closer two-party competition in most states, both South and North. In such states both political parties ought to have a stake in influencing nominations, but there is little evidence that competition has led to endorsements. There are few data that suggest any growing interest in passing endorsement legislation.

There are a few scattered examples of state parties considering or experimenting with endorsements. The Michigan Democratic party recently amended its rules to make endorsements possible. But there was no effort to use this procedure in 1982, despite the large number of gubernatorial candidates. The Maryland Republican party recently rejected a proposal for preprimary endorsements made by a study commission that recommended it as an essential step for overcoming the party's minority status. It is worth noting that in the early 1970s, when Indiana finally abandoned the convention and adopted the direct primary for statewide nominations, it did not retain the convention to make endorsements (unlike New York).

MEASURING THE SUCCESS OF ENDORSEMENTS

What difference does it make if a political party makes preprimary endorsements? What difference does it make whether such endorsements are made through a process authorized by law or through informal party practices? What kind of impact would we expect endorsements to have on the outcome of primaries?

If a party organization endorses a candidate for nomination, this may discourage other candidates from running in the primary, particularly if the endorsee has easier access to the ballot or a favored position on the ballot. One way of measuring the impact of endorsements is to calculate how often the endorsee is challenged in a primary. The second way of measuring impact is to determine, in contested primaries, how often the endorsed candidate wins and how often the endorsee loses.

Neither of these measures can fully answer our questions about the impact of endorsements because they cannot tell us what would have happened in the absence of endorsements. For example, an incumbent governor seeking renomination usually wins endorsement and renomination, often without opposition. But in states without endorsement, the incumbent is usually renominated easily. One way to assess the impact of endorsements is to compare the frequency of uncontested primaries in those that have, and those that lack, endorsements, and we will do that after examining individual state patterns of endorsements.

The details of legal endorsing systems vary from state to state, and the informal endorsing techniques of state parties also vary. There are also differences among state parties in organizational strength and in attitudes of candidates and party workers toward the endorsement process. A comparison among the states and state parties will show how these variables affect the impact of endorsements.

Table 3.3 summarizes information on the effects of endorsements for 13 of the states using either legal or informal endorsements – most of these listed in Tables 3.1 and 3.2. In cases where a state has used legal and informal endorsements at different times (North Dakota and Massachusetts) these two methods are listed separately.

Table 3.3 shows for each state party the number of election years in which the gubernatorial primary was uncontested and those in which it was contested. In those years when data are available, it shows for uncontested races if there was any contest in the convention, and in contested races if the endorsed candidate won the primary. It is difficult to collect information, particularly for earlier years, on the action of endorsing conventions; such data are scattered thinly through newspaper accounts, books and articles, and occasionally party records. That is why Table 3.3 indicates that in some years information on endorsements is not available. In a couple of states (Colorado and Wisconsin), earlier primaries, for which less complete information is available, are listed separately from more recent ones. For some states, the years included in Table 3.3 are all of those during which legal or informal endorsements have been used. But the shortage of information has led to

Table 3.3
Primary Competition and Success of Party Endorsees

State	No. of Elections	Years	Party	Legal or Informal	No Primary Contest				Primary Contest			
					Tot.	Convention		?	Tot.	Endorsee		?
						Uncontested	Contest			Wins	Loses	
Colo.	5	50-58	Dem.	L	4	—	—	4	1	—	—	1
	5	50-58	Rep.	L	4	—	—	4	1	—	—	1
	6	62-82	Dem.	L	5	4	1	—	1	1	—	—
	6	62-82	Rep.	L	3	2	1	—	3	3	—	—
Conn.	7	58-82	Dem.	L	6	5	1	—	1	1	—	—
	7	58-82	Rep.	L	6	2	4	—	1	1	—	—
R.I.	17	50-82	Dem.	L	11	2	—	9	6	6	—	—
	17	50-82	Rep.	L	15	2	—	13	2	2	—	—
Utah	9	48-80	Dem.	L	3	3	—	—	6	6	—	—
	9	48-80	Rep.	L	2	1	1	—	7	4	3	—
N.Y.	4	70-82	Dem.	L	0	—	—	—	4	2	2	—
	4	70-82	Rep.	L	3	3	—	—	1	1	—	—

State		Years										
N.D.	8	50-64	Dem.	I	6	2	1	3	2	—	—	2
	8	50-64	Rep.	I	2	—	1	1	6	2	—	4
	4	68-80	Dem.	L	3	3	—	—	1	1	—	—
	4	68-80	Rep.	L	0	—	—	—	4	3	1	—
N.M.	4	64,66	Dem.	L	1	1	—	—	3	2	1	—
	4	78-82	Rep.	L	1	—	1	—	3	2	1	—
Mass.	8	54-70	Dem.	L	1	1	—	—	7	5	2	—
	8	54-70	Rep.	L	7	5	2	—	0	—	—	—
	1	82	Dem.	I	0	—	—	—	1	1	—	—
	3	74-82	Rep.	I	0	—	—	—	3	1	2	—
Idaho	2	66-70	Dem.	L	0	—	—	—	2	—	2	—
	2	66-70	Rep.	L	0	—	—	—	1	1	—	—
Minn.	8	58-82	Dem.	I	1	—	1	—	7	5	2	—
	7	60-82	Rep.	I	3	2	1	—	4	3	1	—
Wisc.	6	50-60	Rep.	I	5	—	—	5	1	1	—	—
	7	62-78	Rep.	I	3	2	1	—	4	3	1	—
Ill.	8	56-82	Dem.	I	3	3	—	—	5	4	1	—
Calif.	8	54-82	Dem.	I	0	—	—	—	5	5	—	—
	10	46-82	Rep.	I	1	1	—	—	8	6	2	—

Source: Compiled by the author.

the exclusion of data on endorsements in earlier years for the following states: Colorado, North Dakota (informal endorsements), New Mexico, Minnesota (Democrats), Illinois.*

Legal Endorsements

The effectiveness of the endorsement system is obvious in Colorado. The endorsed candidate has only been challenged in a primary one-third of the time since 1950, although Republican challenges have become more frequent in recent years. Since 1928 only one endorsee has been beaten in a gubernatorial primary (Eyre and Martin 1967, p. 51).

In Connecticut, primary competition is discouraged by both the law and party norms. The law requires that a candidate win 20 percent of the convention vote to get on the ballot. Party norms reinforce the principle that losing candidates should support the endorsee rather than entering a primary; some candidates make such a commitment when they seek convention support. Since the primary was established, only two gubernatorial candidates have entered the primary, both unsuccessfully — a Republican in 1970 and a Democrat in 1978. The Republican, who won 22 percent of the vote in convention, criticized the endorsement process in his campaign, but won only 20 percent of the primary vote. The Democratic challenge in 1978 came from the lieutenant governor, running against the incumbent governor; after barely winning 20 percent at the convention, he got one-third of the primary vote. It is worth noting that in 1982, when a Democratic candidate for secretary of state challenged the endorsee, it was the first time in either party that a candidate for one of the lesser statewide offices had made such a challenge.

The Rhode Island endorsement system is another one that has proved to be very effective. Since it was first established as part of the primary law, there have been primary contests in only one-fourth

---

*Newspaper reports were my main sources for information on endorsements in the states. There is detailed information for particular states in the following works: Illinois (Sittig 1962), California (Rowe 1961), and Massachusetts (Barbrook 1973). I received information from the Republican state committee in Minnesota.

of the gubernatorial races. Most of these contests have been in the Democratic primary, including four very close races involving factions and ethnic groups from 1958 through 1964. But in no case has a gubernatorial endorsee in either party been defeated. (Candidates endorsed for other offices have occasionally been defeated, however, including Democratic endorsees in the 1960 and 1976 Senate races.)

The endorsement system mandated by law in Utah gives an absolute advantage to candidates endorsed by the convention; there is no other way to get on the ballot. As originally drafted, the law required the convention to endorse two candidates for the primary — no more and no less. Amendments in 1963 and 1969 provided that there would be only one nominee (and thus no primary contest) if one candidate got 80 percent (the 1963 requirement) or 70 percent (the current requirement).

While endorsement systems in other states may discourage contested primaries and reduce the number of candidates, the Utah law encourages contests (though less completely than it used to) while banning more than two candidates. The next question is whether, with two endorsed candidates, the one getting the most convention votes usually wins. Table 3.3 shows that there have been three cases, all Republican, of a candidate winning the primary after coming in second in the endorsement. Two of these involved J. Bracken Lee, who defeated the top endorsee in 1948, but as the incumbent governor and top endorsee was beaten in the 1956 primary.

New York has had limited experience with preprimary conventions, and the record has been a mixed one. The law provides that a candidate must get a majority of the votes to be endorsed, but that any candidate who can get 25 percent of the vote on any ballot at the convention can get on the primary ballot without having to use petitions. (The voting system in convention is a weighted one, based on the party's vote in the last gubernatorial election in each county.)

Although these rules would appear to give the top endorsee a considerable advantage and restrict the number of candidates, the New York Democratic party, in particular, has developed a practice of giving the 25 percent endorsement to most serious candidates, by shifting support from one ballot to the next. In 1976 the Democratic convention went so far as to give majority endorsement to one senatorial candidate and provide 25 percent support to three others.

One reason why the Democratic convention has followed this practice is that leading candidates often want to avoid the charge that they are trying to dominate the convention and exclude challengers. This suggests that some New York politicians are not very comfortable with the endorsement process. In 1970 the only Democratic endorsee for governor was Arthur Goldberg, but he announced that he would also collect petitions to qualify for the ballot in an effort to avoid the image of being an establishment candidate.

As Table 3.3 shows, the Democratic convention endorsement has not proved to be very influential in New York. The gubernatorial endorsee has always been challenged, and two endorsees have been beaten. The last two governors of New York, Hugh Carey (in 1974) and Mario Cuomo (in 1982) won the governorship after defeating the convention endorsee in the primary. The story of Cuomo's success is discussed further in the next two chapters.

On the Republican side, the gubernatorial endorsements have been much more effective. In 1970, 1974, and 1978 the Republicans endorsed a candidate for governor without any open contest in the convention and with no primary challenge. In 1982 there was a four-way fight for the endorsement, and an unsuccessful challenge in the primary by the candidate who finished second at the convention. This convention will also be discussed in more detail in the next chapters.

Another state where the legal advantage enjoyed by the endorsee seems to have limited value is New Mexico, where any candidate winning 20 percent on the single convention ballot can avoid the necessity of filing petitions to enter the primary. Table 3.3 shows what has happened since 1964 in the four gubernatorial races held when endorsements were used. In six of the eight cases the primary has been contested, and on two occasions (both in 1966) the endorsee has lost. The endorsement process does seem to have accomplished another goal set by its sponsors: limiting the number of candidates and making possible a majority vote for the primary winner. In each of three contested Democratic primaries (1966, 1978, and 1982) the winner has had a majority, and in the first two there were only two candidates. Similarly, the Republican gubernatorial contests (in the same three years) have been won by majority votes with only two or three candidates.

Comparing Legal and Informal Endorsements

North Dakota and Massachusetts are states that would seem to share few political characteristics, but they are both states where it is possible to compare the effects of legal and informal endorsements, and also where the endorsement records of the two parties have been very different.

In North Dakota political parties have been holding endorsing conventions since the primary was adopted in 1907, but it was not until the 1968 primary that endorsing conventions gained legal authority. A full comparison between informal and legal endorsements is not possible because little information is available about early endorsements, but the data shown in Table 3.3 suggest that the establishment of a legal base for endorsements has had little impact on their effectiveness.

The most obvious contrasts in North Dakota are those between Democratic and Republican endorsements. In the 1950-80 period only 3 of 12 Democratic gubernatorial primaries, but 10 of 12 Republican primaries, were contested. Despite the frequency of Republican contests, there is only one example (in 1968) of an endorsee being beaten in the primary. (For the 1950-56 period information is lacking on the success of endorsees.)

The lack of Democratic primary competition in the 1960s and 1970s resulted from the success of Democratic governors. William Guy was elected in 1960 and won reelection in 1962, 1964, and 1968 — never having primary opposition. In 1972 Guy retired; Arthur Link won convention endorsement on the seventh ballot against three opponents, and had only minor primary opposition. Link was renominated without opposition in 1976 and 1980, though losing to a Republican in the latter year.

Republican nominations were much more closely contested in the convention and often in the primary during the same period. In some cases the endorsee was challenged in the primary by one of those who lost in the convention; in other cases the challenge came from someone who had bypassed the convention. There was never more than one challenger in the Republican primary, however. In 1968 there were five candidates seeking endorsement, and it took four ballots for someone to win a majority; the candidate who finished third at the convention won the primary. In 1972 the winner of the 1968 primary bypassed the convention and made an unsuccessful challenge in the primary to the endorsee, who had eliminated four rivals at the convention.

It is unusual for so many candidates to seek the nomination of a party out of power, but during the 1960s and 1970s the Democratic margin in North Dakota gubernatorial races was usually under 55 percent, and Republican prospects always looked strong. The effect of the endorsing convention was to eliminate a number of candidates, though not usually to prevent a primary. The Republican who finally won the governorship in 1980, Allen Olson, defeated two candidates in the convention, and then easily won the primary against an opponent who had scorned the convention route.

In Massachusetts there have been dramatic differences between the Democratic and Republican conventions. During the eight elections with legal endorsing procedures (1954-80), the Republican endorsee was nominated seven times without a primary challenge; in 1958 the endorsee died and the party executive committee selected a replacement. The Democratic endorsee, however, was challenged in seven of the eight elections; the primaries were often close, and two of the endorsees were defeated. After the law authorizing conventions was repealed, the Republican party held informal conventions, but they were much less effective than the legal ones had been. The gubernatorial endorsee was regularly challenged, and in both 1978 and 1982 the endorsee was beaten in the primary.

As noted earlier, the Republican party had taken the initiative in getting the endorsing system approved by the Massachusetts legislature, and the party used the conventions to put together slates that were carefully balanced, both ethnically and geographically. Frequently the gubernatorial candidate was nominated by acclamation; on the few occasions when there was a contest for endorsement, the losers did not enter the primary. One of the very few convention battles that carried over into the primary was a 1962 contest for attorney general between two candidates who went on to greater political success thereafter: Edward Brooke and Elliot Richardson. Brooke won both the convention designation and the primary election.

The first informal Republican convention was held in 1974 and it featured a surprising challenge to incumbent Governor Francis Sargent. Sargent won two-thirds of the convention vote against a right-wing opponent, who carried the fight into the primary. Sargent won the primary by nearly as large a margin, but lost the general election. Four years later the winner of the Republican convention was defeated in the primary, and the Republicans failed to capitalize on Democratic disunity and lost the election. In 1982 the Republican convention endorsee was beaten again — by a candidate who had not even sought the convention's endorsement. The 1982 convention will be examined more carefully in the next chapter.

The Democratic party in Massachusetts for many years has been torn by factional conflicts, rooted in ethnic and geographic factors and ideological disagreements, but often centered around strong personalities. The convention system might have been a technique for negotiating compromises and creating balanced tickets, but it was not. Instead it became an arena in which the preliminary battles were fought leading to the main event — the primary election. Party workers who had supported losing candidates in the convention were often angered by the tactics used and pressures exerted by the winning candidate, and worked even harder for their candidate in the primary.

In the first two Democratic conventions, in 1954 and 1956, the winner of the gubernatorial endorsement also had to win a primary against a candidate who had not sought endorsement. In 1956 an attempt to bind all candidates to accept the decision of the convention failed, and several endorsees for other statewide offices lost in the primary. In 1958 Governor Foster Furcolo became the only gubernatorial candidate whose endorsement was not contested in a primary. Two years later the endorsee, Joseph Ward, had six opponents in the primary and won by only 30 percent (Barbrook 1973, ch. 5).

In 1964 Endicott Peabody won a narrow convention endorsement and an easy primary victory over the third-place finisher in the convention; he also was elected governor. But Peabody succeeded in alienating many Democrats during his two-year term, and was challenged in the convention by his lieutenant governor. Peabody won convention endorsement but narrowly lost the primary to Lieutenant Governor Francis Bellotti, in a campaign that rekindled ethnic divisions in the party. The Democrats lost the election in 1964, and also those in 1966 and 1970, years in which once again the convention fights were repeated in the primary. In 1970 the endorsee lost in a four-way primary where the winner's margin was 34 percent (Barbrook 1973, ch. 7).

It was not surprising that many Democratic politicians believed that the convention system was a liability rather than an asset to the party and that the Democratic majority in the legislature succeeded in repealing the law establishing endorsements. In the next two elections the Democrats elected a governor, Michael Dukakis, and then after four years defeated him in the primary, choosing Edward King in his place. The events that led to the establishment of an informal Democratic endorsing convention in 1982, and Dukakis's success in winning its endorsement, and the primary, will be described in succeeding chapters.

Informal Endorsing Systems

The impact of informal party endorsing systems is difficult to determine in states where the endorsements are carried out privately or where the media pay little attention to the process. In such cases it is difficult to compile accurate information about endorsements. In this section I will review the results of endorsements in four states. Both parties in Minnesota and the Republican party in Wisconsin have held large-scale, well-publicized endorsing conventions for many years. The Illinois Democratic Central Committee has made endorsements for a long time and, although the decision-making process is not public, the results are. Several informal party groups in California have held conventions to make preprimary endorsements.

Although the Minnesota Democratic-Farmer-Labor party (DFL) has made endorsements since its establishment in 1944, the data in Table 3.3 begin with the year 1958; the Republican data begin in 1960, when the party adopted the policy of regular endorsements. The endorsements have seldom prevented primaries, particularly in the DFL, but the endorsees have usually won these primaries by comfortable margins, often against token opposition. Until 1982 there had only been one example of an endorsee losing; that occurred in 1966 when the DFL endorsed a challenger to the incumbent governor. In 1982 the endorsees of both parties were defeated; this breakdown of the endorsing system will be described in future chapters.

The most common pattern in the DFL has been for a candidate to be endorsed without opposition in the convention and to face minor opposition in the primary. One reason for this has been that the endorsee has frequently been the incumbent governor (in 1958, 1960, 1974, and 1978). In 1966, however, the Democratic governor was Karl Rolvaag, whom many Democrats believed to be too weak to win reelection. A bitterly divided state convention required 20 ballots before finally endorsing Lieutenant Governor Sandy Keith for the gubernatorial nomination by the two-thirds margin then required. (A 60 percent vote is now needed.) Governor Rolvaag launched a campaign that was effective enough to win a 68 percent majority in the primary, and obviously picked up a large sympathy vote; but he was defeated in the general election (Lebedoff 1969).

The Republican party has had more close and prolonged contests in its convention, but its gubernatorial primaries (until 1982) have been infrequent and lopsided. The normal pattern has been for those candidates who are beaten in the convention to support the endorsed candidate. In the four contested primaries during this period (1966, 1970, 1978, and 1982) the opposition has come from candidates who did not seek endorsement. The most prolonged convention battle for gubernatorial endorsement occurred in 1966 when 16 ballots were required to select an endorsee in a four-man race. In 1970 five ballots were required in a two-man race. The requirement of a 60 percent vote for endorsement obviously leads to more balloting than would a simple majority requirement. On balance, the endorsing system used by both parties in Minnesota seems to have achieved its purposes with a high degree of consistency, although its failure in 1982 has raised some questions about its future effectiveness.

Since it began making endorsements regularly, the Wisconsin Republican party has usually been successful in avoiding close, divisive primaries and only one of its gubernatorial endorsees has been beaten in the primary. Although details are lacking, during the 1950-60 period most of the convention endorsements apparently were made without significant conflict. (In 1956, however, the Republican convention failed to endorse Republican Senator Alexander Wiley and he defeated the endorsee in the primary.) One of the closest races was in 1962, when the endorsee won a narrow convention victory and had to defeat two other candidates in the primary.

In 1978 the endorsement system proved ineffective. The convention narrowly endorsed U.S. Representative Robert Kasten over

Lee Dreyfus, but Dreyfus challenged Kasten successfully in the primary and was elected governor. As noted earlier, in 1979 the party decided to make endorsements optional, and in 1982 it endorsed no one for governor.

The Cook County Democratic party in Illinois has retained much of its political power in an age when most local political machines were losing their control. Therefore, it is not surprising to find that the leaders of that party have played a vigorous and usually successful role in the state nominating process. For many years the Illinois Democratic State Central Committee has chosen a slate of candidates, and that selection process has been dominated by the members from Cook County. During his years in power, Mayor Richard Daley largely controlled that process.

During the 1956-82 period, there were primary contests in five of the eight elections, but the endorsee was defeated only once. In both 1956 and 1960 the endorsee was challenged in the primary by candidates who criticized the endorsement process; both endorsees won with close to 60 percent of the vote. (In 1956, however, the endorsee was caught up in a scandal after the primary and had to be replaced by the Central Committee.) In the next two elections the endorsements went unchallenged (Sittig 1962, ch. 5).

The most serious challenge to the endorsement system came in 1972 when the endorsee, Lieutenant Governor Paul Simon, was narrowly defeated in the primary by Daniel Walker, who had not sought the endorsement. It was the first time a gubernatorial endorsee had lost since 1936, when the organization refused to endorse the incumbent governor. During his term as govenor, Daniel Walker continued to feud with Mayor Daley and the organization. The Mayor persuaded Secretary of State Michael Howlett to run in 1976, with the organization's endorsement, and Howlett defeated Walker in the primary, by 54 percent.

Since that time, the Illinois Democratic organization has had no difficulty in getting its endorsee nominated, although in both 1978 and 1982 it selected candidates (Michael Bakalis and Adlai Stevenson) who were not clearly allied with the organization but who appeared to be the strongest candidates available. Some political observers in Illinois have criticized the endorsement system in recent years on the grounds that the Cook County leaders have failed to construct well-balanced tickets that would have appeal in other parts of the state.

As noted earlier, preprimary endorsements developed in California because of the weaknesses of the political parties and the havoc created by the cross-filing system. The endorsements have been made, not by the official party organization but by informal party groups. The endorsements served a valuable purpose in their early years, but there is little evidence that they have had much influence in recent years.

During its early years the California Republican Assembly (CRA) was very successful. Most major candidates sought its endorsement; those not endorsed often dropped out; and most endorsees defeated whatever primary opponents they had. The gubernatorial candidates endorsed by the CRA had little difficulty in the convention or the primary. This included such strong candidates as Earl Warren, William Knowland, and Richard Nixon. In 1966 the CRA endorsed Ronald Reagan, who won two-thirds of the vote in the primary, and who was renominated in 1970 without opposition.

Since that time, however, the influence of the CRA has declined. One important reason is that a number of other Republican groups, representing different ideological positions, have sprung up and have made their own endorsements. The California Republican League represents the moderate wing of the party, while the misnamed United Republicans of California represents its right wing. In none of the last three primaries has there been an incumbent running or any other dominant Republican. In 1978 there were seven candidates and the winner managed to get only 40 percent of the vote. The gubernatorial candidates endorsed by the CRA in 1974 and 1978 both lost the primary. In 1982 the CRA was unable to reach the two-thirds majority needed for a gubernatorial endorsement; Lieutenant Governor Mike Curb got 198 of the 200 required votes in the convention, but lost the primary.

In its early years the California Democratic Council (CDC) also played a major role in nominations. Its endorsements frequently led other candidates to drop out, and this helped to block cross-filed Republicans from winning the Democratic primary. The CDC did not lose a primary until a Senate race in 1964. The CDC-endorsed gubernatorial candidates won in 1954, 1958, 1962, and 1966. The voters elected Democrat Pat Brown as governor in 1958 and reelected him in 1962. Although Brown breezed through the 1958 and 1962 primaries, in 1966 he had five opponents and won a bare majority before losing to Ronald Reagan.

The CDC made no gubernatorial endorsements in 1970, 1974, and 1982; its only recent endorsement occurred in 1978, when it supported Governor Jerry Brown in his reelection bid. The repeated failure of the CDC to make endorsements indicates how much its influence has eroded. During the 1960s the organization aroused the resentment of many Democrats, including elected officials, because of its strongly liberal position and its vigorous criticism of the Johnson Administration's policies in Vietnam. Democratic office holders questioned the right of the organization to define the ideological and policy standards that they should adhere to. Many Democratic candidates perceived the CDC endorsement to be more of a liability than an asset.

In 1974 the CDC convention was unable to reach the required 60 percent level of agreement to endorse anyone. One candidate, Jerome Waldie, got 47 percent of the convention vote, and finished fifth in the primary. Jerry Brown, the eventual primary winner, got only 17 percent of the CDC vote. In 1982 Tom Bradley, the obvious Democratic front-runner, decided not to seek the CDC endorsement, and as a result the CDC decided to make no endorsement. It seems unlikely that the CDC will regain any significant influence over the nominating process in California.

Conclusions

What conclusions can be drawn about the effectiveness of endorsements, and the conditions under which they are most effective? The answer, of course, depends on what we mean by effectiveness. The goals of those political leaders who established endorsement systems, either by law or by party rule, differed from state to state. Some were trying to gain control over nominations for the party organization; others were seeking an advantage for a particular group or faction; some were concerned with maximizing their party's chances for election.

It is possible to summarize some of the consequences of endorsements statistically, although we should recognize that averages will obscure important variations among the states. One consequence of endorsements is a reduction in primary competition. If the data in Table 3.3 are summarized, they show that there were contested primaries in 42.3 percent of cases when legal endorsements were in effect, and in 65.7 percent of cases with informal party endorsements. This compares to contested contests in 77.5 percent of all other primaries held in northern states from the 1946-50 period through 1982. (These other cases would include a few elections where endorsements occurred but we lack data on them.) These findings suggest that legal endorsements have greater effects on competition than informal ones.

In several states, notably New York, North Dakota, and Massachusetts the effects of endorsement are quite different in the two parties. If we make comparisons between parties in the states as a whole, we find that in legal endorsement states there were contests in 48.5 percent of Democratic primaries and 35.9 percent of Republican ones. In the states with informal endorsements there were only trivial differences between the parties, but this is misleading because Wisconsin and Illinois had endorsements only in one party.

In those cases where there were primary contests and where data are available on the result of endorsements the endorsed candidate won the primary 77 percent of the time, with no important difference between legal and informal endorsements. This suggests that the endorsement is usually a considerable advantage to a candidate. Many of the endorsements, however, go to incumbents and other strong candidates, who would presumably win without any endorsement machinery.

There is no clear evidence of a trend toward greater or less success for endorsed candidates. There are only two examples of losses by endorsed candidates before 1964, but data on endorsements are available for only a few states during the 1950s. In the four election years, 1964-70, eight endorsees lost; in the 1972-78 period, there were seven losses; none lost in 1980; and four lost in 1982, all in states to be examined more fully in later chapters.

As we have examined endorsements in each state, it has become obvious that the way the endorsement system works, and its consequences, are dependent on a number of variables, such as the strength of the party organization. The principle of endorsement appears to be more solidly established in some states than in others; this is particularly evident when candidates who make a strong showing in the convention but lose decide not to enter the primary.

The best way to understand how endorsement systems work, how they vary among states, and what effects they have is to examine a few systems in more detail. The next chapter examines the

1982 endorsing conventions held in both parties in Massachusetts, Connecticut, New York, Minnesota, and New Mexico. Chapter 5 is an effort to answer questions about the impact of endorsements on primary elections, also using these five states as examples.

4

Conventions in 1982:
Case Studies of State Parties

National political party conventions are familiar to all of us through television: the crowded convention halls, the exuberant demonstrations, the overblown oratory, and the occasionally exciting roll call votes. Those who pay closer attention to national conventions also understand the importance of rules and procedures, the strategy of candidates, and the dynamics of the convention process.

Most Americans, and perhaps most political scientists, have never seen a state political convention – particularly one called to endorse state candidates (rather than nominating delegates to national conventions). The visitor to a state convention finds that it appears to be a smaller and briefer version of the national convention. There is the same atmosphere on the floor, the same demonstrations with bands and balloons, speeches from the podium that replicate the oratory of national meetings, and a larger number of – and more exciting – roll calls. Watching the demonstrations at a state convention, one suspects that delegates have learned their roles from watching national conventions.

There are some differences among the state conventions that are obvious on the surface. One is a matter of size. The 1982 Massachusetts Democratic convention had almost 3,300 delegates, more than attended a national convention, meeting in a large arena. The New York Republican state committee members, numbering about 400, were crowded into a hotel ballroom. There are differences in style. The 1,200-plus delegates to the Minnesota Democratic-Farmer-Labor convention were seated at long tables in the large auditorium so that they could keep track of the stacks of material related to the party platform, which was a major focus of attention. The New York Republican committee skipped over the platform — to be adopted at a later meeting.

The careful observer of the state conventions will discover that they differ from the national conventions, and from each other, in a number of important ways. While the national conventions in recent years have often met to confirm a choice of candidates made in the primaries, the state conventions are the first real test of candidate strength. Moreover, the state convention decisions are subject to challenge in the primary elections that follow, unless the losing candidates are forced out or drop out.

The state conventions differ from one another in important ways. Some conventions have a long historical tradition; some are relatively new. Some have legal foundation; others are informal. Candidates in some states must win a minimum percentage at the convention to get on the ballot; in other states, losing candidates or those who bypass the convention may collect voter signatures on petitions. Some conventions take only a single ballot; others may require many ballots to get a majority or an extraordinary majority such as 60 percent.

In addition to these variations in the institution and its rules and procedures, the conventions held in any year differ from one another because of political circumstances. An incumbent governor may be seeking renomination; there may be a challenge to the endorsee by a well-financed outsider; a convention may be dominated by controversies over issues; there may be serious disagreements over the rules for the convention — with implications for the fate of candidates.

During the spring and summer of 1982 I visited the state endorsing conventions of seven state parties in five states: both party conventions in Minnesota and New York, and conventions of the Connecticut Republicans, the New Mexico Democrats, and the Massachusetts Democrats. I observed the proceedings, interviewed a few party leaders, and exchanged notes with other political scientists. After the conventions, I sent out a brief questionnaire to a random sample of delegates who had attended. I also sent questionnaires to a sample of delegates attending the other three party conventions in these five states.

The analysis of the state endorsing conventions in this chapter and the next one is based on these first-hand observations, press accounts of the conventions and the prior delegate selection process, and the questionnaires sent to delegates. The questionnaires were brief, two- or three-page ones, with a mixture of closed- and open-ended questions. Although some questions were used consistently for most state parties, some were varied to fit particular circumstances of a state convention. Delegates were asked not to put their names on the questionnaires. The response rate for the questionnaires was 48.3 percent, except in New York where it was only 26 percent. Detailed information on the sample is found in the appendix.

This chapter will begin with a description of the process by which delegates were selected to the convention, and a brief summary of information on the political background of delegates. Most of the chapter will be devoted to case studies of the conventions — particularly those that I observed in person. Chapter 5 will be an assessment of the endorsement process and its consequences in the primary in these five states, based on the same sources and (in Massachusetts) on a survey of voters.

THE DELEGATE-SELECTION PROCESS

There are many ways of selecting delegates to nominating or endorsing conventions: They may be selected by voters in primaries, chosen by party activists in local caucuses, or appointed by party leaders or committees. The primary and caucus systems are used for choosing delegates to national nominating conventions. The delegates to the eight state endorsing conventions (excluding New York) were generally chosen by party caucuses open to any member of the party, but attended by those most active in the party and/or most interested in particular candidates. Some delegates were chosen directly by local caucuses; some were chosen at county or district conventions by delegates who had been elected at local caucuses. (Massachusetts Republicans, however, were chosen by local party committees.)

The exact mechanics for selecting delegates is relatively unimportant. It is more interesting to find out how much participation there is in the process and how much conflict is involved. Are the delegates hand-picked by a few party leaders, or is there substantial attendance at caucuses? Do candidates for governor — or other major office — try to recruit persons to run as delegates, or get commitments from those interested in running, before they are elected? How frequently are there contests for delegate positions, and are such contests a result of conflicts among gubernatorial, or other, candidates? To what extent do delegates make commitments to candidates, particularly in the gubernatorial races, before their election? Are conflicts over issues involved to any extent in the delegate selection process?

At the risk of oversimplifying what may be a complicated and varied process, I would suggest two quite different models of selecting delegates. In the first, a party organization model, the local party leaders put together a slate of loyal activists to run for delegate. If party caucuses are held, turnout is limited to the party faithful and there is little or no challenge to the slate. Once elected, the delegates representing a county or city meet with the leadership to reach consensus, if possible, on the candidates they will support — expecting that a united position will enhance the political leverage of the local party.

The second, or candidate organization model, is one in which the candidates for major statewide office seek to elect their own delegates. This may be done by recruiting persons in each local unit who have been active in the party and are likely to become delegates and/or by mobilizing supporters of the candidate to attend caucuses and elect their own people as delegates. To the extent that this model prevails in a state, it may be possible to determine the probable endorsee before the convention meets. Obviously if there are contests for several major offices, such as governor, senator, and attorney general, a number of candidate organizations may have supporters at local caucuses, and may engage in bargaining during the selection process, producing delegates who have commitments to candidates at several levels.

The two models do not exhaust the possibilities. It would be possible to have an unorganized model, in which persons active and interested in politics show up at caucuses and elect delegates without any leadership being exercised by party or candidate organizations. It would also be possible to have a selection process in which candidates for delegate were recruited and supporters mobilized by leaders interested in issues rather than candidates.

How well do the state parties in our sample fit any of these models? We should not expect any selection system to fit any model perfectly, and we should recognize that variations occur within a party from one locality to another. Table 4.1 shows data collected from delegate questionnaires that answer at least some of our questions.

The Connecticut parties best fit the model of delegate selection controlled by the party organization. The first step in the process is the endorsement of a slate of delegates by a local party committee, or a caucus, depending on local party rules. There selections can be challenged in a primary election by others who want to be delegates, but this is relatively rare. Only 4 percent of the Democratic delegates and 11 percent of the Republican ones were involved in a primary election (Table 4.1).

In 1982 candidate organizations made little effort to influence selection of Democratic delegates — perhaps because the gubernatorial nomination was one-sided. On the Republican side, there seem to have been some attempts by supporters of gubernatorial or senatorial candidates to influence the choice of delegates, and among the small number of selections that were decided in a primary, a majority involved such candidate slates. A third of the Republican delegates were asked about their gubernatorial or senatorial preferences (and usually both). More than two-thirds of the Democratic delegates and half of the Republicans reported that their local delegations made some effort to reach consensus on one or both of the major statewide races. Such efforts were much more likely to be successful in the Democratic gubernatorial race — with the governor seeking renomination — than in either of the Republican races; the Democratic Senate nomination was uncontested.

In one sense, the New York state parties fit the party organization model. The delegates, of course, are not elected to an endorsing convention, but are members of the central committee; this means that candidate organizations must deal with these established party leaders. Moreover, more than two-thirds of the Democrats and half of the Republicans reported that some efforts were made by the party organization at the local level to reach consensus on major candidates. When asked why these efforts were made, delegates emphasized several advantages of unity: The local organization would gain political clout or leverage, improve its chances of getting

Table 4.1
Pre-Convention Experiences of Delegates
(in percentages)

Experience	Conn.		Minn.		N.M.		Mass.		N.Y.	
	Dem.	Rep.	Dem.	Rep.	Dem.	Rep.	Dem.	Rep.	Dem.	Rep.
Opposed in caucus or primary	4	11	—	54	70	69	88	43	—	—
Asked to support gubernatorial candidate before election	—	30	—	—	77	81	79	71	—	—
Committed to gubernatorial candidate before election	—	—	41	24	58	65	91	35	—	—
Local party sought unity or commitment from delegate	70	51	—	—	20	22	32	31	70	54
(n)	(89)	(180)	(225)	(217)	(127)	(97)	(250)	(192)	(66)	(69)

Source: Compiled by the author.

74

state patronage, increase its influence on the candidate selection process, and avoid the dangers arising from a split in the local ranks.

The New Mexico delegate selection process is a good example of the candidate organization model. Except in a few counties, the local party organizations do not appear to be strong. Only about one-fifth of the delegates said that local party leaders asked them to support a particular gubernatorial candidate. The candidates for major statewide offices, particularly governor and senator, tried to run slates of delegates as much as possible. About 70 percent of the delegates — a comparatively high figure — said that they had opposition when they ran as delegates. About four-fifths of the delegates said they were contacted by gubernatorial candidates before their election; substantial majorities said they made commitments to gubernatorial candidates before being elected. When the results of the selection process reached the gubernatorial candidates' headquarters, claims were made about the number of delegates won that provided a roughly accurate estimate of the delegate support that each actually gained at the convention.

The best example of strong candidate organizations having an impact on delegate selection is found in the Massachusetts Democratic party, particularly in the case of the organization supporting former Governor Dukakis. The Dukakis forces, many of whom had been active in the movement to establish an endorsing convention, decided to make an all-out effort to win that convention, as part of a broad strategy of building a strong organizational base. Governor Edward King's organization was opposed to the principle of an endorsing convention, and moved much more slowly to mobilize its forces, despite the advantages that an incumbent administration would be expected to have in organizational contests. A third candidate, Lieutenant Governor Thomas O'Neill, also joined the active search for delegates.

It was estimated that some 100,000 Democrats attended nearly 600 caucuses across the state, and when the results were tabulated estimates were published showing that Dukakis had 67 percent of the delegates, King 22 percent, O'Neill 5 percent, and 5 percent uncommitted. At the convention, with O'Neill no longer running, Dukakis won 68 percent and King 32 percent. Delegate questionnaires indicated that almost 90 percent were elected with opposition, and approximately the same number made a commitment to a candidate before they were elected. Less than one-third of the delegates, slightly more for King delegates, reported some effort by their local party leaders to get them to support a gubernatorial candidate. Less than one-third of the Massachusetts Democratic delegates reported holding a party office, the lowest figure reported for any state party.

The situation in the Massachusetts Republican party is quite different. Almost 70 percent of the delegates report holding party office. They were elected by local committees, not open caucuses; 43 percent reported having opposition in their election; and only 35 percent made a commitment to a candidate before being elected. At the time delegates were elected, the leading candidates issued contradictory statements about the number of committed delegates each had, although the estimates made by the top candidate, John Lakian, turned out to be reasonably accurate.

The delegate selection process in the Minnesota Independent Republican party does not fit neatly into either the party or candidate organization model. There were five major candidates seeking convention endorsement for governor, and they seem to have made only limited efforts to run slates of delegates, partly because some of them entered the race late when the front runner appeared to be faltering. Only one-fourth of the delegates reported that they had made a commitment before being elected. In previous years it has been the practice for local party leaders to be elected as convention delegates, apparently with little opposition.

In 1982, however, the Republican precinct caucuses were invaded by large numbers of persons with strong ideological commitments, particularly to pro-life, pro-family, and morality issues. Some were active in pro-life organizations, and many were evangelical Christians, mobilized by local church groups to get to the precinct caucuses. A large proportion of them were also supporting the gubernatorial candidacy of Glen Sherwood, whose platform was based on these issues. When delegates elected at the precinct meetings met at district and county caucuses to choose state convention delegates, a number of compromises were made in order to include more party regulars as delegates. The delegate survey showed that 58 percent had attended the previous convention – a relatively high figure; but 54 percent said that they had won election as delegates with opposition. According to the survey, when they decided to seek election, 14 percent of the delegates were primarily interested in candidates, 25 percent in issues, and 22 percent in both; 38 percent answered neither. Moral and economic issues were most often mentioned.

The delegate selection used by the Minnesota DFL is unique. It is not dominated by party organizations, although two-thirds of the 1982 delegates had attended the previous convention. It is not candidate dominated, although in 1982 some candidates, particularly those running for attorney general, tried to get their loyal supporters elected as delegates. Issues play a larger role in party conventions, and in the delegate selection process, than in the other parties being studied. When asked about their major interest in seeking election, 37 percent of delegates said issues, 11 percent said candidates, and 43 percent said both; only 9 percent mentioned neither. Of those emphasizing issues, 84 percent listed the question of abortion (with a slight majority being pro-choice), but large numbers mentioned ERA, the nuclear freeze, and a variety of economic issues.

Issues are incorporated into the DFL selection process in an unusual fashion. When delegates chosen in precinct caucuses meet at the district or county level to elect state delegates, they usually organize into subcaucuses. Anyone at the caucus can try to organize a subcaucus by attracting enough persons to elect one state delegate. Elections are strictly proportional; if the county is entitled to 10 state delegates and 100 persons attend the caucus, any subcaucus of 10 persons can elect one delegate. Of the DFL delegates who answered the survey, 82 percent were elected by a subcaucus. There are some counties that do not use the subcaucus system, and efforts to organize them may fail in some caucuses.

The organizer of a subcaucus may give it any label he or she chooses: an issue or cluster of issues, a candidate or group of candidates, even a combination of issues and candidates. The organizer may broaden the title to attract more members. According to the delegate survey, the types of caucuses (and the percentage of delegates elected by each) were: one or more candidates only (5 percent), candidate(s) and a broadly defined issue — such as progressive (12), a broad issue only (22), candidate(s) and specific issue(s) (9), a single issue (26), several issues (9), no subcaucus (18). Of the 26 percent mentioning a single issue, 20 percent specified a pro- or anti-abortion subcaucus.

The subcaucus selection process is symptomatic of the extraordinary issue orientation of DFL party activists. It is noteworthy that the precinct, district, and county caucuses also frequently pass resolutions on a variety of issues, and these are forwarded to the next convention level. But the subcaucus also is a mechanism that encourages persons to become active in the DFL in order to win support for particular issues. In recent years it has contributed to escalation of the abortion issue as a dominant question that deeply divides the DFL.

DELEGATES AS PARTY ACTIVISTS

What kinds of persons attend state party conventions? Are they experienced party workers with a long record of party organizational activity? Or are they complete amateurs, drawn to political activity by their interest in a particular candidate or issue? How much experience have they had with political conventions? How familiar are they with the norms and procedures of conventions?

A limited amount of evidence is available to answer these questions in several of the states, based on questionnaires sent to delegates (Table 4.2). In New York, of course, the endorsements are made by members of the state committee, who serve four-year terms and often have extensive experience in party affairs. In most of the other state parties, we find that half to two-thirds of the delegates hold some kind of political party office at the local or state level. The percentages are lower in New Mexico, particularly for Democrats. The lowest proportion of delegates holding party office, less than one-third, is found in Massachusetts. Although the Democratic contest in Massachusetts was often seen as a struggle between old-time professionals supporting King and the new breed of amateurs supporting Dukakis, the proportion of delegates holding party office was almost the same for supporters of the two candidates. The Massachusetts Republican party has the highest percentage (69) of delegates holding party office, perhaps because the delegates were selected by ward and town committee chairmen across the state rather than by caucuses open to all members of the party — the pattern prevailing in other state parties.

Data from questionnaires in three states provide evidence on previous attendance at party conventions (Table 4.2). The most experienced delegates are found in Connecticut, where two-thirds of the Democrats and half of the Republicans attended the 1978

Table 4.2
Party Experience of Delegates
(in percentages)

	Conn.		Minn.		N.M.		Mass.		N.Y.	
Experience	Dem.	Rep.	Dem.	Rep.	Dem.	Rep.	Dem.	Rep.	Dem.	Rep.
Holds any party office	60	53	67	58	36	46	31	69	–	–
Attended past conventions:										
last one	67	52	42	50	–	–	35	–	–	–
last two			21	28			12			
(n)	(89)	(180)	(225)	(217)	(127)	(97)	(250)	(192)	(66)	(69)

Source: Compiled by the author.

state convention. Connecticut remains a state with relatively strong party organizations. In Minnesota half of those attending the Independent Republican convention and over 40 percent of the DFL delegates had attended the 1980 convention; substantial proportions had attended both the 1978 and 1980 conventions. The figure for Minnesota Republicans presumably would have been higher except for the influx of a number of political amateurs from church groups supporting a particular candidate. Although the Massachusetts Democrats had not held a regular convention for many years, it held an issues convention in 1981 and a charter convention in 1979. One-third of the delegates had attended the more recent one and 12 percent had attended both. The questionnaire sent to Massachusetts Republicans did not include this question, but party officials estimated that most of the delegates had attended previous conventions.

CASE STUDIES OF STATE CONVENTIONS IN 1982

Every state convention is different, not only because of variations in legal status, rules, and procedures, but because of different political realities. The purpose of case studies is not to overwhelm the reader with details about particular candidates and issues, but to create a better understanding of the convention process and the reasons for variation in that process. This section includes case studies of eight conventions, including all of those where first-hand observation was possible. Most of our attention will be on gubernatorial races, but occasionally we should examine other contests as well because of the light they shed on the convention endorsement process.

Table 4.3 summarizes the most important legal and procedural characteristics of the conventions and defines the size in terms of the number of voting delegates.

Most of the state conventions met for one and a half or two days. A common pattern is to meet for one long evening and all of the next day; others start one morning and end late the next afternoon. They often meet on Friday, Saturday, or Sunday. The conventions are open to the public, and often held in large arenas, with ample room in the balconies for spectators or nondelegate supporters of candidates. Press and television coverage is extensive although not so pervasive as at national conventions.

Table 4.3
Characteristics of Conventions

Characteristics	Conn.		Minn.		N.M.		Mass.		N.Y.	
	Dem.	Rep.	Dem.	Rep.	Dem.	Rep.	Dem.	Rep.	Dem.	Rep.
Legal (L) or Informal (I)	L	L	I	I	L	L	I	I	L	L
Law or party rule requires candidates seek endorsement	X	X			X	X	X			
Law or rule sets minimum % required to run in primary	20	20					15			
Law sets minimum % required to run in primary without petition					20	20			25	25
Percent required to endorse or only single ballot (S)	51	51	60	60	S	S	51	51	51	51
Number of delegates	1,300	933	1,286	2,025	1,712	750	3,359	1,348	357	390

Source: Compiled by the author.

Connecticut Republicans: The Power of Endorsement

Connecticut is a state with strong party organizations, and the Republican convention provides the best example in 1982 of an effective endorsement process. There were major struggles at the convention over the endorsements for governor and for senator, and in both cases the endorsee went unchallenged in the primary.

The Republicans who gathered in Hartford in late July faced two major decisions: Which gubernatorial candidate had the best chance to defeat the Democratic incumbent? Should the Republican party reject its incumbent Senator Lowell Weicker, and seek to replace him with Prescott Bush, the vice president's brother? The two contests were intertwined in rather subtle ways, although there were no alliances between gubernatorial and senatorial candidates. The endorsement contest was much closer in the governor's race, and much more bitter in the senatorial race.

The two leading candidates for governor were Lewis Rome and Richard Bozzuto, both former members and former floor leaders of the state Senate. Rome had the reputation of being a skillful compromiser, but low-keyed. Bozzuto had the reputation of being more aggressive and sometimes abrasive. Four years earlier Rome had sought the governorship, but accepted the lieutenant governor's nomination and then lost the election. Two years earlier Bozzuto had failed to be endorsed for U.S. senator, and lost a close and expensive primary for that office. A third candidate was a current state senator, Gerald Labriola. A fourth candidate dropped out a few days before the convention.

Senator Lowell Weicker faced a primary challenge for reasons of both personality and ideology. He is a blunt, abrasive man who had feuded with some party leaders and neglected others. He is also an independent, or maverick, in the Senate who had often spoken and voted against the programs of President Reagan. Those Republicans who, for a variety of reasons, wanted to oust Weicker rallied around Prescott Bush, an unlikely choice in several respects. Bush had never been elected to office, except for a seat on a local town meeting over 35 years ago; and he is hardly a charismatic figure or a dynamic speaker. The fact that his brother is George Bush would not appear to be an asset in the eyes of ultra-conservatives; presumably Jesse Helms does not have a brother in Connecticut.

In the weeks and days before the convention political maneuvers and rumors dominated the headlines. The most dramatic development was the endorsement of Weicker by the state party chairman, Ralph Capecelatro, who became convinced that only Weicker could defeat Democratic Congressman Toby Moffett in the Senate race. The maverick Weicker had organizational support, and Bush was cast into the unexpected role of outsider. At the same time Chairman Capecelatro endorsed Rome for governor and continued a struggle with Bozzuto over the selection of a chairman for the convention.

The 933 Republican convention delegates met in a large room with a low ceiling in the lower level of a shopping mall. Delegates seeking relief from the marathon sessions in the warm, crowded room could escape to the shopping center, and would often return licking ice cream cones. Arrayed along one side of the convention hall were several raised platforms where the coordinators for each of the major candidates huddled around phones and directed the floor workers with walkie-talkies.

The first evening of the convention was devoted largely to nominating speeches for both governor and senator. The speeches in the gubernatorial contest were standard political oratory, but those in the senatorial race were hard-hitting attacks on the other candidate. Senator Weicker was repeatedly attacked by Bush speakers for failing to support President Reagan. One of those endorsing Weicker described his opponents as a small band conducting an inquisition. He attacked Bush for his lack of a track record: "A political race is a marathon and you don't take a taxi to the finish line. There is no divine right of brotherhood in Connecticut." He asserted that Bush could not be elected, but would pull the ticket down to defeat with him, and urged him to get out of the race.

To an observer who had spent much of the summer watching state conventions, the most memorable feature of the first night in Hartford was the band. In contrast to others I had seen, the band hired by Bozzuto was a large, well-trained, dramatically conducted band that led the demonstrators onto the floor, moved to the front of the hall, and played with precision and enthusiasm — a performance that aroused and entertained the delegates, whether or not it changed votes. And late in the evening, when the senatorial speeches finally ended, the same band was back reincarnated as the leader of the Weicker demonstration, playing with the same enthusiasm. It proved impossible to read any political meaning into bandmanship, however. There was no alliance between Bozzuto and Weicker, and the events of the next day were to prove that a winning band does not guarantee convention endorsement.

Saturday morning the convention got down to the serious business of endorsing candidates − a process that took 13 hours to complete. The rules of the convention require a personal roll-call vote for the major races; as their names are called, each of the 933 delegates steps to a microphone and announces his or her vote. The rules also provide that at the end of the roll call, it is possible for delegates to change their votes − and ample time is given for this − before the total is announced. This rule is obviously functional because it may prevent a time-consuming second call of the roll. It also affects the endorsement process. A majority vote is required for an endorsement, and a 20 percent vote on any ballot is required to enter the primary. At the end of the roll call, a candidate who is close to a majority is likely to gain endorsement through vote shifting; such shifts may also deprive losing candidates of their 20 percent and thus avoid primary challenges.

The roll call for governor took two and a half hours and failed to produce a majority. No totals were announced, but those who were keeping score realized how close the results were: Rome 414, Bozzuto 392, and Labriola 122. It was clear that Labriola held the balance of power, and it was also obvious that the long-rumored alliance between Rome and Labriola would become reality. It was apparent that Labriola could not win and could not hold his delegates. A Bozzuto-Labriola ticket would have been unrealistic, failing to provide the necessary geographic and ethnic balance. Shortly after the vote shifting began, Labriola appeared at the podium to announce that he was withdrawing from the race, and that Rome was his personal choice. As the vote changing dragged on, and delegates realized that the Rome-Labriola ticket would be a reality, nearly all Labriola delegates shifted to Rome, and he won the necessary majority.

When delegates were asked in our survey what were the main reasons for their preferences in the gubernatorial race, relatively few stressed issues. Three-quarters of the Rome supporters emphasized his personal qualities, one-fourth stressed his record, and almost one-third said he had the best chances of winning the election. Two-thirds of the Bozzuto supporters emphasized his electability, and about 40 percent stressed personal qualities.

With the gubernatorial voting and vote changing finally completed, the delegates entered the next stage of the endurance contest: the vote for senator. Prescott Bush, led by his floor managers, moved across the convention floor talking earnestly with individual delegates who were believed to be undecided or leaning, but there was little evidence that he was changing votes. Repeatedly delegates told him that they agreed with his views, but they did not think that he could be elected.

When the roll call and a few vote changes were finally over, Weicker had won endorsement by a vote of 609 to 321. There had been little doubt that he would win, or that Bush would win the 20 percent needed for a primary challenge.

What was important about the senatorial endorsement was the reasoning behind the delegates' votes. The delegates were performing the classic role of a political party: picking a slate that could win. It was clear that large numbers of them — enough to determine the outcome — shared Bush's views but believed the evidence from polls showing that only Weicker could be elected. When asked in our survey for the main reasons for their senatorial vote, 79 percent of the Weicker supporters and only 4 percent of the Bush delegates said he had the best chance of winning the election. Of the Weicker supporters, 22 percent stressed his incumbency or record, but only 14 percent mentioned his stand on issues. Bush supporters were more likely to emphasize his stand on issues (28 percent), but the most frequent reason mentioned (by over half) was criticism of Weicker.

Half of the Republican delegates in our survey reported that their local delegations had tried to reach consensus on the gubernatorial or senatorial races; of those reporting such efforts, almost half said that agreement was achieved in the governor's race, and more than half made that claim for the senatorial race.

The success of these unity efforts can be measured by examining the voting patterns of the city and town delegations in the governor's race — before vote shifting occurred. There are 27 delegations with 10 or more members, ranging up to 28 members in the largest; they constituted 42 percent of all delegates. Very few of these were totally united. There were ten delegations with at least 85 percent of the members voting for one candidate, and 4 others with at least 70 percent for one candidate. There were 57 other delegations that ranged in size from 4 to 9 members; almost half — 28 — voted with complete unity in the governor's race. Obviously some of this bloc voting might have occurred without deliberate efforts at consensus, simply because of the local campaign efforts or regional contacts of a candidate. The pattern of voting suggests that, in addition, serious efforts were made in some delegations to achieve agreement, but that in the larger cities strong party organizations were not able to impose disciplined cohesion.

Once a decision had been reached in the senatorial race, the rest of the convention was devoted to selecting candidates for other statewide positions. Most of the negotiations went on in private while the delegates waited into the evening for the results. Traditionally the delegates have accorded the gubernatorial endorsee the right to name these running mates. This time there was a floor fight over endorsement of a secretary of state, but it ended when the word finally reached delegates about which candidate Rome preferred. The political leaders, as usual, tried for geographical balance; in addition, one of Bozzuto's advisers was selected in an attempt to appease him. Some delegates felt, however, that the slate-makers had failed to give enough priority to finding well-known, proven vote-getters needed for an uphill battle in the fall campaign. When asked in our survey to suggest ways of improving the convention process, a number of delegates criticized the way the slate was selected.

Any evaluation of the convention's success would depend, of course on one's criteria for success. The convention chose its strongest candidate, the incumbent, for senator, and he won reelection. It probably chose its strongest prospect for governor, though he failed to defeat the incumbent. Most significantly, despite the close gubernatorial race and the bitter senatorial race, the convention's choices went unchallenged in the primary. The reasons for this will be discussed in the next chapter, in the context of our full evaluation of the endorsement process.

Minnesota Democrats: More Issues Than Candidates

The Minnesota Democratic-Farmer-Labor party (DFL) is a proud party, proud of its heritage, its organization, and the men it has contributed to national politics. It is also proud of its commitment to principles, and it is an extraordinarily issue-oriented party.

It is an excellent example of the responsible party model. A major reason why delegates favor the principle of endorsements is to make candidates responsible to the party — and to DFL principles. This can be an important source of strength, but it can also create problems, if issues become deeply divisive and if individuals become active in politics primarily in order to advance particular causes (Marshall 1981).

I have described the phenomenon of the subcaucus, used in the selection of delegates at the county and district levels. Most delegates are elected by a subcaucus, which often carries an ideological label and sometimes indicates a very specific issue commitment. Because issues seem to be so important at the DFL convention, I will look first at the process by which the convention dealt with issues.

The DFL convention in early June was held in a large convention hall in Duluth. The 1,286 delegates were seated at long tables, usually covered with stacks of materials on candidates and issues. The delegates were prepared to devote much of their time to studying, debating, and voting on the platform issues. In past DFL conventions, platform issues had been debated in so much detail that the convention ran out of time, and many issues had to be referred to the state committee for a decision.

In 1982 the DFL tried an experiment to speed up the process without giving up the focus on issues that so many members wanted. As the first step the convention adopted the principle of a continuing platform, and agreed to use an updated version of the 1980 platform as that document. As the next step the delegates were presented with a 38-page list of 175 proposed amendments to the continuing platform. They were asked to fill out ballots (to be machine counted) in which they voted on each one of the 175 items and also indicated whether they wanted a debate held on the amendment. It required a 60 percent vote to adopt an amendment, but only 25 percent to require a debate. The delegates spent an hour and a half Friday afternoon carefully reading and marking their ballots on the 175 items. These were clearly delegates who took issues seriously.

The next day, when the ballots had been counted, everyone was surprised to discover that all 175 amendments had been adopted, and there was no issue on which 25 percent requested a debate. At that point efforts were made to change the rules to lower the percentage needed for debate, with a minority arguing vigorously that the DFL was abandoning the important principle of permitting extensive debate on issues. The proposals, which would have permitted debate on several issues, were voted down.

In addition to the amendments on the ballot, there were three issues scheduled for debate on Friday because of minority reports that had been filed; there were also a number of resolutions (not platform planks) on a wide variety of issues, which the convention dealt with off and on during the convention, whenever there was a break in the action.

The most important platform issue debated on Friday was the question of abortion — the issue that deeply divided the convention. As we noted in discussing delegate selection, 20 percent of the delegates were chosen in either pro-life or pro-choice subcaucuses; 70 percent said that when they decided to seek election the abortion issue was one they were particularly interested in — and a slight majority of these were pro-choice. The majority report from the platform committee recommended a pro-choice plank emphasizing constitutional rights. The minority report recommended that the platform contain no statement on abortion. It had support from the pro-life group, which recognized it lacked the votes to get its proposals adopted, and from some party members who were less interested in abortion than in winning elections and avoiding divisive questions. The convention proved to be almost evenly divided on the issue, and because it required 60 percent to amend the continuing platform, it proved impossible either to adopt the pro-choice plank or the position of no plank. The ironic result of the deadlock was to leave in the continuing platform a pro-choice statement adopted in 1980 by the state committee, not the convention.

The DFL delegates were as serious about candidate endorsements as they were about platform issues. Throughout the long convention, they appeared to be attentive and patient, staying on the floor, listening to the speeches, and voting. Delegates frequently appeared at the floor microphones to raise questions or make procedural suggestions. They were articulate and well informed. When demonstrations for candidates took place they were enthusiastic but disciplined, finishing on schedule to keep the convention moving along.

The DFL delegates believe in the principle of endorsement, and with very rare exceptions DFL conventions have made endorsements for every statewide office. The rules require a 60 percent vote to endorse, and of course that means that multiple ballots are common, even if only two candidates are running. The first step in the endorsement process is a report by a 16-person committee that makes recommendations on endorsement if at least 10 members can agree on an endorsee. Although the candidates work hard to get this committee support, it does not seem to carry much weight when there is a close contest, particularly for one of the top offices.

The endorsement process began with the relatively uncontroversial nomination of Mark Dayton as a senatorial candidate. Dayton, from a wealthy family, had already spent a great deal to become the front runner. Eugene McCarthy, who was absent and was making no effort to win convention support, won only 7 votes.

The gubernatorial endorsement was a curious noncontest. The only serious candidate seeking endorsement was Warren Spannaus, completing his third term as Attorney General. He faced two significant challenges: within the convention, several groups were threatening to withhold endorsement for a variety of reasons; outside the convention, former Governor Rudy Perpich was waiting to run against him in the primary. Spannaus was endorsed by an 81 percent margin, and most of the other votes were cast for "no endorsement." Some of these opposition votes were cast by feminists who were protesting Spannaus's refusal to select a woman as a running mate; some were cast by ardent supporters of the pro-life movement; and some were cast by delegates committed to Rudy Perpich.

Rudy Perpich's role in the convention was a peculiar one, and an unsettling one for Spannaus. Perpich was a lieutenant governor who succeeded to the governorship in 1977 when his predecessor became senator. As governor, Perpich attracted media attention and caught the public imagination because of his informal and unconventional style, his unpredictability, and his personal attention to problems. He is particularly popular in his home base, the Iron Range in northern Minnesota. When Perpich sought election on his own in 1978, he was defeated in the Republican landslide. He took a job as an overseas representative of an American business. When he decided to seek the governorship in 1982, he concluded that he could not afford to leave his job early enough to campaign for convention endorsement. He may have also believed that his prospects of winning endorsement from party regulars were less than his chances in a primary. Perpich was at the convention, but he was not seeking its endorsement. He maintained a hospitality suite, but he made little effort to recruit delegates to his cause, though some were wearing Perpich buttons. He appeared before the convention early Sunday morning (a time of his choosing), where he got a polite response from delegates, who filled about half the hall. He proceeded to deliver a totally nonpolitical speech on his proposals for developing the Iron Range and achieving energy independence by using the state's natural resources such as peat.

Perpich's attitude toward the convention appeared to be ambivalent. He was not seeking its endorsement, for tactical and practical reasons, but he did not criticize the endorsement principle. At the same time, his decision to challenge Spannaus in the primary constituted a threat to the effectiveness of the endorsement system, and his subsequent victory over Spannaus may have undermined that system.

The closest race for a major office at the DFL convention, that for attorney general, deserves attention because it was a focal point for a variety of the significant interests and viewpoints at the convention. One candidate was Hubert H. Humphrey III, better known as "Skip." His name was obviously an asset, particularly in a party that was seeking a comeback from the disastrous 1978 election. Humphrey had campaigned extensively around the state, and had particularly strong backing in rural areas; his position on the abortion issue had also won him support from many pro-life delegates. Tom Berg's support was from the urban and suburban areas, particularly the Twin Cities. When asked in our survey about reasons for support, his delegates overwhelmingly mentioned personal qualifications. The third candidate was Nancy Olkon, whose support came particularly from the Twin Cites and from those delegates who felt it was important for the party to nominate a well-qualified woman. She dropped out after the first ballot and succeeded in swinging most of her support to Berg.

As the balloting progressed the candidates worked their way from table to table, reinforcing support and seeking converts. After the second ballot Humphrey had a margin of 53 percent, a lead of 643 to 575; after the next ballot he picked up only 2 votes, and gained 14 more votes after the fourth ballot. It looked as if the DFL would be unable to make an endorsement. But the purpose of the convention is to make endorsements, and most delegates take that purpose very seriously. On the fifth ballot, a shift toward

Humphrey began, and when Berg recognized it — before the result was announced — he went to the podium and conceded.

The selection of a lieutenant governor was the last endorsement made by the convention. Under state law the governor and lieutenant governor run as a slate in both the primary and general election (with voters casting a single vote). This normally gives the governor considerable freedom in choosing a running mate. Spannaus chose a veteran state legislator, Carl Johnson, but his endorsement proved to be less than automatic. Those delegates seeking a woman rallied behind Arlene Lehto, who proved to be an effective speaker in her appearance at the convention; she also won support from disgruntled labor delegates and some Perpich supporters seeking to embarrass Spannaus. Johnson gained only 56 percent on the first ballot, but on a second ballot he barely got the necessary 60 percent.

In many ways the DFL convention appeared to be a success. The disputes over issues, and specifically abortion, had been somewhat less divisive than in the past. The endorsement fights had left relatively few scars. The ticket was believed to be a strong one, and the chances for recapturing state government seemed good, given the serious condition of the economy and the unwillingness of the incumbent Republican governor to seek a second term. Most endorsees would avoid a primary and could concentrate on the general election. Only the endorsee, Warren Spannaus, faced primary opposition, and that proved to be insurmountable.

Minnesota Republicans: The Many Voices of Conservatism

The Independent Republican (IR) party in Minnesota has had a history of endorsements that have been even more consistently successful than those of the DFL. As noted in the previous chapter, the normal pattern in gubernatorial races has been for candidates who seek the endorsement unsuccessfully to accept the convention's decision. Occasionally other candidates have made a primary challenge but have made poor showings. In 1982 there were five serious candidates seeking the gubernatorial endorsement, and the four losers accepted the verdict of the convention. Once again the challenge came from the outside, but this time it was successful. For the first time since the IR had authorized endorsements, the convention's choice for governor had lost.

The 2,025 Republicans who met in the large convention hall in St. Paul in mid-June were, by any standards, a very conservative group. In some respects they appeared to be as ideologically oriented as the DFL delegates. They debated the platform in detail, section by section, off and on throughout the convention, whenever nothing else was scheduled. They took voice votes or, when necessary, standing votes on each section and on proposed amendments. In addition, they voted by machine-readable ballot on 25 items that the platform committee had decided were most likely to be controversial. If ideology seemed any less important at this convention than it had been at the DFL meeting it was because the issues were less divisive. Even on issues inherently controversial, like abortion, the delegates demonstrated a substantial level of agreement.

The overwhelmingly conservative temper of the convention can be appreciated by sampling a few platform planks. The convention voted to support: the expanded use of nuclear power in Minnesota; the opening of wilderness areas to mining and drilling after the year 2000 with appropriate safeguards; the honoring of our commitments to Taiwan; the right of all law-abiding citizens to keep and bear arms; a requirement that scientific creation theory as well as evolution theory be taught in the school without any reference to religion; and (by a narrow margin) the repeal of state law mandating the fluoridation of public drinking water. The delegates voted on a series of planks related to abortion, and by margins of approximately two-to-one (varying with the exact language) they endorsed a Human Life Amendment to the U.S. Constitution, opposed funding for abortions or freedom of choice regarding abortion; the only exception to a total ban on abortions was when the mother's life is in jeopardy.

It would be an exaggeration to suggest that all IR delegates were strongly committed to conservatism. Roughly one-third of the delegates voted against several of the planks listed above, in addition to the anti-abortion ones; this was true of planks on conservation, nuclear power, and scientific creationism. But on all of these issues, and many others less controversial, the conservative position was in the majority.

The politically significant differences at the IR convention did not concern the position to be taken on issues but the priorities to be given to particular topics. The new element in the 1982 convention was the presence of a substantial number of delegates with fundamentalist church backgrounds, led by a gubernatorial candidate — Glen Sherwood — whose dominant concern was issues of morality, or family issues as the candidate liked to call them. These issues included: the pro-life position on abortion, opposition to pornography, support for raising the drinking age to 21, stricter marijuana laws, revision or repeal of the no-fault divorce law, and opposition to pari-mutuel betting.

Those delegates who stressed these issues were not out of step with the viewpoints of a majority of other delegates; they differed in the emphasis placed on these issues. Other delegates tended to be more concerned with the critical economic problems facing the state and with support for the Reagan administration.

When delegates were asked in our survey about their primary interest in seeking election to the convention 70 percent of Sherwood delegates emphasized issues only or issues and candidates; 14 percent said candidates only; and 16 percent said neither. When the answers from all other delegates are combined, only 38 percent said issues only or issues and candidates; 15 percent said candidates only; and 47 percent said neither. Of those Sherwood delegates who expressed such an interest in issues, two-thirds mentioned abortion (usually specifying the pro-life position), one-third mentioned morality issues, and one-sixth specified family issues. (As many as three issue areas were coded.) Among those supporters of other candidates who expressed a major interest in issues, about one-fourth mentioned abortion and very few mentioned other morality or family issues; most of their answers concerned economic matters (which interested Sherwood supporters somewhat less).

In order to understand why the field of gubernatorial candidates was so crowded, it is necessary to review the political developments that preceded the convention. In 1978 a veteran Republican congressman, Albert Quie, was elected governor. When he took office, Quie found a large surplus in the treasury, and persuaded the legislature to enact a substantial tax cut. Then came the recession, which hit Minnesota particularly hard, partly because the Iron Range region of the state is so dependent on the steel industry. By 1981 the state faced a deficit of about $700 million, and Quie was forced to raise taxes and cut spending. As his standing in the opinion polls tumbled, Quie became a serious liability to the Republican party, and in late January 1982, he announced that he would not seek a second term.

Lieutenant Governor Lou Wangberg immediately jumped into the race, with the full endorsement of most top Republican office holders, led by the governor. At first Wangberg seemed to be far in front of the pack, but he soon began to encounter problems. It was not easy to separate himself from the unpopular governor while serving in his administration and enjoying his endorsement. Wangberg, who was holding his first elective office, lacked both name recognition and a dynamic campaign style.

As it became apparent that Wangberg did not have the nomination sewed up, other candidates entered the fray. One was Robert Ashbach, a twenty-year veteran of the legislature and the minority leader in the Senate, widely regarded as an expert on government finances. He was the only candidate on record in favor of the legal right to abortion, a position that was certain to handicap him in the convention. A second candidate was Paul Overgaard, a former legislator who more recently had developed a strong reputation in Republican circles as an expert campaign strategist and fund raiser. A third candidate was David Jennings, a second-term legislator who led a "new right" faction in the House and had recently been elected minority leader; at age 33 he was regarded by many observers to be simply laying the groundwork for more serious campaigns in later years.

When the convention met in June, the front-runner was none of these; it was Glen Sherwood, a five-term member of the legislature who had served as House minority leader, and whose base of support consisted of fundamentalist church members and others who shared his views on the importance of morality issues. Sherwood, a low-keyed campaigner with little name recognition, had been lightly regarded by most political observers until the fundamentalist groups mobilized their members to attend caucuses and produced a large bloc of loyal supporters. Despite Sherwood's lead among delegates, there were doubts about whether he had enough second-choice support among backers of other candidates to reach the 60 percent required for endorsement.

At the grass-roots level, the Sherwood campaign mobilized large numbers of persons who had never been active in politics before. Of those Sherwood supporters who won election as state convention delegates, the proportion of party activists was larger, but still less than among other delegates. The proportion of Sherwood delegates holding party office was 46 percent; it ranged from 57 percent for Ashbach and Jennings delegates to 71 percent for Wangberg delegates, in our sample survey. The proportion of delegates who had attended the 1980 or 1978 conventions was only 35 percent for Sherwood delegates, compared to 52 for Jennings and for Overgaard, 72 for Ashbach, and 81 for Wangberg.

There were also some significant and not surprising differences among the delegates in the reasons they gave in our survey for supporting specific gubernatorial candidates. Almost 60 percent of the Sherwood supporters mentioned his pro-life or pro-family position; about half mentioned other issues. Wangberg's supporters most often emphasized his stand on issues, his personal qualifications, and his experience; one-third said that he had the best chance of being elected. Overgaard's supporters overwhelmingly (70 percent) stressed that he had the best chance of being elected, and they also stressed his experience and personal qualifications. Ashbach was regarded by his delegates as being strong in experience and issues. Four-fifths of Jennings supporters mentioned his position on issues. Except in the case of Sherwood delegates, no particular emphasis was given to abortion or morality issues.

In a five-way race for an endorsement that requires a 60 percent majority, it is obvious that a candidate's strength cannot be measured by the number of delegates who rank him first on the first ballot but by the staying power of these delegates and his second-choice support among those backing other delegates. In other words, how broad is the candidate's potential strength? Another possibility, of course, is that the outcome will be determined by an alliance between two candidates, with one candidate offering a place on the ticket to the other. This was the pattern in the Connecticut Republican party, but it was not in the scenario for Minnesota.

A crowd of over 2,000 delegates makes possible large-scale demonstrations, with the delegates often being joined by supporters brought in from outside the hall. The Sherwood supporters carried signs with evergreens, thus turning the hall temporarily into a Sherwood forest. Each of the candidates got a chance to speak as part of the nominating process; few, if any, of them turned out to be spellbinders.

The voting for governor lasted for seven ballots. It was conducted very efficiently; the use of machine-readable paper ballots for the largest counties facilitated the process. It was also a nonstop process. As soon as the totals were announced for one ballot, the next ballot commenced — except when candidates came to the platform to drop out of the race. As a consequence, the candidates were forced to make decisions and communicate them to supporters in a hurry.

Table 4.4 shows the results of the voting, in percentage terms, for each of the seven ballots. At the end of the first ballot Sherwood was ahead, as predicted, but with a smaller margin than the 40 percent that his supporters had claimed and many observers had expected. It was anticipated that Sherwood's delegates would stick with him until released. If he had captured 40 percent, he might have been in a position to block the endorsement of anyone else — except on his terms. It was difficult to believe that he had nearly enough second-choice strength to win endorsement. Wangberg was solidly entrenched in second place, waiting to pick up votes from those who faded.

For the next two ballots, Ashbach and Jennings gradually lost votes, some of which went to Wangberg and most of which went to Overgaard. Sherwood gained virtually nothing — a net addition of 3 votes out of almost 2,000. At the end of the third ballot, Ashbach and Jennings both appeared on the platform to announce their withdrawal; neither one announced their support for other

Table 4.4
Votes for Gubernatorial Candidates in Minnesota
Republican Convention
(in percentages)

				Ballot			
Candidate	*First*	*Second*	*Third*	*Fourth*	*Fifth*	*Sixth*	*Seventh*
Wangberg	26.5	27.3	28.2	33.1	35.2	55.9	67.9
Overgaard	21.1	24.6	26.7	33.8	35.7	40.4	28.4
Sherwood	30.5	30.8	30.7	32.0	28.3	—	—
Ashbach	9.6	6.0	4.3	—	—	—	—
Jennings	11.5	11.0	9.6	—	—	—	—
Other/Pass	0.8	0.3	0.5	1.1	0.8	3.7	3.7
Total	100	100	100	100	100	100	100

Source: Compiled by the author.

candidates. The fourth ballot produced a virtual deadlock among the three remaining candidates. Although Sherwood gained a few votes, Overgaard and Wangberg were the clear beneficiaries of the dropouts, and were in a virtual dead heat.

The fifth ballot was a crucial one. Overgaard and Wangberg continued to gain ground, separated now by only nine votes, and Sherwood for the first time lost a significant number of votes − more than 10 percent of his delegates. It was now obvious that there were only two candidates with a chance of endorsement: Wangberg and Overgaard. Wangberg was the lieutenant governor, supported by the governor and other party leaders, who had failed to keep his front runner status. Overgaard was the campaign strategist, well respected in the party and regarded as a likely compromise choice.

As the fifth ballot progressed, Glen Sherwood watched the results with growing dismay. He became convinced of two things: he could not win the endorsement, and Overgaard was gaining strength faster than Wangberg and appeared more likely to be endorsed. Wangberg and Overgaard were both conservatives, but Sherwood perceived an important difference between them. Wangberg was staunchly conservative on economics and on the family issues that Sherwood considers so important. Sherwood perceived Overgaard to be less staunchly conservative and specifically less dependable on the pro-life and pro-family issues to which Sherwood is so deeply committed.

After a frantic conference with his advisers, who were urging him to stay in the race, Sherwood went to the podium and announced that he was withdrawing from the race. He endorsed no other candidate by name, but urged his supporters to vote for a pro-life, pro-family candidate; his delegates got the clear signal that he preferred Wangberg. Sherwood's decision to pull out and support Wangberg was not based on any deal or any desire to be slated on the ticket; it was a simple decision to support the most conservative, pro-family candidate available.

On the sixth ballot it became clear that most Sherwood supporters were following their leader's advice. (Our survey showed that nine-tenths of the Sherwood delegates in our sample supported Wangberg after Sherwood dropped out.) Wangberg surged ahead, and on the seventh ballot, with some Overgaard delegates making a shift, Wangberg got two-thirds of the votes. At 1:30 in the morning the gubernatorial endorsement process was completed.

The endorsement of Wangberg resulted from an alliance between some of the most experienced and some of the least experienced party activists at the convention who shared a strong commitment to conservative causes. There is no way of determining which of the five candidates would have been the most electable − in the primary or the general election, but it is clear that the Sherwood supporters who shifted to Wangberg did so because they approved of his policy positions rather than because they believed he was most electable.

How successful was the convention? It succeeded in reaching 60 percent agreement on a gubernatorial endorsement − no small achievement with so many candidates running. It reached this agreement without leaving deep scars among the delegates. None of the losing candidates at the convention chose to challenge Wangberg in the primary. What the convention failed to do was to endorse a candidate capable of winning the primary election.

There was one candidate missing from the convention: Wheelock Whitney, a wealthy businessman and social activist who had been a small-town mayor in the 1960s and had been the Republican nominee for senator against Eugene McCarthy in 1964. Whitney supported the principle of endorsements, but he did not seek the convention endorsement for several reasons: He was out of touch with party activists and local organizations; he was out of step with the conservative mood of the delegates − more specifically he favored legalized abortion; and he had the resources necessary to mount a media campaign in the primary. Before the convention, he had run an extensive television advertising campaign, but he suspended it for several weeks leading up to the convention, saying he did not want to appear to be trying to influence the delegates. Whitney did not appear at the convention; there were no Wheelock Whitney buttons or banners in evidence. There was only a single one-page sheet distributed to delegates in which Whitney reaffirmed his intention to run in the primary and indicated why he thought an open primary would be healthy for the party.

There was no evidence at the convention that delegates were concerned about Whitney. The threat of a primary challenge was not mentioned in speeches. More specifically, the majority of delegates clearly did not give priority to selecting a candidate who, because of campaign skills or a moderate position on issues, would be best able to defeat Whitney. In the next chapter we will confront the question of why the IR endorsee lost the primary, and whether a different choice would have produced a different outcome.

New Mexico Democrats: A Successful Convention

The New Mexico conventions that met in 1982 were only the second ones to make gubernatorial endorsements since passage of the law reestablishing the endorsing system. That law requires candidates to seek convention endorsement, gives a place on the primary ballot to anyone getting 20 percent on the convention ballot, and also permits candidates to qualify for the primary by petition. This means that, unlike the situation in Minnesota, for example, it is impossible for a candidate to completely bypass the convention. It also means that only a single ballot is taken at the convention. The major impact of these rules is to focus attention at the convention not on the question of who will get the most votes — though that is important — but which candidates will get the 20 percent necessary to qualify for the ballot.

Qualifying by petition is not unusually difficult, although it does require signatures totaling 3 percent of the number of votes cast in the party's last gubernatorial primary. But failure to get a 20 percent vote at the convention is a clear indication of weakness within the party organization, and is damaging to the momentum of a campaign. Moreover, the number of votes won at the convention determines position on the primary ballot, and those who fail to get 20 percent are listed below those who meet that minimum. Obviously ballot position can make a difference in an election.

The 1982 New Mexico Democratic convention met in Albuquerque in mid-March. The 1,712 delegates met in a large semicircular auditorium in a convention center, which provided plenty of room for both delegates and spectators but which lacked the aisle space that would make possible large-scale demonstrations. Much of the informal activity of the convention took place in a large open area just outside the auditorium where delegates mingled, talked with candidates, and listened to the mariachi bands hired by candidates. Some of the candidates for governor, and for other offices, spent much of their time meeting the delegates one at a time.

The first afternoon of the convention was devoted to the party platform, and most attention was focused on the right-to-work issue, one that sharply divided the party. A substantial number of delegates were union members, and the unions had worked hard to win support on this issue. By a vote of 1,098 to 607 the convention adopted a plank opposing right-to-work legislation. As the debate over other planks dragged on, delegates drifted out of the hall, and by the time the platform was adopted in late afternoon most of the delegates had left.

The convention worked through the next day endorsing candidates for a number of statewide and congressional offices. It followed the unusual procedure of voting first on lesser offices, then the gubernatorial, congressional, and senatorial races. (In congressional endorsements, only delegates from the specific district voted.) This was a system apparently designed to keep delegates from leaving early. It would also appear to prevent those who fell short in the governor's race from running for a lower office, but this was also precluded by the requirement that candidates get preliminary petitions signed (1 percent of the primary vote) to run for an office before the convention.

I have earlier described the selection process for this convention as being candidate oriented: Most local party organizations were not powerful, and candidate organizations made a strong effort to mobilize their supporters to run as delegates and to convert persons who had a good chance of becoming delegates. Of the delegates who answered our survey, 70 percent were elected with opposition, and 58 percent had made a commitment to a gubernatorial candidate before being elected. (In some counties certain local party officials automatically were chosen as delegates.) Presumably as many or more of the delegates had made commitments to candidates for other offices as well. There was a very close race for the senatorial nomination and contests for several other offices. When asked if they were particularly interested in supporting candidates for individual offices, 58 percent mentioned the gubernatorial race, 49 percent senatorial, 27 percent a congressional race, and as many as 20 percent some other statewide races.

There were four candidates seeking endorsement for governor. The heavy favorite was Toney Anaya, the former attorney general, a Hispanic candidate with strong support from organized labor; when returns from county conventions were complete, he claimed to have 60 percent of the delegates. The other candidates only claimed that they had, or expected to get, the 20 percent necessary to enter the primary. The second strongest candidate was expected to be Aubrey Dunn, a former state senator with a reputation as a conservative, particularly in fiscal affairs. Two other contenders with past or present records in the state Senate were Fabian Chavez and Les Houston. Chavez had a long political record, including a gubernatorial race in 1968, but was not well known to younger voters. Houston had a record as a maverick and a relatively narrow base of political support.

The state constitution prohibits successive gubernatorial terms, and incumbent Governor Bruce King appeared to play no significant role in the convention. His administration had been plagued with a number of problems, and the gubernatorial candidates did not publicly seek his support, although he was believed by some observers to be providing help to Dunn behind the scenes. When King spoke briefly to the convention, the delegates appeared to pay little attention to the speech.

Each of the gubernatorial candidates spoke to the convention following brief demonstrations on their behalf. Anaya was greeted by chants of *"Toney, Toney"* as he appeared at the platform. He launched immediately into an aggressive, angry speech charging that efforts were being made to manipulate the delegates. He was referring to rumors sweeping the convention that both Dunn and Houston were trying to shift enough of their delegates to Fabian Chavez to assure that Chavez would get the 20 percent needed to appear on the ballot. Because Anaya and Chavez would appeal particularly to Hispanic voters, the obvious purpose of the tactic was to erode Anaya's support in the primary.

Chavez spoke next to the convention, proclaimed himself a unity candidate, and urged the convention to give him — and all other candidates — the needed 20 percent. Dunn was a dignified, competent, dull speaker, who made no mention of Anaya's charges. When Houston appeared before the delegates, he got no demonstration, only a scattering of applause. He announced that he obviously lacked the 20 percent of convention support needed, that he would follow the petition route to the primary, and that he was asking his delegates to vote for Chavez — an announcement greeted by cheers quickly drowned out by boos.

As the roll call for governor progressed, the major question to be decided was not how large a majority Anaya would get, but whether Chavez could pick up enough support to meet the 20 percent requirement. He could not. Anaya got 56 percent, Dunn 26, and Chavez only 18. No one seemed to know how many votes Houston controlled (probably less than 5 percent) or whether most of them voted for Chavez as requested. In reality, Chavez could not have reached his goal without votes, or more votes, from Dunn. Why did Dunn not shift enough votes (another 35 or so) to Chavez to meet the 20 percent goal? The answer seems to be that Dunn did not have an accurate enough head count, or close enough communications with his delegates, to carry out such a delicate maneuver effectively. His 26 percent total gave him little margin for error. Dunn had complete control only in his home county, and it would have been damaging to appear weak in that delegation, which he carried 33 to 8 over Anaya. As the roll call progressed, Dunn stood with his aides at the side of the hall and watched his tactic fail. Perhaps the obvious lesson of this episode is that delicate maneuvers cannot be carried out very effectively when only a single ballot is used.

The roll call revealed that there was very little bloc voting in the larger counties, with the exception of Rio Arriba county (a unanimous 67 votes for Chavez), where the party organization was reputed to be powerful. One reason for this was that the party operated with an elaborate proportional representation system for electing delegates at the local level.

Our survey of delegates showed that both Anaya and Dunn supporters were most likely to mention their candidate's stand on issues in explaining their vote (86 percent of Anaya supporters and 69 percent of Dunn delegates). Nearly half of each group indicated personal contact with the candidate was a major reason. A majority of the Anaya supporters and over one-third of those for Dunn said he would be more electable. The small number of Chavez and/or Houston supporters stressed issues and personal contact.

The other major race, for the senatorial nomination, was more closely contested. Attorney General Jeff Bingaman defeated former Governor Jerry Apodaca by a margin of 50 to 48 percent, with the rest going to minor candidates. There seemed to be no linkage between the two races, but there may have been some trading among individual delegates. Although both Anaya and Apodaca are Hispanic, an analysis of the county-by-county roll-call vote failed to show a similar pattern of voting for the two. Anaya won 62 percent of the vote in the largest county — Bernalillo; Apodaca had only 42 percent of the vote there. Anaya apparently appealed to younger, more urban, and more liberal Hispanics than did Apodaca.

A major reason why New Mexico readopted endorsing conventions was to reduce the number of candidates running in primaries and increase the chances of the winner getting a majority. Based on these criteria, the Democratic convention was successful. There were only four candidates for governor and three for senator in the primary. Although both Chavez and Houston entered the gubernatorial primary via the petition route, they got less than 10 percent of the vote between them, and Anaya was nominated with 56.6 percent (and elected). Bingaman won the primary with 53.5 percent and was elected.

Massachusetts Democrats: A Candidate-Controlled Convention

An understanding of the events that transpired at the Massachusetts Democratic convention in May 1982 requires a summary of the struggle within the party over the previous four years. In 1978 the incumbent Democratic Governor Michael Dukakis was defeated in the Democratic primary by Edward King, who went on to win the election. During the primary campaign, King had supported cutting local property taxes but had placed most emphasis on his support for capital punishment, tougher treatment of criminals, and raising the drinking age to 21, and his opposition to abortion. Dukakis fundamentally disagreed with King on these issues. Surveys showed that King and Dukakis voters disagreed significantly on these issues. The differences in views reflected variations in socioeconomic background; specifically, the Dukakis supporters tended to have substantially higher levels of education than King supporters (White 1982).

During the latter part of the Dukakis administration, a movement was under way to revitalize the state Democratic party. It was not led by Dukakis, but was developed by a number of liberal party activists. After a series of hearings around the state, a charter commission was appointed in the fall of 1977. One of the major proposals of that commission was to revive the endorsing convention; it was to be modeled on the Connecticut challenge primary and would require candidates to get a minimum convention vote in order to run in the primary. The commission also proposed an issues convention in odd-numbered years (Mileur 1981).

It was not until after the 1978 election that a charter convention was held; it met in May 1979 and reconvened to finish its work in November. The convention adopted the new charter after prolonged debate and consideration of many amendments. Most of the support for the charter came from outside of the Boston area and from liberal Democrats — although liberals were concerned about some provisions, particularly a so-called loyalty oath. The provision for an endorsing convention barely won the necessary two-thirds vote — after the percentage of convention votes required to run in the primary was reduced from 20 to 15 (Mileur 1981).

Early in 1981 Michael Dukakis began his campaign to recapture the governorship. He made a particular effort to win support from a variety of liberal, union, and public employee groups that had become disillusioned with his fiscal conservatism during his first term but that were more upset by Governor King's record. Dukakis campaigned intensively, building a strong grass-roots organization and seeking convention delegates. He decided to use the new endorsing convention as a vehicle for recruiting a large number of workers, developing a strong organization, and — he hoped — demonstrating his strength by winning the endorsement. Most of those in the party who had been active in the movement to revitalize the party and reestablish the convention became Dukakis supporters.

There was a second challenger to King who decided to work for convention support: Lieutenant Governor Thomas P. O'Neill III, son of the Speaker of the U.S. House of Representatives. O'Neill raised considerable money and campaigned extensively to win convention delegates, but failed to compete effectively with Dukakis for the anti-King vote.

Governor King also began his campaign early, but concentrated on raising money and developing an extensive television and radio advertising campaign, well in advance of the other candidates. He was obviously concerned about opinion polls that showed him far behind Dukakis. King was very reluctant to seek the convention endorsement and join the campaign for delegates because he believed that Dukakis would be able to control the convention. The preferred King strategy was to concentrate on the primary election and his extensive media campaign.

The problem faced by King was the provision of the party charter requiring candidates to win 15 percent of the convention vote in order to enter the primary. When the charter convention had approved the principle of an endorsing convention with the 15 percent provision, its supporters had expected to be able to win legislative authorization for the plan. But the legislators, like a number of other elected officials, were unenthusiastic about endorsements; those who were loyal to the governor recognized that the convention would not serve his purposes. In the absence of legislation, the Democratic party went ahead with plans for a convention. But a puzzling legal question remained: Could Democratic party rules impose a prerequisite for a place on the primary ballot, beyond the petition requirement in the law?

In part because it did not want to risk a judicial ruling that could jeopardize access to the primary, the King organization began to mobilize its supporters for the mid-February caucuses that would choose convention delegates. Obviously an incumbent governor has considerable resources in any organizational effort. In the last few weeks before the caucuses, King's campaign staff contacted state and local officials and loyal party workers to organize the caucuses. He sent a letter to members of pro-life groups urging them to participate actively in the caucuses. The King organization had no illusions that this last-minute effort would win the endorsement; it hoped to make a respectable showing and get at least the required 15 percent.

The caucuses were an overwhelming victory for Dukakis. One reason was a heavy turnout, some 100,000 persons at nearly 600 meetings, demonstrating the organizational effectiveness of the Dukakis campaign. It was estimated that Dukakis captured 67 percent of the delegate positions, with King getting 22 percent and O'Neill only 5 percent – leaving 5 percent uncommitted. It was a setback for King not only because the governor won less than one-fourth of the votes but also because O'Neill's campaign appeared doomed, and King wanted O'Neill to stay in the race to take away votes from Dukakis.

One other remarkable event occurred before the state convention met. The legislature passed a law to make it clear that a candidate could run in the primary without getting 15 percent in the Democratic convention. Governor King, before signing the bill, asked the Massachusetts Supreme Judicial Court for an advisory opinion about whether such a law would supersede the Democratic party charter. The court held that such a law would "abridge the constitutional rights of the Democratic party and its members to associate by allowing candidates to be placed on the Democratic State primary ballot in contravention of the party's charter." The court argued that the party had a substantial interest in ensuring that its members could have an effective role in determining who would be the party's candidate in the general election. Similarly it had a legitimate interest in reducing the number of candidates, to eliminate voter confusion, and in limiting candidates to those with significant party support. The court held that the state had no compelling interest in interfering with these interests and thus with the party's freedom of association.

In the short run, the decision had no impact on the governor's race. O'Neill decided to drop out of the race, not because of the 15 percent requirement, but because he lacked the public support and the funds to continue. The rule did have a significant effect on the lieutenant governor's race, as we shall see; candidates who fell short of 15 percent lost a court ballot to get on the primary ballot. In the long run the court decision was more important, because it gave the Democratic convention greater legitimacy, and meant that future candidates would not be able to bypass it, even if the legislature continued to refuse to give it legal sanction.

When the Democratic convention met in Springfield in late May, the opponents of the 15 percent rule tried to get that body to abandon the rule — at least for 1982. The rules fight was the main order of business on the first evening. The King forces hoped to gain support from O'Neill backers, and also from delegates supporting some of the eight candidates for lieutenant governor who might be jeopardized by the rule. Their tactic was to deluge the leadership with a large number of charter amendments (39 in all) in order to tie up the convention and harass its leadership — and perhaps win some compromise.

The tactic failed, partly because the Dukakis delegates were in the majority and would not support any amendment that might damage their candidate. Our survey showed that the 15 percent rule had the support of 84 percent of Dukakis delegates and 25 percent of King supporters. Moreover, the convention leadership handled the onslaught of amendments skillfully. They started by challenging the signatures on many of the petitions for amendments, and they selected for a roll-call vote one of the more radical amendments, which would have the effect of abolishing not just the 15 percent rule but the entire endorsing convention. It was beaten by a three-to-one margin. The two sides then compromised and agreed to vote on one more amendment: a proposal to delay implementation of the 15 percent rule until the next convention. Though a more reasonable proposal, the amendment was defeated by an overwhelming voice vote. The Dukakis forces were clearly in control.

The Massachusetts Democratic convention had all the trappings of a national convention – more than 3,300 delegates, a large convention hall, full-scale demonstrations, candidate bands in the gallery, and even thousands of balloons gathered in a net high above the floor, ready to be released during the Dukakis convention. It even had Ted Kennedy, in person, to speak after he had won easy endorsement for senatorial renomination.

The convention gave every appearance of being dominated by Dukakis forces. They ran the convention from the podium; they had won the rules fight; and they put on by far the largest demonstration. When the roll-call vote was taken, Dukakis defeated King by a 68-32 percent margin. It appeared that some of the O'Neill supporters voted for King, and others did not vote.

A survey of delegates conducted by two political scientists, John White and Jerome Mileur, showed that the Dukakis and King delegates differed sharply on a number of issues, particularly in the social area.* On the question of state funding for abortions for low-income women, 72 percent of Dukakis delegates and only 16 percent of those for King were in favor. Capital punishment had much more support from the King group (74 percent) than from Dukakis delegates (38 percent). ERA had the support of 89 percent of Dukakis supporters and half of King supporters. There were also substantial differences on such issues as spending priorities for environmental protection, education, and defense; support for a federal balanced budget amendment; and attitudes toward President Reagan – with Dukakis delegates consistently taking the more liberal position.

---

*I am indebted to John White and Jerome Mileur for making available the results of this survey. They distributed questionnaires to delegates at the convention, and succeeded in collecting 646 responses.

Our survey showed that, in explaining their vote, two-thirds of the Dukakis supporters mentioned his personal qualifications, 43 percent stressed his record as governor, and 42 percent his stand on issues. Of the King supporters, two-thirds mentioned his record as the incumbent, half mentioned his stand on issues, and only 20 percent emphasized his personal qualifications. About one-fifth of the supporters of each candidate explained their vote in part by criticizing the other candidate. Virtually none of the delegates emphasized the candidate's electability — in sharp contrast to the results in other state conventions. Presumably the reason is that to an extraordinary degree these delegates were committed to a candidate rather than to the party; finding the candidate most likely to get elected was not their concern. This reflects the delegate selection process, the deep divisions within the party, and the weakness of the Massachusetts Republican party, which seemed unprepared to capitalize on Democratic divisions.

The race for lieutenant governor deserves our attention, not only because it was characterized by the drama and excitement lacking in the governor's race, but also because it showed some interesting implications of the 15 percent rule. There were eight candidates for lieutenant governor, and five of these could be serious contenders. Evelyn Murphy had served as Environmental Affairs Secretary in the Dukakis administration. Samuel Rotondi was a state senator. Louis Nickinello was a state representative. John Kerry had been a county assistant district attorney. Lois Pines had served in the legislature.

When eight persons are being nominated for lieutenant governor, it is difficult for any single candidate to make much of an impact on the delegates. The normal procedure was for one delegate to make a nominating speech from the podium, followed by a very brief statement from the candidate to finish up the allotted five minutes. Evelyn Murphy, and her campaign managers, had a better idea. When her turn came, the auditorium lights dimmed, and a curtain opened to display a large screen on which slides from synchronized projectors, with a sound track, summarized the candidate's accomplishments. The presentation was slick and professional, and as it ended, Evelyn Murphy appeared in the spotlight at the podium to ask the delegates for their support. As she spoke for half a minute, the theme music from *Chariots of Fire* began in the background;

and when she concluded, the music, with its symbolic theme of the long-distance runner, pulsated through the auditorium.

More than 7 hours and 5 ballots later the delegates endorsed Evelyn Murphy by a margin of 12 votes out of 2,666. It would be impossible to estimate how many votes were swayed by her dramatic presentation, but at the very least it demonstrated to the delegates her ability to campaign and to use effective media techniques. Perhaps equally important, it enabled her to stand out in the crowd.

The search for votes in the lieutenant governor's race did not begin until after the delegates had been chosen. For the most part delegates were recruited and elected because of their commitment in the governor's race and not any other candidate preferences. Almost one-third of the delegates in our survey said that they decided on a choice for lieutenant governor before being elected; half said after election and before the convention; and 17 percent decided at the convention. Murphy, Pines, and Nickinello picked up more of their support at the convention.

Table 4.5 shows the votes cast for lieutenant governor on four ballots. (The third ballot was aborted because of protests that resulted when two candidates withdrew while the balloting was going on.) One candidate (Pressman) withdrew before the voting

Table 4.5
Votes Cast for Candidates for Lieutenant Governor
in Massachusetts Democratic Convention
(in percentages)

| Candidate | *Ballot* | | | |
	First	*Second*	*Fourth*	*Fifth*
Murphy	20.2	24.0	41.7	50.2
Rotondi	23.9	25.3	43.3	49.8
Kerry	15.3	14.4	15.0	—
Pines	14.8	18.3	—	—
Nickinello	18.9	17.9	—	—
Geary	5.3	—	—	—
Langione	1.4	0.2	—	—

Source: Compiled by the author.

began; Geary dropped out after one ballot; and Langione was forced out after the second ballot by rules designed to drop those with little support. The table shows that the delegates gave at least 15 percent to the remaining five candidates. After the first ballot four of the candidates had reached the required 15 percent. At that point, Kerry agreed to shift enough delegates to Lois Pines to assure that she would qualify for the primary. He believed that having a second woman running in the primary would reduce Evelyn Murphy's vote. Pines and Nickinello dropped out during the third ballot, and Kerry withdrew after the fourth; all three made it clear that they would stay in the primary.

After two ballots Murphy and Rotondi each had about one-fourth of the vote; after five ballots they each had about half, with each having picked up more than 500 votes. One reason for their percentage gain was that about 570 delegates had left, or at least stopped voting, between the second and the fifth ballots. Obviously Murphy had slightly more second-choice strength than Rotondi; our survey showed her picking up most of the Kerry and Pines supporters, while Rotondi got more Nickinello delegates. Some shifts probably reflected the calculations of candidates about which opponents would be toughest to beat. Before the convention Rotondi had been a slight favorite, along with Kerry; a shift of votes to Murphy could be a way of assuring that no front runner got too far ahead.

Most observers believed that Murphy had gained a great deal from the endorsement because she had emerged from back in the pack. Her endorsement did not carry her to victory in the primary, however; she lost narrowly to Kerry in a five-person race. In the next chapter we will assess more fully the advantages of endorsement gained by both Murphy and Dukakis.

Probably the most significant accomplishment of the Massachusetts Democratic convention was survival. The institution designed to be given a legal foundation by the legislature survived as an informal party body — with its 15-percent rule intact. The courts decided, and the majority of delegates agreed, that candidates must seek convention support and gain 15 percent of the votes to run in the primary. There was no way to bypass it. This did not, however, have the effect of significantly reducing the number of candidates for lieutenant governor. It was not evident that delegates made any serious effort to provide a slate that was balanced geographically or ethnically. (One of the criticisms of Murphy was that she would not bring balance to the ticket.) The convention did not overcome or moderate the deep divisions in the party that were epitomized by the governor's race. The convention did succeed in endorsing a gubernatorial candidate who could win the primary and the general election.

Massachusetts Republicans: The Search for a Winner

A familiar characteristic of state primaries in recent years has been the nomination of candidates who lack an established record as party leaders and officeholders, but who have the financial resources to gain name recognition through large-scale media advertising. Established political leaders should be in a better position to win the endorsement of delegates in a convention, and that endorsement may be of some value in a primary contest — even against a well-financed outsider. In the Minnesota Republican primary, however, we saw an example of a well-financed outsider — for a variety of reasons — being able to defeat the convention endorsee. In the 1982 Massachusetts Republican convention, we find an example of the well-financed outsider defeating established political leaders for the endorsement. We will also see the well-financed, and party-endorsed outsider losing the primary to an established political leader who ignored the convention.

The Massachusetts Republican convention that met in Boston in early March was the party's third informal gubernatorial endorsing convention since repeal of the law sanctioning such meetings. The 1978 convention had been an untypical one for the Republican party. The convention had been bitterly divided, and its gubernatorial endorsee had been defeated in the primary. This year the party was determined to avoid such divisiveness, and to find a candidate who would win the primary and have a serious chance of beating the Democrats in November. After years in the minority, the party wanted to be able to capitalize on the sharp split within the Democratic party.

The delegates to the convention were local party leaders (two-thirds of them) and other activists rather than advocates of particular candidates or causes. They had been chosen, not by caucuses open to all Republicans, but by local party committees. Only a third of those in our survey professed to have made a commitment to a candidate before being chosen, though most had been contacted by several candidates.

Given their backgrounds, these delegates might have been expected to support experienced party leaders rather than outsiders, but a majority of them voted to endorse John Lakian, a 39-year-old businessman, and a millionaire who demonstrated a willingness to use his funds lavishly for campaigning. By the time the convention met, he had already spent $200,000, much more than any other candidate. He had spent a full year campaigning and courting prospective delegates.

Delegates appeared to be impressed not only by Lakian's lavish parties for Republicans but also by his willingness to contribute enough funds to make possible a large-scale, professional campaign for the November election. Most of the Lakian delegates in our survey (83 percent) said they supported him because he had the best chance of winning; 71 percent mentioned his stand on issues; 29 percent emphasized the importance of having a fresh new face or a charismatic personality. Very few mentioned his ability to fund much of the campaign, but this may have been a reason why most stressed his electability.

Lakian won 57 percent of the vote on the first ballot. His only serious challenger, with 34 percent, was William Robinson, an 18-year veteran of the legislature and the House minority leader. Robinson's supporters in our survey emphasized his stand on issues and his experience; half of them also said he had the best chance of being elected. A majority of the delegates, however, decided that the party's best chance was to select a new face, a candidate with campaign skills and the resources to launch a strong media campaign.

After losing the endorsement, Robinson dropped out of the race; on the other hand, Andrew Card, a four-term legislator with a record as a moderate, decided to stay in the primary despite getting only 7 percent of the convention vote. The third candidate in the primary was John Sears, a Boston city council member with a long record in politics who started the campaign better known than any other candidate. Sears was unenthusiastic about the endorsement process, and decided to bypass it entirely.

In some respects the Massachusetts Republican convention was a success. It avoided bitter fights over candidates or ideology, and it chose a candidate largely on the basis of electability. It failed, however, in two respects. It was unable to prevent a major candidate, John Sears, from bypassing the convention and challenging the endorsee. And it misjudged the political skills of John Lakian. He got only 27 percent of the vote in the primary, finishing far behind Sears and barely ahead of Andrew Card. Lakian's loss was caused in large part by doubts raised in the press about the accuracy of statements in his campaign literature about his record and background. We will return to this story in later chapters.

New York Republicans: Endorsing a Winner

For the classic example of the well-financed outsider winning convention endorsement, we turn to the New York Republican party and the saga of Lew Lehrman. Lehrman was a multimillionaire without a political record, who won convention endorsement over three experienced political leaders after spending millions on television advertising — and went on to win the primary election and almost win the election.

The New York endorsing conventions of both parties differ from the other conventions we have been examining because they are actually meetings of the state central committee. This results in a much smaller convention. It also means that the delegates have not been elected just for this purpose, but are the local party leaders serving a four-year term on the state committee. They are the most active party workers, presumably concerned more about selecting winning candidates than helping a candidate or an ideological cause.

Another important aspect of the New York delegates is that they are members of local party organizations, some of which may be powerful enough to influence the votes cast by the delegates. Members of a county delegation may vote together out of a sense of loyalty to the organization, a desire to get or keep patronage, or for other reasons. Delegates to such a convention are less likely to be free agents than those at the other conventions we have surveyed.

The survey of convention delegates provides some evidence about the importance of local organizations. (The results from the New York surveys should be analyzed with some caution because the sample of delegates in both parties is smaller, both proportionately and in absolute terms, than in other conventions.) Over four-fifths of the delegates said that the county party organization attempted to take a united position on the governor's race, and only a few said that the effort failed. When asked what were the advantages to the local organization in voting as a bloc on endorsement, the most frequent answers were: It gives the organization clout or leverage in the party; it prevents divisive splits in the party; it helps the party in getting patronage if it unites behind a winner; and it enhances the organization's influence over choice of a candidate. It is also worth noting that three-fourths of the delegates said they consulted active party workers in their county or district in making their choice.

Lewis Lehrman is a multimillionaire, who made his fortune from a chain of drug stores. He brought to the campaign for governor his financial resources, an intense style of campaigning, and doctrinaire conservative views. At convention time he had already spent $3 million and become the best-known candidate through an advertising campaign that saturated the television channels. Delegates arriving for the mid-June convention in New York City were greeted by a poll of Republican voters in the New York *Post* showing that Lehrman had 43 percent, each of his three rivals had 5 or 6 percent, and 41 percent were undecided. The poll showed that 72 percent of the voters could identify Lehrman; the recognition level for other candidates ranged from 19 to 49 percent.

Lehrman's three opponents were experienced Republican leaders, though not well known to the voting public. Paul Curran had served in the legislature and in the mid-1970s had been U.S. attorney in Manhattan, but he had not been active in political affairs for several years. James Emery was an eighteen-year veteran of the state Assembly and currently its minority leader. Richard Rosenbaum was a veteran political leader and former state party chairman, long associated with Nelson Rockefeller.

The Republican party establishment, and specifically the leaders of local party organizations, were dismayed by Lehrman's candidacy. They viewed him not only as an independent, nonorganization man, but also as one who, if elected governor, would challenge the power of county leaders. They sought to find a candidate who could stop him. Joseph Margiotta, the leader of the largest and most tightly organized local party, in Nassau County, endorsed Curran, who also picked up support from leaders of two other large counties: New York and Erie. But the Curran campaign failed to make much headway with other local leaders. James Emery came to the convention with the support of 22 county leaders, a large number of whom were reported to be on Emery's Assembly payroll. Rosenbaum claimed support from three county leaders. Lehrman announced that he had the support of 15 county chairmen, most importantly the leader of the Kings County (Brooklyn) organization.

The New York conventions of both parties differ from the other conventions we have studied because of the role played by county leaders. Only in this state did candidates announce in advance which county chairmen were supporting them. This obviously reflects the stronger organization of party organizations in the state, but also the consequences of having the state committee, rather than an elected convention, make the endorsement.

The nearly 400 Republican delegates (along with nonvoting county chairs) met in a long, narrow, and often crowded ballroom in a New York City hotel. After conducting routine business the first afternoon, the convention was scheduled to convene promptly at 10 the next morning, and most of the delegates were in their seats. An hour later the party chairman announced that the start of the session would be delayed because of negotiations among party leaders. When the session finally began, at about 2, the delegates were told simply that the discussions had not been successful.

The negotiations had been undertaken by state chairman George Clark, who believed that a compromise could be worked out if Emery was persuaded to take second place on the ticket. Emery balked at this, however, because other candidates would not guarantee him nomination as lieutenant governor, nor were they willing for a convention vote to be taken on that race before the gubernatorial contest. One obstacle was that Curran had already picked someone else to be his running mate.

When our sample of delegates were asked about whether it was desirable to engage in such negotiations, 58 percent agreed that it was; most stressed the need for a strong ticket and the desirability of weeding out weak candidates. On the other hand 36 percent argued that the decision should be left to the delegates.

The four candidates were placed in nomination, and each was entitled to a demonstration. For the most part delegates stood and watched, or waved posters, while demonstrators marched in from the lobby and encircled the delegates. Lew Lehrman, in shirtsleeves and his well-known red suspenders, joined his own demonstration.

The roll call voting was a laborious process because each committee member voted individually, or in some cases had a designated alternate vote. It was also complicated because each delegate cast a different number of votes, based on the number of Republican votes cast in the last gubernatorial election in the district he or she represents.

At the end of the first ballot, Lehrman had 27.5 percent, Curran 26.6, Emery 25.8, and Rosenbaum 20. The first three had qualified for the primary, and were in virtually a dead heat. The second ballot brought little change, although Emery lost some votes and Rosenbaum gained enough to pull even with him. It was obviously time for more negotiations. This time there was only a brief delay, and then Chairman Clark announced that the morning's negotiations had been an effort to get Emery to run for lieutenant governor, and that Emery now had an announcement. Emery appeared, announced he was withdrawing from the gubernatorial race and would make himself available for nomination as lieutenant governor. The third ballot then began, but was interrupted to permit Rosenbaum to announce his withdrawal from the race. At the end of the third ballot Lehrman had 69 percent of the vote for endorsement. He had picked up virtually all of the Emery delegates and some of the Rosenbaum ones.

It was now nearly midnight, and Chairman Clark was telling an exhausted and rebellious convention that because they were behind schedule they should stay in session to take up the next agenda item: the attorney general's race. At that point a motion was made to suspend the rules and nominate Emery for lieutenant governor by acclamation. The proposal caught the gubernatorial candidates and the convention leadership by surprise, but it was obviously popular with the delegates and it was soon passed enthusiastically.

Because of the publicized claims by candidates about commitments by county chairmen, it is worth looking at the extent of bloc voting by county delegations. There were 43 counties where a candidate had publicly claimed to have the chairman's support; 33 voted for that candidate with complete unity; 4 provided majority support, and 6 were sharply divided. Most of the largest county delegations voted with complete or almost total unity, including Nassau, Erie, and New York for Curran; Westchester for Emery; Onondaga for Lehrman; and Monroe for Rosenbaum. Emery had united support in a number of small counties, while Lehrman had all or most of the votes in a number of medium-sized and small counties whose chairmen supported him.

When asked their reason for voting for each candidate, about one-third of all delegates, except those for Lehrman, mentioned organizational pressure or the need for unity in the group. Supporters of Curran and Lehrman often either said he was more electable or mentioned specific political advantages, such as effective television advertising, a well-organized campaign or help for the local ticket — the types of reasons seldom given by delegates in other states. Delegates also stressed personal qualities of all candidates, the experience of Curran and Emery, and the fact that Emery and Rosenbaum came from upstate. It is worth noting that Lehrman's doctrinaire conservatism was barely mentioned as an asset.

At the end of the second ballot, it appeared that there might be a deadlock with no endorsement possible, as Lehrman had been predicting. There seem to have been several reasons why the convention majority at that point turned to Lehrman rather than Curran. It was obvious that Lehrman was going to run in the primary, with or without majority endorsement, and was prepared to invest as much money as needed for a winning campaign. Lehrman already had a huge lead in the polls. Moreover, Lehrman was prepared to use his own resources in the general election, and the party was badly in need of campaign funds. Curran lacked the personal resources and apparently the fund-raising ability to mount an effective challenge. In effect, most of those party leaders not committed to Curran decided that Lehrman should be endorsed because he could not be beaten. They proved to be correct. Lehrman outspent Curran 20 to 1 in the primary and beat him by an 88-20 margin.

Lehrman had one other advantage. It was obvious by the time the convention met that, whatever the Republicans did, he would be endorsed by the Conservative party. If he were defeated in the Republican primary, he could still run in November on the Conservative line, almost certainly drawing enough votes from the Republican nominee to ensure a Democratic victory. It seems clear that, though he sought the endorsement and very much wanted to meet the 25 percent standard, Lehrman did not consider endorsement by a majority of delegates either likely or essential for his campaign.

In assessing the Republican endorsing convention, one should remember that this was the party's first experience with a contest for governor, or a gubernatorial primary, under the current law. It is significant that the convention succeeded in making an endorsement, despite the early three-way deadlock. It clearly nominated its strongest candidate, who won a landslide in the primary and came surprisingly close in the general election. It accomplished this by nominating an outsider, a candidate who seemed likely to win the primary with or without the endorsement. The record of the convention was hardly one of success for the party organization — except success in recognizing political strength.

New York Democrats: The Mayor's Convention

The battle for the Democratic gubernatorial nomination began on January 15 with Governor Hugh Carey's surprising announcement that he would not seek a third term. The *New York Times*, in covering the story, listed nine plausible candidates for the nomination, headed by Lieutenant Governor Mario Cuomo, who was described as "all but certain to try." Nowhere in the story was there any mention of New York City Mayor Edward Koch. Ten days later Koch startled the other candidates by admitting to reporters that he was considering running for governor, despite repeated statements in the past that he would complete his term as mayor and his assertion that living in Albany would be a "fate worse than death." By late February, Koch was officially in the governor's race and everyone else had pulled out except Mario Cuomo.

Koch, starting with a strong base, but not absolute control, in New York City, set out on a personal trip to win over delegates in upstate New York, and to overcome the effects of numerous comments he had made about the dreariness of life outside his city. Koch's campaign was well organized, under the direction of famed campaign manager David Garth. By early April the press was reporting that Koch had secured majority support from state committee members, including the endorsement of four New York City county chairmen and the Erie county chairman.

The convention that met in Syracuse in late June was clearly dominated by Mayor Koch. The only interesting questions were how large his margin would be and what candidates he would select as his slate. The 357 voting committee members (plus those county chairmen who were not members) met in a theater in the Civic Center. The theater was designed with several levels of boxes along the sides of the horseshoe, and these were used by some of the major television stations and newspapers. During the 6 p.m. news hour delegates could watch Mayor Koch scurrying from box to box for live TV interviews.

Koch and Cuomo were nominated quickly. The brief "demonstrations" consisted of some delegates standing and waving posters while 30 or 40 supporters in the gallery, out of sight of most delegates, waved signs and tooted horns. For connoisseurs of demonstrations, these were a total flop. Of course there were no marching bands, though a tuxedo-clad orchestra at the side of the stage played music whenever the convention proceedings were dull or a candidate was introduced.

On the gubernatorial roll call Koch won 61 percent of the vote, and Cuomo 39. The Cuomo total was larger than some had expected, but it did not really diminish Koch's comfortable control of the convention. The roll-call voting system was like that in the New York Republican party, with votes weighted according to the party strength in each district. The actual distribution of votes was different from that in the Republican convention because of greater Democratic voting strength in New York City. The delegates from the five boroughs of New York City had 39 percent of the total vote, and those from the three largest suburban counties around the city had 21 percent.

In responding to our survey, 64 percent of the Koch delegates and 46 percent of Cuomo supporters said that their county delegations tried to take a united position on a gubernatorial candidate. As was the case for Republican delegates, they emphasized the importance of giving the local organization leverage and a share of patronage, supporting a winner, and avoiding divisive splits. Over 90 percent of delegates said they consulted local party workers in the process of making a decision about candidates.

In fact there was somewhat less perfect cohesion in the larger Democratic delegations than had been true in the Republican convention. Among the largest counties, Suffolk was united and Bronx almost united for Koch, and he had large margins in several of the others (Queens, Kings, and Erie); Cuomo had united support in Albany and large margins in Westchester and Monroe. Many of the upstate counties had only two or three delegates, making unity less of an accomplishment.

When asked reasons for their support, very few mentioned organizational pressure. Among the Koch delegates, 55 percent said he was more electable; nearly half mentioned his record and nearly half stressed personal qualities. Cuomo supporters most often referred to his stand on issues, his interest in upstate New York, his personal qualities, and the preference of local voters for him. Koch supporters almost never mentioned issues; Cuomo supporters rarely said he had the better chance of being elected.

After the balloting for governor had ended, the convention devoted its attention to making endorsements for the rest of the slate. It is a well-established practice for the gubernatorial endorsee to put together a balanced slate, one designed to help him in the fall election, and Koch devoted much time and effort to the negotiations for such a slate. Cuomo decided not to engage in slating, because he lacked the votes to make it effective and because he might benefit from a hands-off policy. In our survey most Koch delegates, but only half the Cuomo supporters, approved of the principle of slate-building by the gubernatorial candidate. Those who responded favorably were more likely to mention geographic balance (53 percent) than ethnic balance (28 percent); some also noted the governor's need to have a lieutenant governor he could work with.

There is another tradition that has developed in the New York Democratic endorsing convention: assuring that serious candidates for all races get the 25 percent vote necessary to enter the primary without petitions. It is a practice criticized by some party leaders, including the state chairmen, because it has the effect of undermining the impact of the endorsement. In our survey 71 percent of the respondents favored the practice of encouraging competition by giving 25 percent support to serious candidates — with Cuomo supporters more likely than Koch supporters to agree. Those responding favorably generally emphasized that primaries were healthy for the party and that serious candidates should be spared the nuisance of collecting signatures.

In the roll calls for both comptroller and lieutenant governor (the only contested races), the delegates gave the required 25 percent to three candidates, and then many of them shifted on the second ballot to give comfortable majorities to Koch's candidates. In some cases delegates who were supporting Koch agreed to accept his choice for another office on the second ballot after fulfilling commitments to others on the first ballot. The Koch organization, which was equipped with a computer recording the first and second choices of delegates, apparently engaged in considerable maneuvering to make sure that other candidates gained their 25 percent while Koch's candidates maintained a secure lead and gained a second-ballot majority.

When the balloting finally ended, each of the candidates who had met the 25 percent standard was entitled to address the convention, with the endorsed candidates speaking first. Fearful that he would be speaking to a half-empty hall, Cuomo negotiated a compromise under which he would speak after Koch, to be followed by endorsed candidates for other offices, and then those others with a 25 percent vote. Koch and Cuomo in turn were greeted enthusiastically by their partisans; Cuomo appeared to be the more effective speaker. As the other candiates took their turn one by one at the podium, the crowd diminished. Delegates who had a particular interest in a candidate for lesser office stayed long enough to cheer his speech, and then left in his wake. When the last speaker for comptroller was introduced, the hall was almost empty except for a few reporters typing their stories and one patient political scientist. In fact, the final candidate for comptroller had also gone home, leaving a substitute to speak for him. And so the New York Democratic convention ended, not with a bang, but a whimper.

The convention had selected the gubernatorial candidate who was ahead in the polls, in organization, and in financing, the strangely charismatic mayor of New York who did not want to live in Albany. It had endorsed his slate of running mates despite the views of many delegates and political observers that he had not picked wisely. No one seemed to doubt that the state committee had picked the strongest gubernatorial candidate, but it had not prevented — or tried to discourage — the lieutenant governor from challenging him. Three months later, on September 23, Mario Cuomo defeated Edward Koch for the nomination by a margin of 53-47 percent, or nearly 75,000 votes. We will try to explain that curious result in later chapters.

CONCLUSIONS

It is difficult and potentially misleading to generalize from a few case studies about variations in convention practices and the consequences of endorsements. The purpose of such case studies is to show the variety of variables that can affect conventions. In

Connecticut both the provisions of the primary challenge law and political tradition discourage nonendorsed candidates from entering the primary; but in 1982 gubernatorial candidate Bozzuto was deterred partly by shortages of funds, and senatorial candidate Bush gave up because of political realities and the poll results. An incumbent governor should be able to maintain enough influence over the party to win endorsement, as O'Neill did in the Connecticut Democratic convention; King's failure to do so in Massachusetts has a wide variety of explanations. In Minnesota, where gubernatorial endorsees were beaten in both party primaries by candidates bypassing the convention, the explanations for these losses are quite different.

The model of an endorsing convention as an organization of party activists, primarily interested in winning elections and enhancing organizational strength can be eroded by strong candidate organizations that influence delegate selection, as in the New Mexico parties and the Massachusetts Democratic party. It can also be undermined by issue-oriented delegates, as in both Minnesota parties.

The purpose of this chapter has been largely descriptive: to show how conventions operate and how and why they vary among the states. The purpose of the next chapter is to examine the effectiveness of endorsements. Under what conditions and for what reasons do endorsements affect the outcome of primaries, or prevent contested primaries? What are the major obstacles to successful endorsements? Fortunately, the 1982 examples provide us with a wide range of political situations and results.

5

The Impact of
Convention Endorsements

What difference do convention endorsements make? Does the endorsed candidate usually win, and if so, does the endorsement contribute significantly to that victory? Under what conditions, and in what political situations, does the endorsee win — or lose? Chapter 3 summarized the results of convention endorsements over some thirty years in those states where such data were available. Table 3.3 showed how often the endorsee was challenged in the primary, and how often beaten. Chapter 4 described the circumstances under which endorsements were made at several 1982 conventions, and then reported the fate of the endorsee. The purpose of this chapter is to analyze the 1982 endorsements in an effort to understand their impact on the political process, and specifically on the electoral outcomes.

The most obvious impact that an endorsement might have is to contribute to the victory of the endorsee in the primary, either by persuading other candidates to withdraw or by providing various forms of tangible or intangible help to the endorsee in defeating challengers. A second electoral impact of an endorsement might be to contribute to success in the general election through the selection of a candidate, or a slate of candidates, capable of winning in that race. There may also be indirect effects of endorsements, contributing to the strength of party organization or arousing the interest of party activists. There could also be negative impacts. The fight over an endorsement in a convention might be more divisive than a primary battle, or the convention delegates might choose a candidate less able to win the general election than others who might have entered and won the primary in the absence of an endorsement.

The most direct and obvious consequence of an endorsement is to eliminate other primary candidates. In a few states, such as Connecticut, nonendorsees may be forced out of the primary if they fall short of a minimum percentage of votes in the convention. A nonendorsee may drop out because of a sense of party loyalty or a commitment made in advance not to challenge the endorsee — a commitment usually made under the pressure of party norms. Finally, a nonendorsee may drop out because a poor showing at the convention convinces the candidate that victory in the primary is unlikely.

If other candidates challenge the endorsee in the primary, what kinds of advantage might the endorsee have? The advantage might be largely psychological, a matter of momentum and a demonstration that one has the organizational and campaign skills necessary to win. It might be more tangible, if those who work in and contribute to campaigns are more likely to support the endorsee. In a few states there may be tangible advantages because the party organization contributes various kinds of material assistance to the endorsee.

It is also possible that the endorsee will benefit in the primary because voters are more likely to support the endorsee. In those states where the endorsee has top place on the ballot, it is likely that some voters who know relatively little about the candidates will vote for the name at the top, without knowing what the top position implies about party endorsement. It is also possible that some voters will be aware of the endorsement and will consciously vote for the endorsed candidate. There is, of course, the possibility that some knowledgeable voters will deliberately vote against the endorsed candidate. Voters who would deliberately support the endorsee would presumably be those with a strong sense of loyalty to the party or specifically to the party organization. In recent years there has been a decline in the proportion of voters who identify strongly with the party and of those who vote consistently with the party in general elections. This fact should make us very cautious in testing the hypothesis that endorsees benefit from the deliberate action of primary voters.

One indirect, but important effect of the convention endorsement system may be to revitalize the political party structure and provide incentives for campaign participation to political activists. V. O. Key (1956 ch. 6) suggested that the growth of the direct primary and the consequent elimination of caucuses and conventions contributed to the atrophy of party organization, particularly in the minority.

One major source of evidence for answering these questions is the responses of delegates to our questionnaires. It is mostly perceptual evidence, but it comes from a large number of persons very much involved in the political process. They are in a position to evaluate not only electoral consequences of endorsements but also the effects on party organization. There is very limited evidence available in a few states from surveys of votes. Part of this analysis will rest on a review of events that followed the endorsing conventions summarized in the previous chapter.

DELEGATE EVALUATIONS OF
THE ENDORSEMENT PROCESS

The delegates who responded to our survey were asked several questions about the endorsement process. The specific questions were not identical in all states because of variations in the way the endorsement process works. Most were asked a simple question about whether convention endorsements were desirable, or good for the party, and were asked an open-ended question about their reasons for that evaluation. Most were also asked an open-ended question about the advantages that a gubernatorial candidate gains from being endorsed, in the event of a primary contest.

Table 5.1 summarizes responses in three states to the question about whether the practice of endorsements is good for the party. We would expect to find the strongest support for endorsements in those parties where the tradition is most solidly established, but it would also be plausible to find less support among those delegates whose candidate was not endorsed. In Connecticut, where the practice of endorsements is very well established, there is very strong support among Democrats, but among Republicans the level of support depends on candidate preferences. New Mexico is a state

Table 5.1
Views of Delegates about Whether Endorsements Are Desirable by Party and Candidate Preference
(in percentages)

Connecticut

Are Endorsements Good?	Democrats	Republicans					
	Total	Total	Rome	Bozzuto	Labriola	Weicker	Bush
Yes	86	64	71	59	52	72	45
No	7	32	24	37	48	24	51
It depends	7	4	5	4	0	4	4
(N)	(89)	(174)	(82)	(71)	(20)	(117)	(53)

New Mexico

Are Endorsements Good?	Democrats				Republicans		
	Total	Anaya	Dunn	Others	Total	Irick	Sego
Yes	47	54	41	40	55	58	38
No	46	36	56	53	43	42	52
It depends	7	9	3	7	2	0	10
(N)	(89)	(33)	(34)	(18)	(87)	(68)	(25)

Massachusetts

| | Democrats | | | Republicans | | | |
	Total	Dukakis	King	Total	Lakian	Robinson	Others
Yes	80	92	48	79	89	72	42
No	17	5	50	17	6	28	42
It depends	3	3	2	4	5	0	16
(N)	(241)	(174)	(56)	(179)	(102)	(53)	(20)

Source: Compiled by the author.

127

where endorsements are an off-again-on-again process, and this ambivalence is reflected in the attitude of delegates, only about half of whom favor endorsements. There is less support for endorsement among the backers of winners in New Mexico than in the other states. The Massachusetts Republican party has a long record of successful endorsements, which may explain the strong record of delegate support for the endorsement practice. In the Massachusetts Democratic party, as we would expect, support for endorsement is very high among the Dukakis delegates; what is surprising is that half of the King delegates support endorsement, despite King's adamant opposition.

In Minnesota, where the principle of endorsement appears to be well established in both parties, delegates were asked whether the convention should make endorsements in every race or whether there are circumstances that justify no endorsement. In the DFL, 57 percent of the delegates recognized circumstances that would make endorsement undesirable or perhaps impossible; among IR delegates the figure was only 40 percent. Delegates most often mentioned the following: None of the candidates is good enough or none supports the party platform, the convention is deadlocked, or there is a close contest among equally good candidates. Minnesota delegates were also asked if all the party's candidates for state office should seek convention endorsement and abide by the result. Almost two-thirds of DFL delegates and just over half of IR delegates believed that they should.

The endorsement law in New York permits anyone getting 25 percent in any ballot in the convention to enter the primary without further requirements, and in the Democratic party it is common to manipulate voting so that most serious candidates can get 25 percent. Delegates in both parties were asked whether candidates not getting a majority should be encouraged or discouraged from running in the primary. Among Democratic delegates, 71 percent favored encouraging other candidates; among Republicans the comparable figure was 52 percent. There was greater support for such an inclusive policy among delegates committed to Mario Cuomo, who came in second and among Republicans backing Lehrman, who — though the winner — was the outsider who appeared dubious about the endorsement process, and his supporters seemed to share those doubts.

Those delegates in our survey who responded that convention endorsements are good — or are not good — were asked, in open-ended fashion, the reasons for that evaluation. The results are summarized in Tables 5.2 and 5.3. Specific answers have been coded to fit into broad categories, and only the more frequent answers are included. In addition to Connecticut, New Mexico, and Massachusetts, where this question was asked, results are included from Minnesota to the question about whether every candidate should seek, and abide by, convention endorsement, because it produced similar responses. (Reasons for negative responses are omitted for Connecticut Democrats because there were so few.) The figures given are percentages of all delegates favoring endorsement (Table 5.2) and opposing it (Table 5.3); they add to more than 100 percent because of multiple responses. No breakdown is given by candidate support because the numbers for each subgroup of delegates are small and the reasons emphasized by each tend to be similar.

Convention delegates, particularly those who have been active in a variety of political activities, ought to have a realistic perception of the advantages and disadvantages of endorsement for the party system. One purpose of asking these questions is to find out how much that perception differs among the state parties.

The most common recurring theme in the positive responses of delegates in all eight state parties relates to the role played in endorsements by party activists. Endorsement is a desirable practice because it gives the hard-working, well-informed activist a chance to play a significant role in the political process. Within this broad theme, several specific points emerge repeatedly in the responses. One is that party activists are well equipped to make endorsements, more so than the average voter in the primary election: "Party activists have insight and experience, and can usually avoid candidates who do not have a broad party base." "Delegates constitute the backbone of campaign committees. They are the best and hardest-working campaigners. They have the best knowledge of a candidate's background and are more likely to pick a winner."

Another aspect of this theme is the argument that the delegate-selection process is representative — at least of those persons with an active interest in the party: "The convention process works because it forces people who want a say in government to become actively involved. Anyone could have been elected as a delegate in

Table 5.2
Reasons Why Delegates Say Endorsement System Is Good
(as percentage of those with positive response)

Reasons Why Good	Conn.		N.M.		Mass.		Minn.	
	Dem.	Rep.	Dem.	Rep.	Dem.	Rep.	Dem.	Rep.
Participation by active workers	64	51	33	39	59	39	34	42
Helps party unity	10	6	5	11	15	23	39	49
Other party-building reasons	15	12	10	13	33	38	35	28
Eliminates weak candidates	13	14	36	26	19	10	3	—
Gets better candidates	14	22	17	22	25	24	—	—
Helps voters decide	—	—	—	—	5	6	—	—
Critical of primaries	17	41	—	—	—	—	7	10
(N)	(72)	(109)	(42)	(46)	(180)	(142)	(140)	(119)

Source: Compiled by the author.

Table 5.3
Reasons Why Delegates Say Endorsement System Is Bad
(as percentage of those with negative response)

Reasons Why Bad	Conn.		N.M.		Mass.		Minn.	
	Dem.	Rep.	Dem.	Rep.	Dem.	Rep.	Dem.	Rep.
Convention is not representative	—	17	58	37	42	19	26	22
Causes party disunity	—	—	28	47	14	14	—	—
Waste of money	—	—	5	37	33	22	—	—
Good candidates left out	—	—	28	47	—	—	17	16
Let voters decide	—	73	—	—	19	19	32	54
Issue-related answer	—	—	—	—	—	—	18	21
Meaningless, not binding	—	3	15	11	28	46	—	—
(N)		(59)	(40)	(38)	(43)	(37)	(65)	(87)

Source: Compiled by the author.

Massachusetts. There was a real grassroots involvement in our Democratic caucuses and in the convention itself. It was not backroom politics. Delegates were not appointed."

Some of the delegates emphasized the linkage between this role for the party worker and the development of the local party system: "The convention system strengthens the local party structure and provides an opportunity for participation by party members who work in the business of politics day in and day out." "This convention is the only thing that has reawakened our local town committee. It gives local Republicans something to do. Primaries are actually destroying grass-roots party organization."

If these delegates are correct, the effects of the endorsement process on a political party cannot be evaluated only by looking at the success of nomination; the process may provide incentives for party workers and strengthen the local organizations. The convention itself may be a vehicle for building contacts at the state level among local party workers.

There is, however, another side to the story. The most common theme of those delegates who criticized the endorsement system was that the convention, and the delegate selection process, were unrepresentative. These critics did not generally dispute the value of involving party activists in the process or strengthening local organizations, but they questioned whether the process for selecting delegates adequately represented party activists, or (in the case of some critics) rank-and-file voters who are loyal to the party. While some critics spoke generally about poor representation, others defined specific distortions in the process — some pertinent to one state party.

One of the specific criticisms repeated by a few delegates in several states was that the process is unrepresentative because it is controlled by machine politicians. A New Mexico Democrat said: "Most ordinary Democrats knew nothing about the initial ward/precinct meetings, and understood less about the complicated voting system. And so the delegates were pretty much party hacks and part of the old Democratic machine — a few exceptions, of course."

A more common complaint concerned the ability of special interests to dominate the selection process. One delegate said, "It is too easy for special interest groups, that do not represent total party membership, to control delegates." A different perspective on special interests came from a Minnesota DFL member: "Political parties are 'Good Old Boy Systems.' Too often, in reality, the system excludes women, minorities, and other interests."

Earlier in this book, I made the distinction between conventions that appeared to be dominated by party organizations and others dominated by candidate organizations. If candidate organizations are able to mobilize their supporters at the caucuses, they may displace persons with a stronger record of party activity. The convention may not, in fact, be representative of party activists. A Massachusetts Democratic delegate who supported Dukakis and generally approved of the endorsement principle nevertheless raised a question about the selection process: "Many of us were at the convention primarily as Dukakis supporters, with no previous involvement in local party affairs. In our town, for example, nearly all of the party 'regulars' were on the King slate, and the Dukakis candidates swept the caucus, leaving the experienced politicians at home."

A final criticism of the representative quality of the convention makes a distinction on ideological grounds between the most active party members and rank-and-file delegates. A Massachusetts Republican said: "The convention process is controlled by a very small minority of the registered voters in Massachusetts. These individuals tend to be of a more conservative strain than the general electorate of the state as well as what I would consider to be the mainstream ideology here. To allow this group to dictate the nominees for the party when votes from both Independents and Democrats are needed to ensure success strikes me as political suicide."

This last criticism was not a common one among delegates, but it is a very perceptive one. Numerous studies by political scientists have shown that party activists such as convention delegates are usually more extreme in their views than rank-and-file voters; Democratic activists are more liberal, and Republicans more conservative. There is some evidence that voters who participate in primaries are less moderate than those who vote only in general elections, but the differences are smaller (and less supported by empirical research) than the findings about convention delegates. This suggests an intriguing dilemma for political parties. Delegates to an endorsing convention have the knowledge and political skill to make a wiser choice of candidates who are electable, but they may be handicapped in making such a choice if they are out of touch, or out of step, in an ideological sense with those voters most likely to support the candidates of their party.

A major theme of delegates in some states, particularly Minnesota, is the need for party unity. The argument is an obvious one: If the party is united, it is more likely to win, and if the convention — by endorsing a candidate — can prevent or reduce serious primary competition, the party will be more united. This reason may not be mentioned more frequently because endorsements often do not produce unity. In Table 5.2 several types of responses are lumped together as "other party-building reasons"; the common thread is the explicit assertion that the party benefits from endorsements. One Minnesota DFL delegate summarized an argument repeatedly made by members of that party: "The primary system has decimated local and state political parties. The precinct caucus/endorsement process has the best chance of building a strong, issue-oriented party system which can hold political officeholders accountable after they are elected."

The emphasis on issues is also reflected in this comment from a Massachusetts Republican: "A political party is, or at least should be, a group of people united to promote a specific political philosophy. People who join political parties and are active tend to be more ideological than the general population and support candidates that reflect the principles of the party. The state convention provides a means of preserving and articulating the party's principles through the endorsement of a candidate." It is interesting to find a similar argument coming from a different perspective — from a Massachusetts Democrat: "The Republican party in Massachusetts, with occasional exceptions, is an insignificant force in state government. The Democratic party often serves as a flag of political convenience to any and all office seekers. Without some forum to test candidate positions, Democratic voters can be buying a pig-in-a-political-poke." Another Massachusetts Democrat used a different analogy to emphasize the need for cohesion in the party: "The Massachusetts Democratic party traditionally operates in a fashion that was popular in the Middle Ages. The party consists of a multitude of feudal baronies even to the local city, town, and precinct level. There is no unity of purpose or program. Each candidate carves out his own limited portion of the electorate to insure his election. The endorsing convention is a limited first step in creating a Democratic party in Massachusetts — a first step in breaking out of the Middle Ages."

Some delegates articulated more specific party-related reasons for endorsements. A number of Massachusetts Republicans, noting the party's minority status and its difficulty in attracting public attention, suggested that the convention served a valuable purpose because it attracted media attention, at least for a brief period. Delegates in several state parties asserted that victory in the November election required a balanced ticket, which only a convention could achieve.

A pair of closely related themes are found consistently in the positive responses of delegates from New Mexico, Connecticut, and Massachusetts (Table 5.2): The endorsement process helps to eliminate weak candidates and concentrates support behind those candidates who have the best chance of winning both the primary and the general election. We have noted that this was one of the reasons for reviving the endorsement system in New Mexico; moreover, the single-ballot system focuses attention on eliminating candidates who fall below 20 percent in the convention. The Connecticut parties and the Massachusetts Democrats have systems that exclude from the primary those who fall short of a minimum vote in convention.

One response from a delegate summarizes well the virtue of endorsement as a screening device: "It is true of course that some otherwise excellent candidates slip through the grates, at least for a while if not permanently, as the convention seeks to sift out live coals from cooling ashes. But those persons who can make it through the convention are, for the most part, those most likely to be able to repeat that success in a statewide election."

A comparable criticism of endorsement would be that it eliminates good candidates who may lack the head start, organizational contacts, or funds to win convention support but who might do well at the polls. This argument was frequently mentioned by critics in New Mexico and Minnesota.

Except for a few Massachusetts delegates, there is no evidence of the argument that endorsements provide valuable advice to the voters. In a state like Connecticut, of course, the endorsement system usually prevents primaries entirely. We will return to this question when we examine the perceived advantages enjoyed by the endorsee.

Supporters of endorsements often criticized primaries, particularly in Connecticut and in Minnesota, where there was particular concern about the fact that the primary was open to participation by members of either party and independents. One frequent criticism of the primary is that voters are not well enough informed about the candidates. Another is that primaries are costly and reward the candidate with resources. A Connecticut Republican said: "A direct primary puts too much emphasis on the ability to raise money for the advertising required in a primary. A candidate can win a convention with far less expenditure."

Another criticism of the primary concerns the problem of ideology also raised by critics of the convention. A Connecticut Republican argues: "In a straight primary it is the extremists — the one-issue people, the far left or the far right — who work the hardest to get out the vote; it is not a true representation, and turnout is low." Similarly, a Connecticut Democrat believes: "Primaries tend to produce more liberal candidates who are extremely difficult to elect. The convention process is generally reflective of the dominant party philosophy; conventions generally nominate 'moderates,' i.e. liberals that look and sound like conservatives."

The simplest, most direct criticism of the endorsement process is that the voters should be permitted to make the decision in the primary; a related argument is that a primary contest is good for the party.

While the endorsement process is defended as less costly than primaries, some Massachusetts and New Mexico delegates perceive the convention as costly. Some argue that well-financed candidates have an advantage in mobilizing support in the caucuses; others assert that the endorsement system increases the costs of campaigning because candidates must spend money on conventions in addition to the costs of the primary campaign — assuming that the convention does not make a primary unnecessary.

While primaries are criticized because they may be dominated by nonmoderate voters or manipulated by single-issue groups, some Minnesota delegates in both parties believe that it is legitimate and necessary to challenge the endorsee in a primary when issues are at stake — for example, if the convention nominates a candidate who does not support the principles of the party.

Finally, a substantial number of Massachusetts delegates and some in New Mexico criticize the endorsing convention as being meaningless, because the endorsee can be challenged in a primary, and — in New Mexico — the only result is to eliminate the weakest candidates. Almost half of the Massachusetts Republican critics, and one-fourth of those who supported endorsements, argued that the convention should be binding. Presumably this means not merely a legal convention, but one that would replace the primary. This was partly a reaction to the fact that in 1978, for the first time, the gubernatorial endorsee was defeated in the primary. Massachusetts Democrats who called the convention meaningless were King supporters, however, who did not want it to be binding.

DELEGATE PERCEPTIONS OF ENDORSEE ADVANTAGES

All of the convention delegates (except Massachusetts Republicans) were asked what advantages the endorsee gains from endorsement if there is a primary challenge. The answers are summarized in Table 5.4. The figures are percentages of all those who responded (including those who said there was no advantage); figures add to more than 100 percent because of multiple responses.

We would expect to find substantial differences among the states, and this is borne out by the responses. Perhaps the most important difference among the states is the proportion of delegates who believe that the endorsement makes little or no difference in the primary. Very few delegates gave that response in Minnesota (where both gubernatorial endorsees were to lose) and in Connecticut (where the endorsees were unchallenged, as usual). In New York, a number of Democratic delegates believed endorsement was no advantage or was even a liability, because the endorsee was perceived as being the choice of party bosses. In New Mexico and in the Massachusetts Democratic party a substantial minority of the delegates (particularly those who did not support the endorsee) doubted that the endorsement would help the endorsee in the primary. It should be recalled that in New Mexico less importance is attached in the convention to selecting the top choice than to eliminating weak candidates.

The greatest contrast among state parties in the advantages gained by the endorsee concerns tangible support from party headquarters (Table 5.4). This is mentioned most often by delegates from both Minnesota parties and both Connecticut parties, and never mentioned in New Mexico or Massachusetts. A Connecticut Democrat said that the party machinery means "money (in good times), expertise, manhours, telephone banks, and possibly the

Table 5.4
Delegates' Perceptions of Advantages Enjoyed by Endorsee
(in percentages)

Perceived Advantage	Conn.		N.M.		Mass.	Minn.		N.Y.	
	Dem.	Rep.	Dem.	Rep.	Dem.	Dem.	Rep.	Dem.	Rep.
Tangible campaign resources received from party	66	48	–	–	–	61	67	17	23
Other tangible campaign resources	34	27	11	27	22	28	20	40	31
Ballot position	6	17	17	8	–	–	–	–	–
Publicity from endorsement	11	8	25	27	19	10	16	16	14
Psychological, campaign momentum	3	11	30	–	33	3	6	27	9
Demonstrates candidate strength	6	11	11	19	25	6	7	10	9
Voters will support endorsee	13	17	–	20	–	29	17	10	37
None or very little	2	8	35	25	25	2	3	16	8
Disadvantage to endorsee	–	–	–	–	–	–	–	14	–
(N)	(82)	(165)	(84)	(83)	(237)	(218)	(217)	(65)	(63)

Source: Compiled by the author.

use of town party headquarters." A Connecticut Republican said that endorsement would mean that the state committee would support the endorsee, and "therefore all the town committees would have to fall in line and all the 'organization' people would support him."

One DFL delegate in Minnesota spelled out a lengthy list of benefits from endorsement: "DFL assistance in campaign funding; appearance on the DFL 'Sample Ballot' statewide; communications (DFL mailings, newsletters, and media coverage); statewide party workers (phone banks, doorknocks, literature drops, voter identification, and get-out-the-vote efforts); and the campaign services of the DFL state office staff, including voter surveys and computer facilities." Several IR delegates in Minnesota mentioned a number of these items as well.

A number of other delegates in Connecticut, New York, and Minnesota mentioned as advantages for the endorsee the access to tangible campaign resources, without specifying that these would be provided through state or local party organizations. Many suggested that it would be easier for the endorsee to attract campaign funds and to recruit campaign workers. This implies that contributors and workers are more likely to help the endorsee either out of a sense of party loyalty or a belief that the endorsee is likely to win the primary. This does not necessarily mean that persons who have worked for another candidate will abandon that person in the primary to support the endorsee, but that the endorsee may pick up support from uncommitted delegates. Obviously it would require much more extensive research to confirm the accuracy of delegate perceptions, but it is significant that in three of the states a large proportion of delegates believed that the endorsee would gain tangible campaign advantages. In New Mexico and Massachusetts, however, relatively few delegates mentioned such advantages.

Another advantage that might be considered tangible is the publicity that the endorsee receives by virtue of endorsement. Obviously it is difficult to estimate the advantages and the lasting impact of publicity. A similarly elusive factor is the advantage of campaign momentum, or the psychological boost that an endorsee receives. Why should it be much more important in some state parties than others, or is it simply a response of delegates who can think of no more tangible advantages? (These reasons were mentioned more often in states where few tangible campaign resources were mentioned.) If we combine the supposed advantages of publicity and momentum, we come close to asserting that endorsements are important if people think they are. This may, in fact, be true, but it is difficult to assess or measure such an assumption.

The responses of some delegates did not so much define the advantages of endorsement as assert that the endorsement was a demonstration of the endorsee's strength. This may, in fact, be one of the less obvious benefits of endorsement — related to the factor of momentum: It demonstrates the organizational and vote-getting abilities of a candidate. In Massachusetts, where Dukakis's endorsement became a near certainty after the caucus results were tabulated, many delegates felt that the fact of endorsement was less important than the demonstration of organizational skill by the Dukakis camp.

The most difficult question to answer regarding the effects of endorsement is the impact on the voters. To what extent are primary voters aware of endorsements and likely to follow the lead of the party convention? Some delegates in most of the state parties suggested that this is an asset; New York Republicans and Minnesota Democrats were most likely to make this claim. The delegates did not provide any evidence to support this assumption about voting behavior, and there is no obvious reason for the variations in answers among the state parties. When delegates say that endorsees get specific, tangible campaign advantages, or help from party headquarters, they probably have some first-hand experience; when they say voters will support a candidate because he or she has convention endorsement, we may wonder what evidence they have.

Let us summarize the advantages that an endorsee might have in seeking to be nominated:

1. Other candidates may drop out after the convention, because they fail to get a required minimum vote, or because of the pressure of party norms to support the endorsee, or because the outcome of the convention convinces them that they cannot win.

2. The endorsee may receive tangible campaign help, such as funding, manpower, and technical assistance, from the state and/or local party organizations.

3. The endorsee may receive such campaign help from other sources.

4. The fact of endorsement may be less important than the process because it forces a successful candidate to create a strong organization; this demonstration of organizational success in turn attracts campaign resources.

5. The endorsement may provide publicity and momentum for the endorsee's campaign, which may help to attract campaign resources and may even influence the voters.

6. In addition to the indirect effects on voters of the factors listed above, some voters in a primary election may be knowledgeable about endorsements and deliberately vote for the endorsed candidate.

ASSESSING THE IMPACT OF ENDORSEMENTS ON PRIMARY ELECTIONS

In 1982 the convention endorsees for governor in the ten state parties we are studying had a mixed record in the primary elections:

Both Democratic and Republican endorsees in Connecticut went unchallenged in the primary; in the Democratic case the potential challenger failed to get the minimum votes required in the convention. Both party endorsees in New Mexico were nominated, defeating primary opponents some of whom had met the 20 percent requirement in the convention. The New York Republican endorsee easily defeated the one (of three) convention opponents who entered the primary. The Massachusetts Democratic endorsee won the primary, defeating the incumbent governor – who had entered the convention reluctantly. Four endorsees lost in the primary. The New York Democratic endorsee lost to the lieutenant governor, who had met the 25 percent requirement in the convention. The Massachusetts Republican endorsee was beaten by a candidate who had bypassed the convention. Both endorsees in Minnesota were beaten by candidates who had bypassed the convention.

My purpose in this section is to assess the impact that endorsements had on these outcomes. Did endorsements contribute to victories? Why were endorsements ineffective for losers? What difference did endorsements make. This is not an attempt to fully explain the outcome of primaries; that effort will be postponed to Chapter 9, when other variables in the campaign are evaluated. This is simply an effort to estimate and explain the effects of endorsements in these ten nominations.

The Success of Endorsements

Any assessment of the Connecticut endorsement process must begin with a recognition of the traditional political norms in the state, norms that discourage candidates in either party from entering the primary election to challenge an endorsed candidate. It may be difficult to measure the influence of such norms, but it would be a mistake to discount their importance.

In the Democratic party in 1982, however, it was not norms but legal rules that prevented a primary challenge. The only challenger to the incumbent governor fell far short of the necessary 20 percent at the convention. The Democratic convention demonstrated the ability of an incumbent governor to control his party and win endorsement, even though he had succeeded to that position in mid-term rather than being elected.

The Republican scenario in Connecticut was quite different. Lewis Rome had won the gubernatorial endorsement by a margin of only 52 to 47 over Richard Bozzuto. Bozzuto was an experienced political leader who had run and nearly won a primary race for the U.S. Senate in 1980. Why did he sidestep a challenge to Rome in 1982? Newspaper reports suggest that one problem was financial; by convention time, he already had a campaign debt of $90,000, and he believed that it would be more difficult to raise funds as a challenger than it would have been as the endorsee. He also was concerned that the loss of a second statewide primary would be very damaging to his career. He seems to have recognized that the opposition of the party organization would be a serious obstacle.

Bozzuto faced another difficulty resulting from the slating system used in Connecticut. During the closing hours of the convention, while Rome put together a slate of candidates for lower offices, Bozzuto did nothing. He made no effort to organize a slate and try to win enough votes for it to get candidates on the primary ballot. Consequently, if he won the primary, he faced the prospect of a general election campaign with Rome's slate, including a lieutenant governor from the same area and ethnic background as Bozzuto. Although Bozzuto had personal reasons, such as his campaign debt, for avoiding a primary, several of the most important deterrents were directly related to the endorsement system and the political norms supporting it.

In New Mexico the endorsing convention has been utilized intermittently, and our survey shows that many delegates question its desirability. There is no party norm discouraging primary competition, and in fact the major purpose of the convention is to discourage weak candidates from running rather than to select a single endorsee. Despite these facts, in 1982 the top gubernatorial endorsee in each party won the primary. The endorsement system failed to completely eliminate weak candidates from the primary; two Democrats and one Republican who failed to get 20 percent in convention filed petitions to enter the race, but they did poorly (one Democrat withdrawing a month before the primary), and both primaries were largely two-man contests won by a majority vote.

There is little evidence to suggest that the endorsements contributed significantly to the primary victories of either Democrat Toney Anaya or Republican John Irick. Before the convention, it appeared that Anaya was ahead in the public opinion polls and had the strongest political organization among Democratic contenders. There was no sign of his public support increasing significantly after the convention. It is possible that the convention provided Anaya with an incentive and opportunity to build his organization, which was very active in the caucuses to select delegates. On the Republican side, polls suggested a near deadlock between Irick and Sego before the convention; therefore it would be more plausible to suggest that Irick's large majority (71 percent) at the convention strengthened his campaign. While New Mexico delegates in our survey generally emphasized the intangible benefits to the endorsee, one-fourth of the Republicans suggested that Irick would gain tangible campaign resources.

There is one piece of hard evidence on the reaction of voters to the endorsement — or more exactly, the lack of such reaction. In a statewide survey of registered voters conducted a few weeks before the primary, respondents were asked which candidates they expected to vote for and the reasons for that choice. Not a single voter in either party mentioned the convention's endorsement as a reason for their candidate preference.*

---

*The data on New Mexico came from the following source: F. Chris Garcia, Zia Research Associates, Survey Conducted for KOAT-TV, Albuquerque, New Mexico. I am indebted to Professor Garcia for agreeing to include this question in the survey.

The respondents were also reminded that party conventions had been held, and were asked if they knew whether their preferred candidate was the first or the second choice or was not endorsed at all. Two-thirds of the respondents did not know the convention's choice. Only 35 percent of Anaya's supporters knew that he was the top choice; 22 percent of Dunn supporters knew that he was the second choice; 25 percent of Chavez backers knew that he did not get convention support. Republican voters were also poorly informed; 73 percent admitted that they did not know the results of the convention. Only 11 percent of Sego supporters knew that he placed second, while 6 percent more knew that he was not the top endorsee. Irick supporters were a little more knowledgeable; 40 percent knew that he was the top choice for endorsement. The fact that more than one-third of the Anaya and Irick supporters knew they were endorsed suggests there may be some publicity value in endorsement, but the data on reasons for preferences suggest that voters were not deliberately following the party convention's lead.

Probably the best example of the endorsement process having an impact on the outcome of a contested primary is in Massachusetts, where Michael Dukakis won the Democratic convention and defeated Governor Edward King in the primary. The problem is to determine in what way the endorsement helped Dukakis. Dukakis did not win because, as the endorsee, he could utilize the campaign resources of the state party or command the loyalty of local party organizations. The state party is not a strong organization; it does not provide tangible help to the endorsee; and Dukakis could not count on support of local party organizations. The endorsement process did not become a vehicle for uniting the party behind the endorsee; the party remains as fragmented as ever.

One campaign technique available to primary candidates is advertising on television and the other mass media. Another is organization: recruiting large numbers of workers to perform a variety of services at the local level. Governor King put priority on television advertising; he raised large sums of money and started an extensive television campaign early. Although he also used television, Dukakis put great emphasis on the development of a strong grass-roots organization. The endorsement system puts a premium on organization because a candidate must recruit delegates and organize supporters for the caucuses that select delegates. Dukakis had two reasons for emphasizing organization: it was an integral part of his strategy, and it was essential for winning convention endorsement. Dukakis's utilization of the new convention system reminds one of McGovern's use of the new delegate-selection rules in the 1972 Democratic convention. In both cases the candidate recognized the importance of changes in the political institutions. Dukakis had not been directly identified with the movement to revive the convention, but the type of party activists most likely to support Dukakis had been the proponents of that movement. Many of the liberal, college-educated Democrats had become disillusioned with Dukakis during his first term, but were much more unhappy with King. Dukakis needed to win back this group of active Democrats and to prove that he had done so to rank-and-file voters. The endorsement process provided him with an ideal vehicle for doing so.

Dukakis achieved his greatest victory at the party caucuses by proving that he had a strong organization and that he had succeeded in enlisting this group of Democrats who were essential to his success in the primary. The convention was important in confirming this victory and proving the ineffectiveness of King's late organizational efforts. But we should not exaggerate the importance of the endorsement. It did not mean that party activists were uniting behind Dukakis or that the deep split within the party was beginning to be healed; it only meant that Dukakis had efficiently mobilized one faction of the party — his natural constituency. There is no evidence that any of King's loyal supporters deserted him because King lost the endorsement.

The King administration had been embarrassed by a number of scandals, and King's conservative policies had alienated a number of liberal Democrats. Dukakis had succeeded in rebuilding bridges to the liberal wing of the party. As a consequence, before the caucuses and the convention, Dukakis held a huge lead over King in public opinion polls. There is no evidence that this lead increased following, or as a result of, the convention. Instead, as the primary approached, King gradually gained on Dukakis in the polls, though never catching him. King's media campaign evidently had some effect.

In the ten days immediately following the primary election, I conducted a statewide survey of registered voters in Massachusetts. One of the questions asked those who had voted in the Democratic primary was what they liked and disliked about the two candidates.

In answering this question, no voter mentioned that Dukakis had the party's endorsement. Voters were asked if they knew whether the Democratic convention had endorsed a candidate for governor, and 46 percent knew that it had. Among that group aware of the endorsement, 86 percent knew that Dukakis was the endorsee, and 12 percent thought it was King. Those who named either Dukakis or King were asked if the endorsement made them more or less likely to vote for the endorsee; 7 percent said more likely, 1 percent said less, and 92 said it made no difference. This suggests that the endorsement had very little direct impact on voters. All Democratic primary voters (not just those aware of the endorsement process) were asked, "Do you think the party convention ought to endorse a candidate for the primary, or should it stay out of the primary?" There was little enthusiasm for endorsements: 28 percent favored them, 55 percent were opposed, and 17 percent had no opinion.

My candidate for the endorsee who won the primary but gained least from endorsement is Republican Lewis Lehrman of New York. He came to the convention riding the crest of a $2.9 million media advertising campaign and, consequently, a huge lead in the polls. Republicans faced the certainty that, whatever their endorsement decision, Lehrman would remain in the primary and outspend any challenger; moreover, should he lose the primary, he would stay in the general election as the Conservative Party candidate. Before the state committee met, local leaders had spent months trying to find, and agree on, one candidate with a good chance of beating Lehrman in the primary – and they had failed, coming up with three relatively weak opponents. The decision of the state committee to endorse Lehrman seems to have been based on a very simple theory: "If you can't beat him, join him."

The decisions of the committee had some effect. It served to reduce the field of candidates from four to two, because the leaders persuaded Emery to accept second place on the ticket and because Rosenbaum's poor showing discouraged him from running. By endorsing Lehrman over Curran, the committee undermined Curran's chances to build a strong organization for the primary effort, and may have contributed to the lopsided result in the primary.

It may have been more important for Lehrman to get 25 percent at the convention than to get endorsed. Getting nominating petitions signed in New York state is a large and expensive chore; by avoiding the need for petitions, Lehrman was able to concentrate resources on his media campaign. Moreover, the 25 percent support, and even more the endorsement, established his legitimacy as a New York Republican candidate, in the face of criticism that he was an outsider and an amateur.

The major reason for Lehrman's 4-1 margin in the primary, however, was that Lehrman had a huge advantage in resources, and used them to wage an aggressive, skillful media campaign against Curran. One of the strongest arguments for the principle of endorsement is that it provides the party with a counterweight against well-financed political amateurs who seek to win primaries through media blitzes. The 1982 New York Republican convention can never be used as an example to support that argument. Lehrman did not win the primary because he had won the endorsement. He won the endorsement because committee members believed he was going to win the primary — whatever action they took.

The Failure of Endorsements

Democratic Mayor Edward Koch of New York is the only convention endorsee who lost the primary to a candidate who had also sought convention endorsement; the others lost to persons who bypassed the convention. It should be recalled that Mario Cuomo won a respectable 39 percent of the vote in the state committee. Given the strength of local party organizations in New York, the state committee vote measures the support that each candidate has generated in these local groups.

This was the second time in four New York Democratic gubernatorial contests that the endorsee had lost the primary, suggesting that endorsement is of limited value to the candidate who wins it. One-third of the delegates in our survey perceived endorsement to be of little value or an actual liability.

It appears that the organizational efforts of local party units are not great enough to determine outcomes, particularly if one candidate holds only a 6-4 lead among these units. Media analyses following Cuomo's unexpected primary victory emphasized that he had an unusually large and well-organized group of volunteers working for him across the state, largely mobilized by labor unions. This apparently overshadowed the organizational advantage Koch enjoyed among local party groups. The turnout was unusually heavy for a

New York primary — another factor that could weaken the impact of local party organizations; it appeared to be particulary heavy among groups supporting Cuomo, such as black and Hispanic ones. Ironically, the two other members of Koch's slate who had opposition won in the primary, producing a ticket quite different from what Cuomo would probably have selected.

In Massachusetts, the primary defeat of John Lakian was the second straight loss of a gubernatorial endorsee, in a party where endorsements had traditionally gone unchallenged. It raises the obvious, but unanswerable, question of whether the informal convention has less prestige or influence than the legal ones did. It is certainly significant that John Sears, a man with long experience in politics and extensive contacts with party activists, chose to ignore the convention and concentrate on winning voters in the primary, even though he faced the prospect (which became a reality) of being outspent.

If Lakian had won the primary, it would have been very difficult to estimate how much his victory was due to the endorsement. Lakian outspent Sears by a margin of more than 4-1, spending much of it on media advertising. A Lakian victory would have resembled the victory of Lehrman in the New York Republican primary. If the contribution of party endorsement to a Lakian victory would have been small or uncertain, the endorsement had nothing to do with his defeat. Less than a month before the primary election, the Boston *Globe* published an article alleging that there was a pattern of discrepancies between Lakian's campaign literature and his actual record, regarding his personal background and accomplishments. The rest of his campaign was downhill; polls showed that he lost his modest lead over Sears and was never able to recover.

The Republican primary was completely overshadowed by the King-Dukakis race in the Democratic primary, and only 13 percent of all primary votes cast for governor were in the Republican primary. Our poll showed that voters who were registered as Republicans were more interested in the Democratic than the Republican gubernatorial primary, by a 2-1 margin. Because of the small vote in the Republican primary, our voting survey included only 55 persons who cast a ballot for a Republican primary candidate. None of them mentioned the endorsement as a reason for voting for Lakian. In this small sample, one-third knew that the Republican convention had made an endorsement, and almost all of these knew it was

Lakian; a handful of persons aware of the endorsement (4 of 14) said it made them more likely to vote for Lakian. Though the voting sample is too small to be reliable, the data are compatible with surveys in other state parties suggesting that few voters are directly influenced by endorsements.

The Minnesota endorsement system in both state parties, though an informal one, is one of the strongest and most effective in the country, with endorsees rarely facing serious challenges in the primary. Prior to 1982, the only upset of a gubernatorial endorsee occurred when the DFL convention refused to endorse an incumbent governor. The 1982 defeat of both DFL and IR gubernatorial candidates by others who had not sought the endorsement has raised questions about the value of the endorsement and the possibility that it is declining in importance. The DFL endorsement process appeared to be more seriously jeopardized because in 1978 its endorsed senatorial candidate had been beaten in the primary.

There are several reasons for both upsets in 1982: On the Democratic side, Perpich's personality and his record during two years as governor; on the Republican, Whitney's expensive media campaign, and the weak organizing and fund-raising efforts of Wangberg. These factors will be explored more fully in later chapters. The immediate question concerns the tangible and intangible benefits of endorsement to the candidates who receive it.

Obviously the surest way to make endorsements effective is to prevent or discourage other candidates from challenging the endorsee in a primary. The Minnesota endorsements have no legal base, and the only restraint on primary competition is the norm that candidates will seek the endorsement and abide by the decision of the convention. How strong is that norm, and is it being eroded?

Until 1982 the norm was very strong in the Republican party. In those years when there was a contest for the gubernatorial endorsement, the losers accepted the result — even though several convention battles were close and prolonged. The only primary challenges were ineffective ones from minor candidates. The DFL norm was almost as strong, but there were some notable exceptions. Convention decisions were often unanimous or nearly so, and frequently involved incumbents. There was a close six-candidate convention in 1970, but no primary challenge. The only primary challenges came from minor candidates. The outstanding exception was in 1966 when the incumbent governor made a successful primary challenge after losing the convention endorsement on the twentieth ballot. In 1978, however, the endorsement process failed in a senatorial race. The DFL endorsee, Congressman Donald Fraser, was beaten in the primary by Bob Short, who had not sought convention endorsement, but who ran an aggressive, well-financed race. One measure of the strength of this political norm is our survey of delegates; two-thirds of the DFL respondents and slightly over half of IR respondents agreed that every statewide candidate should seek convention endorsement and abide by the results. Obviously there is no consensus on this norm. Despite the closeness of the Republican gubernatorial contest for endorsement in 1982, there did not appear to be any serious prospect that any losers would enter the primary; despite the size and loyalty of his bloc of supporters, Sherwood consistently promised to abide by the convention's decision. In the DFL convention, the endorsing committee expected candidates to commit themselves to abide by the convention, and announced that commitment in each case to the convention. Nevertheless, Hubert Humphrey III, narrowly endorsed for attorney general, was reported to be ready to enter the primary if he lost the endorsement.

The two primary winners in 1982 both had good reasons for avoiding the convention. Both believed that they were unable to develop the close contacts among party activists that were needed to win delegates — Perpich because of his job commitment in Europe, and Whitney because of his long absence from direct involvement in party politics. In Whitney's case there was another factor: his belief that his views on issues would not be acceptable to a majority of delegates. Perpich attended, and spoke to, the DFL convention, and made it clear he was not criticizing the endorsement system. Wheelock Whitney stayed away from the IR convention. Both men had important assets that they could bring to a primary contest against the endorsee: Perpich's record as governor and his unique version of charisma, Whitney's large financial resources.

If the convention results are challenged in a primary, the endorsee can expect considerable help from state party headquarters, as delegates who were surveyed emphasized. In the DFL this includes a computer listing of registered voters, which identifies Democrats (a considerable asset in an open primary state), lists of local organizations, party officials, and campaign contributors. The state party will also hand out sample ballots in the polls on primaries.

The state party contributed $30,000 to the gubernatorial campaign of Spanaus. The IR also has a computerized voting list with Republicans identified, and provides some other central services, but it did not make a direct cash contribution to Wangberg's campaign. It seems unlikely that local party organizations consistently provide the same kind of disciplined support for the endorsee that is found in Connecticut. Generally the support of party activists for the endorsee in Minnesota is voluntary, growing out of a sense of party loyalty, rather than compulsory, resulting from organizational pressures.

Although the organizational support from party headquarters and from rank-and-file party activists may be very valuable, it is obviously not an unbeatable combination. An unendorsed candidate may be able to appeal directly to the voters, if he has name identification, campaign skills, the resources for a large media campaign, or some combination of these assets — as the challengers did in 1982.

The strength of an endorsement system, particularly one like the Minnesota system that lacks a legal base, rests on rather fragile foundations. The convention endorsement systems of the DFL and IR are clothed in tradition and party norms; but after the endorsement has been successfully challenged a few times, candidates — like the child in "The Emperor's New Clothes" — will be saying, "But he hasn't got anything on." It would be premature to classify the DFL and IR endorsement systems as naked, but they are thinly clad.

CONCLUSIONS: THE IMPACT OF ENDORSEMENTS

What is the impact of endorsements on nominations, and of the endorsement system on the political parties? Under what conditions do endorsements have the greatest effort? In trying to answer these questions, we should look not only to our recent case studies, but also to the longer record of convention endorsements. The impact of endorsements will be evaluated in terms of several broad purposes: restoring the influence of the party over nominations, increasing its chances of winning elections, strengthening the party as an organization, and making candidates accountable to the party.

The first purpose, a prerequisite to others, is to enhance the party's role in selecting nominees. It seems obvious from reviewing the recent record in a number of states that the surest way to control nominations is to discourage nonendorsed candidates from entering the primary. If the effectiveness of endorsements were to be measured by a single criterion, it would be how often the endorsee goes unchallenged in the primary. Whenever serious candidates who have either lost the endorsement or bypassed it enter the primary, the party's control over the nomination is endangered.

The surest way to avoid or minimize challenges is a law (or a party rule, in Massachusetts) requiring a high minimum vote in convention for a candidate to enter a primary. Obviously that law is less effective if the option exists of getting on the primary ballot by petition. While the legal requirement for a minimum vote is important, it may also be important whether party norms make it hard for candidates to achieve that minimum (as in Connecticut) or relatively easy (as in the New York Democratic party) through tactics of vote changing at the end of or between ballots.

In state parties where challenges can be discouraged only by party norms or pressures, it is more difficult to prevent other candidates from running. Norms are perishable; each time an endorsee is challenged successfully, the norm of supporting the endorsee becomes weaker. This pattern is evident in both Minnesota parties and the Massachusetts Republican party; even in Connecticut and Rhode Island, challenges to endorsees have become more acceptable in recent years. Whether a candidate challenges the endorsee — and whether he succeeds — may depend on his or her political base, financial resources, and ideological commitments, but it may also depend on the attitudes of political activists, their belief about the legitimacy of such a challenge. Our surveys have suggested that there is little consensus but much ambivalence among delegates about whether it is legitimate for candidates to challenge the endorsee, with the attitude depending partly on the delegate's commitment to a candidate.

If an endorsed candidate faces a primary challenge, the endorsement provides momentum and a psychological boost — as does any political victory during a campaign. But the major advantages to a candidate are organizational. In a few states, notably Connecticut and New York, the endorsee gets the disciplined support of local party organizations. If these are strong groups that command loyal voters, this can be a major advantage. In some states, such as Minnesota and Connecticut, the endorsee gains tangible campaign resources from that state party headquarters. When state laws or party rules permit such assistance it can be important, and may grow more important as state parties acquire computers, mailing lists, and the other attributes and skills of modern campaign management.

Endorsement may help a candidate to get campaign resources, such as workers and funds, in addition to whatever may be provided by party organizations. These may become available because the endorsee is perceived as the front runner, or because party activists believe in helping the endorsee — but the strength of such perceptions and beliefs are hard to assess, and it may decline if the endorsement system is eroded by a pattern of successful challenges.

The convention system (except in New York) forces candidates to mobilize delegate support, to get thousands of supporters to attend caucuses, and to recruit potential delegates or win commitments from persons likely to be elected as delegates. The system is one that rewards the successful political organizer, and the reward is not only winning the endorsement but acquiring a grass-roots organization that can be used during the primary and general election campaigns. This is a very important consequence of the endorsement system.

There is no evidence to support the hypothesis that a major advantage of endorsements is its direct impact on the voter. Despite the perceptions of some delegates, the limited evidence from voter surveys suggests that only modest numbers of voters are aware of endorsements, and very few are influenced positively by them. This should not be surprising. Everything we know from survey data about the attitudes of voters toward parties and toward politicians would lead us to doubt that endorsements would carry much weight with voters. Those voters who are influenced presumably would be those with strong personal ties to party organizations.

I conclude that the major advantages of endorsement are organizational ones. The endorsee can gain manpower, funds, and other organizational components; the strongest endorsement systems provide the most organizational assistance. There are, of course, other ways for challengers to build organizations; and the candidate with a weaker organization may still win a primary with greater funding, better media advertising, and better campaigning skills.

A second broad purpose of endorsements is to enable the party to select candidates who are electable. It is difficult to measure the success of endorsement systems in this respect; in states where either both parties or neither party makes endorsements, obviously one party will win and one will lose each election. It would be possible to measure only how well each party utilized the system. An endorsement system may facilitate election victory if it avoids divisive and expensive primaries; we have already discussed this possibility. It may help a party to win if the convention is more successful than primary voters in picking candidates who are electable and a ticket that is balanced. In the long run, an endorsement system can lead to electoral success if it contributes to a stronger party organization.

Why should delegates to an endorsing convention be more successful than primary voters in choosing electable candidates? The answer is that party activists should have a greater commitment to the party, greater political skills, and more information about the candidates. The decisions of Connecticut Republicans to nominate Weicker for senator and of New York Republicans to nominate Lehrman for governor might be cited as examples. On the other hand, New York Democrats were less skillful in perceiving Koch as a winner. There is some uncertainty about the effectiveness of the ticket-balancing exercises carried on in the New York and Connecticut conventions of both parties.

What are the flaws in the argument that convention delegates are better able to choose electable candidates? We know that convention delegates usually are less moderate ideologically than the voters in their party, and that a moderate candidate has some advantages in a general election. If there are ideological differences between leading candidates in convention, the delegates may choose unwisely. The Minnesota IR convention may be an example, though the Connecticut Republicans deliberately chose a senatorial candidate whose philosophy of government many distrusted.

Another flaw in this argument is that party organizations are very permeable — by candidate organizations. Convention decisions are made not often by delegates objectively making tactical choices among candidates, but at least in part by delegates already committed to candidates. The ability to win delegates is, of course, a good test of a candidate's campaigning skills. But party activists who attend caucuses are less moderate ideologically than voters identified with the party (and independent voters); therefore the candidate who can win delegates cannot necessarily win comparable proportions of voters. Moreover, the party organization is permeable by single-issue groups, which are less concerned with helping the party to win elections than with putting the party on record regarding issues and choosing a candidate who takes the correct stand on those issues. The conventions of both Minnesota parties provide examples of this phenomenon.

If the endorsement system strengthens political organizations, it enhances their ability to win elections. Stronger party organizations may also be viewed as intrinsically important goals of endorsing systems. Many political scientists and other observers of the political scene would argue that stronger party organizations are desirable, in the face of increasingly powerful interest groups and PACs and the rise of high-priced media advertising.

According to our surveys, many delegates believe that the convention endorsement system is valuable because it gives the political activists and local organizations a meaningful role to play, and an incentive for participation. Those who help to elect candidates get a chance to nominate them. Party activists enjoy political work, and they find conventions exciting as well as meaningful — with their demonstrations and parties and chances to meet candidates and express their views on candidates and issues. The old-fashioned political organizations were built on discipline and patronage (and New York and Connecticut parties have some of these characteristics). The new organizations are built on voluntary effort, and the chance of participating in the nominating process is an important incentive for such volunteers.

I have said that party organizations are permeable institutions, that it is relatively easy for persons committed to candidates and issues to compete for delegate seats. Does this conflict with the incentive structure for party activists? I would argue that it does not because the permeability or openness of a party organization is one of its strengths. That is how you recruit party activists. A large proportion of those who remain active in the party over a number of years were first attracted to party activity by their commitment to a candidate and/or an issue.

Some of those who believe in party endorsements are seeking to build not only a strong party but also one that is based on principles. They want an endorsement system because it will make the candidates accountable to the party; the convention can choose candidates committed to the party's platform. The Minnesota DFL and IR parties are deeply concerned about policies and accountability. The party charter drafted by Massachusetts Democrats included a separate issues convention, and many delegates to the 1982 convention were critical of Edward King because he did not believe in the liberal policies that they associated with their party.

There are serious risks to a political party in emphasizing its commitment to issues. As already noted, delegates are likely to be ideologically less moderate and more extreme than voters. If they demand that candidates take doctrinaire positions to win endorsement, an accountable candidate may not turn out to be an electable one.

As we have said, political parties, and conventions, are permeable by single-issue groups, who intend to hold candidates accountable on a particular issue. The DFL delegate-selection process is organized by subcaucuses — a method that facilitates election of delegates committed to a single issue. Social issues like abortion are particularly divisive because they cut across the normal political alignments that separate Democrats from Republicans. But there are issues that unite the parties. In the DFL convention, there was strong, virtually united support for job support and social welfare programs, the revival of ERA, and a nuclear freeze; Minnesota Republican delegates were nearly unanimous in support of conservative economic policies.

The concept of accountability is not always in conflict with the goal of electability of candidates. Perhaps a perfect endorsing convention system would maintain some continuity of delegates but remain open to new delegates with candidate and issue commitments. It would also be structured in such a way as to sublimate, or paper over, differences and to make the convention a vehicle for uniting the party behind its candidates. The techniques for creating unity range from compromises on issues and balancing of tickets, to the emotional drama of demonstrations in support of the endorsed candidates.

Part III
Who Votes
in What Primaries?

6

Voting Turnout

The purpose of this chapter is to find out who votes in primaries, and why — and, of course, who does not vote in primaries, and why not. The goal of the following chapter is to determine how voters choose between Democratic and Republican primaries. This chapter has more specific purposes; one is to determine whether the variables that motivate voting in primaries are different from those that lead to voting in general elections. Another purpose is to explain why the level of voting in primaries varies so much from state to state.

Voting, of course, is an individual act, but it is useful to distinguish between individual and institutional variables that affect the decision to vote. Individual variables are characteristics such as age, education, and socioeconomic status, and personal attitudes toward parties and politics. We know from studies of turnout in general elections that these variables affect voting. A person who is older and better educated, with a stronger interest in politics and a higher sense of political efficacy is more likely to vote than persons ranking lower in these qualities — whether the voter lives in Oregon or Georgia and whether the election is a presidential or local one. We assume that these characteristics and attitudes affect voting in primaries as well, but there may be specific variables, such as party identification, that have particular effect on voting in primaries.

At the same time institutional factors affect voting in both general elections and primaries. Persons are more likely to vote in states where laws and procedures make voting easy and where competition is usually close. They are more likely to vote in specific elections where the office (or issue) is perceived by them as important and the race appears to be close — in other words, where their vote matters. This should be true for primaries as well as general elections, but we need to find out exactly what aspects of the primary election system have the greatest impact on turnout in such elections. We need to find out why turnout in primaries varies substantially from state to state, and within states from one party to the other.

There are two kinds of sources for information on voting turnout; voting surveys and aggregate data. In this chapter I will use surveys conducted following the gubernatorial primaries in three states in 1982 as well as national surveys in 1978 and some previous years that have included information on voting in primaries. Aggregate data on voting in gubernatorial primaries in all states from 1951 through 1982 will be analyzed. While aggregate voting data can tell us nothing directly about the motivations of voters, it can tell us how much voting turnout varied under different conditions, such as higher or lower levels of primary competition.

It may be useful to speculate about the relationships between personal and institutional variables that explain voting. Presumably a person who is highly motivated and strongly interested in politics will vote in nearly every election, even if the election is one-sided or unimportant. At the other extreme a person who is totally unmotivated will not vote even in close presidential elections. Institutional variables ought to have their greatest effect on persons who have a moderate motivation and interest in politics.

Primary elections add new dimensions to this speculation. If voters regard voting in a primary election as a form of participation in partisan activity, those whose partisan identification or loyalty is greatest should be most likely to vote. Those who consider themselves independent should be least likely to vote — even if they vote often in general elections. In some states, however, the primary is an open one, with no party registration required. It is possible that voters in such states are less likely to regard primary voting as a partisan action; if so, the strength of party identification would have less impact on the motivation to vote. It is also possible that voting in a primary appears to be a less partisan activity in those states which are dominated by one party and in which the primary is more important than the general election. In fact, we know very little about how voters perceive primary elections.

SURVEYS OF INDIVIDUAL VOTERS

The surveys of primary voting in California, Michigan, and Massachusetts were conducted by telephone immediately after the gubernatorial primaries in those states. Only persons who said they were registered voters were interviewed. Therefore primary turnout in these states, as reported by respondents, is measured as a percentage of registered voters.

In this survey, as in most, the reported rate of voting is higher than what actually occurred in the states. The comparison of reported and actual primary voting (as a percentage of registered voters) is as follows:

	Reported Vote	*Actual Vote*
California	75%	51%
Massachusetts	63%	46%
Michigan	51%	26%

There are two reasons for these discrepancies. National surveys have shown that from 10 to 12 percent of those who claim to vote in general elections do not actually do so; in 1978 the figure was 11.7 percent. If these corrections were applied to our data in 1982, there would still be a large discrepancy between reported and actual voting. This is because those persons who can be located in a telephone survey and agree to answer questions include a disproportionately high percentage of persons who have the characteristics of voters (age, education, residence, and so forth). This can be illustrated by using data on voting in the general election in 1978. In that year, when 58.2 percent of all registered voters actually voted, the proportion of registered respondents in the National Election Survey who actually voted was 69.7 percent, and the proportion claiming to vote was almost 76.5 percent.

In this survey of primary voting we are primarily interested in political and institutional reasons for voting and nonvoting in primaries; therefore, it is not a serious problem if the sample underrepresents persons who fail to vote because of personal characteristics, such as age and education.

Another source of information on primary voting is the 1978 National Election Study (NES) conducted by the University of Michigan. As part of that study, local registration and voting records were checked to determine whether each respondent in fact was registered and had voted in the 1978 primary and general elections. This information is particularly valuable because it is based on the record rather than a claim of having voted. This will be supplemented by information from the 1958, 1964, 1966, and 1968 National Election Studies, in which respondents were asked if they had voted in a primary (or specifically in congressional primary in 1958). These data are less reliable because primaries in some states had been held several months before the survey, focusing on the general election, was taken.

In 1978 only 36 percent of repondents in the NES survey voted in a primary. The figure is much lower than those in our 1982 surveys presumably because many states in 1978 did not have contested statewide primaries in both parties for major offices. In contrast, both parties had contested gubernatorial races in the three states surveyed in 1982. In the earlier national surveys, 30 percent of respondents reported voting in congressional primaries in 1958, while those who reported voting in primaries in 1964, 1966, and 1968 were 39 to 40 percent.

Effects of Personal Characteristics

Previous studies (Wolfinger and Rosenstone 1980, chs. 2 and 3) have suggested that education and age are more important than other socioeconomic characteristics in explaining voting in general elections. Consequently, it is logical to begin our examination of voting in primary elections with an examination of these variables.

The National Election Surveys have consistently shown that both age and education have substantial effects on voting in primaries, and similar effects are found in the three state surveys in 1982. Table 6.1 shows the combined effects of age and education on reported primary voting in California, Massachusetts, and Michigan, and actual primary voting in the 1978 national survey. The total numbers are not large enough to expect a perfect progression from one cell to the next, but generally speaking the greater one's age and the higher one's education, the greater the likelihood of voting. Age

Table 6.1
Proportion of Respondents Who Voted in Primary, by Age and Education
(in percentages)

Age	California (N = 596) Education			Massachusetts (N = 629) Education			Michigan (N = 695) Education		
	Up to 12 Yrs.	Some Coll.	College Grad.	Up to 12 Yrs.	Some Coll.	College Grad.	Up to 12 Yrs.	Some Coll.	College Grad.
18-29	38	50	71	40	67	63	25	38	48
30-39	57	83	74	29	67	68	38	59	60
40-49	69	74	82	67	67	87	46	51	42
50-69	73	87	83	61	63	78	64	68	67
70 +	84	88	92	46	64	86	64	64	100

National Election Survey, 1978

Age	Education				
	Up to 8 Yrs.	9-12 Yrs.	Some Coll.	College Grad.	(N)
18-29	20	22	26	30	(263)
30-39	14	27	38	37	(304)
40-49	20	32	45	50	(224)
50-69	21	43	51	55	(452)
70+	31	39	70	44	(148)
(N)	(159)	(677)	(286)	(269)	

Source: Compiled by the author from 1982 telephone surveys and from 1978 National Election Survey.

is a less important predictor in Massachusetts for some reason. As might be expected, in some cases there is a drop for those who are 70 and over (though that drop would appear greater if education were not controlled). The effect of age is generally greater among those with less education, a relationship also found in studies of voting in general elections (Wolfinger and Rosenstone 1980, pp. 58-60).

Respondents in the three state surveys were asked a question designed to test their knowledge about politics: Which party has a majority in the state legislature? Those who answered accurately were more likely to vote in primaries, compared to those who answered inaccurately or did not know, by margins of 80-69 percent in California, 68-51 in Massachusetts, and 64-46 in Michigan.

One of the best predictors of voting in primaries is interest in campaigns. Table 6.2 shows that voters who were very much interested in the primary campaigns in each of the three states, and particularly in Michigan, were much more likely to vote in the primaries than those not much interested. A similar relationship is found in the 1978 national surveys for those with varying interests in political campaigns.

As we would expect, persons who are better educated and those who are older have more interest in election campaigns, but within any education or age level those persons most interested in campaigns are most likely to vote. This is shown in Table 6.3, which reports 1978 NES data.

Standard questions on civic duty asked in the 1978 NES poll have a substantial effect on voting in the primary. Questions on political efficacy have less effect on primary voting, except for one on parties' interest in the opinions of people.

Effects of Political Variables

Studies of national electorates have consistently shown that persons with stronger party identification are more likely to vote in general elections. Presumably strong identifiers have more interest in politics and a stronger commitment to a party and its candidates than other persons. In a seven-way classification of party identification, however, those weakly identified with a party and independents leaning toward that party vote in nearly the same proportion.

Table 6.2
Proportion of Respondents Who Voted in Primary,
by Interest in Campaign
(in percentages)

Level of Interest in Campaign	California %	(N)	Massachusetts %	(N)	Michigan %	(N)	National Survey %	(N)
Very much	81	(188)	77	(268)	78	(193)	50	(375)
Somewhat	78	(207)	61	(256)	51	(302)	36	(672)
Not much	53	(153)	39	(133)	28	(219)	20	(345)

Source: Compiled by the author.

Table 6.3
Proportion of Respondents Who Voted in Primary, by Interest in
Campaign, Age, and Education: 1978 National Election Survey
(in percentages)

Level of Interest in Campaign	Age						
	All	18-29	30-39	40-49	50-69	70+	(N)
Very much	50	42	52	52	52	48	(375)
Somewhat	36	24	31	39	43	48	(672)
Not much	20	18	21	13	25	21	(345)
(N)	(1,392)	(263)	(305)	(226)	(450)	(148)	

	Education				
	All	Up to 8 Years	9-12 Years	Some College	College Grad.	(N)
Very much	50	28	48	64	51	(374)
Somewhat	36	33	34	35	41	(673)
Not much	20	16	22	17	25	(345)
(N)	(1,392)	(159)	(679)	(286)	(268)	

Source: Compiled by the author from 1978 National Election Survey.

Party identification ought to be more strongly and consistently related to voting in primaries than in general elections because the decision to vote in a primary election would appear to be more of a partisan commitment than a vote in a general election. Independents might be uncertain about which party primary to vote in, and in closed primary states they might be reluctant to register with either party.

Figure 6.1 shows that in the 1978 election there was a sharper, more consistent relationship between party identificaton and voting in primaries than in general elections. Specifically, independents leaning to a party were less likely to vote in primaries than were those weakly identified with a party. A comparison of reported voting in the 1958, 1964, 1966, and 1968 national surveys shows a pattern of voting for primaries and general elections very similar to that in Figure 6.1.

More evidence of the importance of party identification in primary voting is found in Table 6.4, which provides controls for age, education, and interest in campaigns, based on the 1978 NES data. A disproportionate share of independents are younger persons, and it is particularly important to note that party identification has the greatest impact on primary voting among those under 40. It affects voting at all levels of education. Persons who are strongly identified with a party have more interest in election campaigns than other categories. Table 6.4 shows that strength of party identification affects voting in primaries at all levels of interest — but particularly among those who are not very interested.

Recent studies of party identification have suggested that this concept may not be unidimensional but may incorporate two or three separate dimensions (Dennis 1981, Weisberg 1980, Valentine and Van Wingen 1980). For our purposes, the most important aspect of this research is the suggestion that one may perceive oneself as an independent and at the same time be supportive of a party; the two perceptions may be independent. The three state surveys in 1982 did not use the traditional party identification questions; instead they included questions used in recent national surveys designed to tap these two dimensions:

- In your own mind, do you think of yourself as a supporter of one of the political parties?

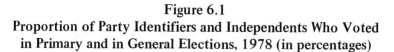

Figure 6.1
Proportion of Party Identifiers and Independents Who Voted in Primary and in General Elections, 1978 (in percentages)

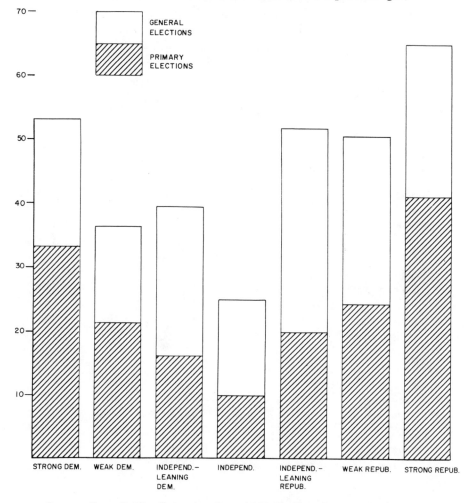

Source: Compiled by the author from 1978 National Election Survey.

Table 6.4
Proportion of Respondents Who Voted in Primary by Party
Identification, Age, Education, and Interest:
1978 National Election Survey
(in percentages)

Characteristics	Party Identification				
	Strong	Weak	Leaning	Independent	(N)
All voters	48	35	29	22	
(N)	(371)	(535)	(333)	(139)	
Age					
18-29	41	27	20	11	(256)
30-39	47	37	24	4	(302)
40-49	46	38	27	33	(224)
50-69	52	39	36	35	(452)
70+	46	30	55	33	(144)
Education					
Up to 8 years	35	16	19	18	(156)
9 to 12 years	48	36	26	18	(671)
Some college	57	33	35	29	(283)
College grad	52	49	31	35	(269)
Level of interest in campaign					
Very much	53	49	49	41	(376)
Somewhat	49	39	24	20	(669)
Not much	33	19	16	14	(334)

Source: Compiled by the author from 1978 National Election Survey.

- [If no or not sure] do you ever think of yourself as closer to one of the two parties?
- Do you ever think of yourself as politically independent or not?

The first two questions provide a five-way measure of party identification, as well as a three-way measure of strength of party identification. The third question provides an entirely separate measure of political independence.

Table 6.5 shows the proportions of registered voters in each of the three states expressing varying degrees of party support and

Table 6.5
Voting in Primary by Party Support and Registration
(in percentages)

Attitude toward Party (N)	Percentage of Registered Voters in Each Category			Percentage in Each Category Who Voted in Primary		
	Calif. (607)	*Mass.* (645)	*Mich.* (712)	*Calif.*	*Mass.*	*Mich.*
Support party	47	42	49	80	74	61
Democratic	23	33	30	75	80	62
Republican	24	9	18	82	53	61
Closer to party	25	25	22	78	66	46
Democratic	15	17	13	75	70	41
Republican	10	8	10	82	57	53
No party support	28	33	29	62	47	35
Consider self independent?						
Yes	86	82	66	76	64	50
No	14	18	34	64	62	54
Party registration						
Democratic	53	46	—	72	77	—
Republican	37	17	—	80	45	—
Independent	8	37	—	—	56	—

Source: Compiled by the author from 1982 telephone survey.

describing themselves as independent, as well as the proportion registered with each party in the closed primary states. It also shows the proportion in each category who voted in the primary. As we would expect, those who describe themselves as supporters of a party are most likely to vote in the primary, and those who are neither supporters nor closer to a party are least likely. The contrasts among these groups are smaller among California voters and quite small among Massachusetts Republicans, presumably because the Republican primary in that state attracted little interest.

It is difficult to interpret the question about political independence because it has only been asked in very recent national surveys. In California and Massachusetts we find that over 80 percent of the respondents consider themselves to be politically independent; in California independents are more likely to vote in the primary, while in Massachusetts it makes little difference. In Michigan two-thirds of the respondents say they are independent, and they are slightly less likely to vote in the primary. If we compare answers given to questions on party support and independence, we find that in California those in all categories of party support have nearly the same high level of independence; in Massachusetts strong party supporters (particularly Republicans) are somewhat less likely to be independent; and in Michigan strong Democratic supporters are much less likely to consider themselves independent, but there is little relationship on the Republican side.

Table 6.4 showed the effects of party identification on primary voting in the 1978 national sample, controlling for age, education, and interest in elections. An analysis of the impact of party support, controlling for the same three variables, shows similar results in California, Massachusetts, and Michigan (although the smaller numbers in some cells obscure some relationships). The data (not shown here) indicate that the effect of party support is particularly strong among younger voters, but affects all age groups. Party support also affects the vote for all educational levels and all interest levels, although the impact is greater at lower levels of interest. As noted above, the impact of party support on voting is less in California than in the other states, and this is of course evident when controls are added.

One of the advantages of conducting surveys in individual states is that one can examine the effects of political institutions and developments peculiar to that state. In the 1982 primary elections

Michigan had competitive and well-publicized gubernatorial primaries in both parties, but the actual turnout was relatively low (26 percent of the registered vote). Our survey shows (Table 6.5) that, among party supporters, Democrats were just as likely as Republicans to vote. In California, Republican primaries for both governor and senator were much more interesting than those in the Democratic party and turnout among registered Republicans was 8 percentage points higher than among registered Democrats. Our survey shows that turnout was higher, by comparable amounts, among registered Republicans and among those who supported or were closer to the Republican party.

The Massachusetts primary is unusual because those enrolled as independents can vote in either primary, while those enrolled as Democrats or Republicans are limited to that primary. In 1982 the close Democratic gubernatorial primary between the governor and the former governor completely overshadowed the three-way Republican race. In the gubernatorial primary 87 percent of all votes were cast in the Democratic race. Our survey shows (Table 6.5) that 77 percent of enrolled Democrats and only 45 percent of enrolled Republicans voted in the primary; 56 percent of those enrolled with neither party voted, and of this group 87 percent chose to vote in the Democratic primary. The figures in Table 6.5 for party support also show Democrats much more likely to vote than Republicans. Massachusetts respondents generally expressed more interest in the Democratic than the Republican campaign — even enrolled Republicans by a 48-21 percent margin (with the rest interested in both). Those more interested in the Democratic primary were much more likely to vote than those interested in the Republican primary or in both.

Earlier in this chapter it was suggested that the effects of party identification or support on primary voting might be greater in states with closed primaries, where the act of voting in a primary would appear to be more of a partisan act. Voters who perceive themselves to be independent of party should be more willing to vote in primaries in states where they can vote in either primary without registering with a party.

It is a plausible theory, but not one supported by the available data. It is evident from Table 6.5 that party support is a little more strongly related to primary voting in an open primary state (Michigan) than in a closed primary state (California). In Massachusetts, which has a mixed system, party support strongly affects voting among Democrats, but not among Republicans — presumably because the Republican primary attracted so little interest.

A national sample of voters provides a better test of this hypothesis because it is less affected by particular circumstances of primaries in individual states. In Table 6.6, based on the 1978 NES data, the states have been divided into those with closed and those with open primaries, and, because most southern states have open primaries, these have been distinguished from northern open primaries. Contrary to what we might expect, strength of party identification has more impact in northern open primary states than closed primary states. Independents are much less likely to vote in primaries in open primary than in closed primary states. Party identification has the least apparent impact in open primary states in the South, perhaps because the Democratic primary has been traditionally more important than the general election in these states. Even in a national sample, the numbers are so small that the findings must remain rather tentative.

On the surface it might appear that the simplest way to find out why persons who are registered do not vote in primaries is to ask them, but in practice the answers to that question are of limited use. Respondents in the three states who met the registration

Table 6.6
Proportion of Respondents Who Voted in Primary by Party Identification and Type of Primary in State: 1978 National Election Survey
(in percentages)

Party Identification	Type of State Primary				
	Closed	Open: North	Open: South	All States	(N)
Strong	49	42	51	48	(372)
Weak	38	25	39	35	(537)
Leaning	32	23	30	29	(334)
Independent	25	11	33	22	(140)
(N)	(839)	(323)	(221)	(1,383)	

Source: Compiled by the author from 1978 National Election Survey.

requirements for voting in the primary (including party registration in California) and who said they had not voted in the primary were asked why not. By far the largest number (from 59 percent in Massachusetts to 73 percent in California) said they were unable to do so. A number of specific excuses were given: They or a family member was ill, they were out of town, they had to work, and so forth. Undoubtedly many of these excuses were legitimate, and we should recognize that many persons lead such busy, complicated lives that it may be a real inconvenience to find time to vote.

The other frequently used reasons for not voting were: They were not interested (7 to 12 percent in the three states), they disliked the candidates (4 to 13 percent), or it makes no difference (up to 6 percent). Very few said that they never voted in primaries. The largest number who said they disliked the candidates (13 percent) was in Massachusetts, where each of the two Democratic gubernatorial candidates had aroused controversy and opposition. In Massachusetts 6 percent of those not voting believed incorrectly that as registered independents they could vote in a party primary.

One way of judging the validity of these answers is to run cross tabulations between the reasons given for not voting and variables that affect voting, such as interest in the primary campaign and support for the party. In all three states the percentage of nonvoters who said they were unable to vote was substantially higher for those very interested in the campaign than for those not much interested. There are similar differences between those who support the party and those who do not. In Michigan, for example, 85 percent of nonvoters very much interested in the campaign said they were unable to vote, compared to 76 percent who were somewhat interested and 42 percent of those not much interested. (The contrasts are less clear cut in the other two states.) In Michigan 38 percent of those who said they were not much interested in the campaign explained their nonvoting by saying they were not interested, did not like any candidates, or the election makes no difference; only 2 percent of those very interested gave one of these answers. It seems likely that many of those who do not vote despite an interest in the campaign and/or strong party support are actually unable to do so. Persons who are uninterested or who have little or no commitment to a party are less likely to say they were unable to vote, and that is probably often an invalid excuse.

Weighing the Effects of Many Variables

The best method of evaluating the multiple effect of variables on a dichotomous variable such as voting is discriminant analysis, a method that measures the relative contribution of each variable and the combined effects of several variables in dividing cases into several groups — in this case voters and nonvoters. Table 6.7 shows that the variance explained by a combination of the variables we have analyzed is relatively low.* The percentage of cases correctly predicted increases from just over 60 percent to about two-thirds if interest in campaigns is included. This is not very impressive when we recall that 50 percent could be predicted by chance.

Age is particularly important in California and Michigan, education in California and Massachusetts, strength of party support in California and Michigan. When interest in campaigns is added to the calculations, it becomes the most important variable; it obviously has the most immediate impact on voting. Interest is related to these variables; adding interest to the calculations reduces but does not eliminate the effect of the other variables, and in Massachusetts party support becomes considerably more important. In neither California nor Massachusetts does party registration have much effect on voting.

A similar analysis was done for the 1978 national election data. It shows that strength of party identification and interest in election campaigns have much more effect on primary voting than age and education, but the combined effects of these variables is quite small. This is presumably because in a national survey many other things affect voting in primaries, including the presence or absence of important, competitive primaries in the states.

---

*The canonical correlation squared can be interpreted as the proportion of the variance explained, while the percentage predicted tells us how many of the cases can be correctly assigned to groups (as voters or nonvoters) based on the variables being used. The standardized canonical discriminant function coefficients are similar to betas in a regression analysis, measuring the importance of each variable taking into account the effects of the others.

Table 6.7
Discriminating between Primary Voters and Nonvoters

Variables	Standardized Canonical Discriminant Function Coefficients							
	California		Massachusetts		Michigan		1978 National Survey	
Age	.728	−.496	.323	−.199	.700	−.411	−.201	−.081
Education	.511	−.381	.646	−.351	.247	−.128	.532	−.256
Party support	−.482	.247	−.079	.468	−.660	.336	.872	.555
D/R registration	−.201	.152	−.158	.125	—	—	—	—
Campaign interest	—	.666	—	.665	—	.757	—	.725
Canonical correlation	.316	.402	.280	.357	.302	.430	.198	.277
Canonical correlation squared	.100	.161	.078	.127	.091	.185	.039	.077
Classification:								
% correctly predicted	61.1%	68.1%	62.2%	66.5%	62.0%	67.9%	59.9%	63.0%

Source: Compiled by the author.

175

Profile of the Primary Voter

In summary, primary voters are very much like voters in general elections. They rank even higher in the characteristics that distinguish voters from nonvoters in general elections. Primary voters are better educated and older than others. They have more knowledge of politics, more interest in campaigns, and a stronger sense of civic duty than those who do not vote in primaries. This is exactly what we would expect to find because in most states turnout is lower in primary than in general elections; in other words, the primaries attract a subset of general election voters who are particularly motivated to participate.

A more interesting question is whether primary voters have some characteristics that do not explain general election voting, or do not explain it as well. In fact, primary voters are particularly likely to have a strong sense of party identification or party support. While these measures of party loyalty affect voting in general elections, they have a stronger and more consistent impact on voting in primaries. Party identification or support is particularly important in determining which persons who are younger or less interested in politics will actually vote in primaries. It is also true that persons are more likely to vote in primaries if they belong to the majority party or to the party that most often has competitive primaries — a point to be examined more carefully in our analysis of state-level data.

PRIMARY VOTING IN NORTHERN STATES

In order to understand how the level of voting turnout in primaries is affected by the characteristics of state political systems, it is necessary to examine all of the states over a period of years. This will enable us to measure the effects of differences among states and between parties in a state, and differences resulting from varying political situations, such as the closeness of primary competition.

Data have been collected on voting turnout in all contested gubernatorial primaries held in each state from 1951 through 1982. Only contested primaries are included in the analysis for both theoretical and practical reasons. There is little theoretical reason for finding out why persons vote in elections where there is no contest. The practical problems result from the fact that in many states when there is no competition no primary is held or else no votes are recorded. This analysis will deal separately with voting turnout in northern and southern state primaries, because of differences in both the substantive questions to be examined and the methods of measuring turnout.

Comparing the States

Voting turnout is generally calculated as a percentage of voting-age population, although this has the effect of depressing turnout because many persons, such as those in hospitals, mental institutions, and prisons, may not actually be able to vote. It is also useful to compare voting turnout in primary and in general elections. Table 6.8 shows for each northern state the total turnout in both primaries as a percentage of voting-age population and as a percentage of the vote cast in the general election, and also the turnout for general elections as a percentage of voting-age population. The data in this table are necessarily limited to those election years in which both parties held contested primaries for governor.

The most obvious conclusion is that primary turnout is much higher in some states than in others. There are six states in which turnout (as a percentage of voting population) ranged from 41 to 49 percent, and twelve where it averaged less than 25 percent. Most states with very low turnout had relatively few contested primaries. Similarly there is a large variation in primary turnout measured as a percentage of vote in the general election. The states with high turnout in primaries are not consistently the same ones having high turnout in general elections.

Throughout the rest of this analysis, primary voting turnout will be measured as a percentage of the party's vote in the general election, rather than a percentage of voting-age population. There are both theoretical and practical reasons for this choice. My purpose is to identify and measure the impact of those institutional variables that particularly affect voting in the primary, as distinct from those that affect general election voting. These may include requirements for party registration (or their absence), patterns of competition within each primary, party organizational influence on nominations, and each party's prospects for electoral success.

Table 6.8
Vote in Gubernatorial Primaries Compared to Vote in General Election and Voting-Age Population in Years When Both Primaries Contested, 1951-82
(in percentages)

| State | No. of Yrs. | Total Primary Vote as Percent of: | | Total General Election Vote as Percent of Voting-Age Population |
		Voting-Age Population	Total General Election Vote	
W. Va.	6	48.5	68.2	71.4
Mont.	4	45.9	67.4	68.0
Wyo.	6	42.3	75.3	56.4
Ha.	6	41.6	89.4	48.2
Ak.	6	40.9	91.1	47.4
Wash.	8	40.9	61.4	66.4
Utah	5	39.2	56.2	71.7
Idaho	4	38.0	63.2	60.9
Okla.	7	37.8	90.1	42.0
Calif.	7	37.1	75.4	49.5
Ore.	8	36.1	66.3	54.6
S. D.	4	34.0	55.6	62.0
N. D.	1	31.5	46.1	68.3
Nev.	6	31.0	74.1	41.8
Minn.	6	30.3	48.3	62.9
Mo.	8	30.2	47.7	63.6
N. M.	7	29.9	60.2	49.9
Neb.	11	29.8	53.1	57.6
Ky.	8	29.0	69.9	41.3
Ill.	4	28.3	42.5	67.0
N. H.	3	27.3	48.6	57.0
Mass.	3	27.0	60.1	44.8
Penn.	6	25.9	50.4	51.9
Ks.	7	25.4	49.1	51.5
Md.	6	24.6	62.7	39.1
Ariz.	4	24.3	56.4	42.4
Wisc.	4	24.0	46.3	53.0
Vt.	4	23.1	44.3	52.3
Maine	6	22.9	51.0	47.6
R. I.	1	22.9	37.0	62.0
Mich.	2	21.6	45.6	47.7
Ohio	8	21.1	44.7	48.3
Colo.	1	21.0	43.9	47.9
Iowa	4	18.9	31.9	59.5
N. J.	7	17.4	37.2	47.4
N. Y.	1	14.2	36.2	39.3

Source: Compiled by the author.

There is a serious practical problem with measuring primary turnout as a percentage of voting-age population: It is impossible to determine what proportion of that population is Democratic and what is Republican. The two party primaries are quite separate elections, and distinctly different forces may affect voting in each of them. If we calculate only the total vote cast in both primaries, however, it is impossible to measure these effects. Moreover, the total vote can be computed only in those years when both primaries were contested, as is done in Table 6.8. This affects our ability to measure the effect on turnout of patterns of low competition in one or both party primaries in a state.

It is not feasible to calculate primary voting turnout as a percentage of the registered Democratic and Republican vote, for several reasons. In open primary states, of course, voters are not registered by party. In many states party registration data are not available for the early years covered in this study. Finally, some of the variables affecting why persons vote in a primary may also affect why they register with a party rather than registering as independents, and the impact of these variables would be understated by using party registration in calculating turnout.

Table 6.9 makes it possible to compare levels of voting turnout in both party primaries in each state. In years when both primaries were contested, it shows the average percentage of the total vote that was cast in the Democratic primary, and the states are arranged on this scale from the most Democratic to the most Republican. It also shows, for each party, the average vote cast in all contested primaries as a percentage of that party's vote in general election races. The denominator used in calculating that percentage is the average number of votes cast for that party's candidates in the same year in general election contests for the following offices: the governor, U.S. senator (if scheduled that year), and the total of all U.S. House races in the state. The purpose of averaging elections for two or three offices is to avoid distortions caused by particularly strong or weak candidates in a given year. I am measuring the primary vote as a proportion of the normal vote for the party in the same year. (For those states that elect a governor in odd-numbered years, the average includes the vote for governor as well as the vote for U.S. senator and congressmen in the year immediately preceding or following, whichever one was not a presidential election year.)

Table 6.9
Comparison of Turnout in Democratic and Republican Primaries, 1951-82
(in percentages)

State	Democratic Primary Vote as Percent of Vote in Both Primaries When Both Contested	Each Primary Vote as Percent of That Party's Vote in General Election	
		Democratic	Republican
Okla.	85.4	136.1	34.4
Mass.	81.4	63.8	29.2
Ky.	80.9	108.9	34.9
Md.	80.4	92.0	31.1
Ha.	79.7	103.3	50.5
R. I.	76.5	43.6	16.8
N. M.	74.5	85.6	32.4
Mo.	69.3	61.2	32.8
N. Y.	69.3	43.8	28.3
W. Va.	65.9	79.8	65.1
Nev.	65.5	80.6	64.6
Ill.	61.3	56.4	37.0
Mont.	60.2	100.9	72.9
Minn.	58.6	52.5	42.2
Ariz.	57.7	78.2	45.7
Colo.	56.8	41.8	38.2
Calif.	56.2	82.9	71.0
Wisc.	55.5	44.6	52.8
Wash.	54.2	63.1	64.8
Mich.	53.5	43.6	46.6
Ohio	52.4	47.6	43.8
Ore.	52.3	69.1	64.6
Penn.	50.2	51.7	49.8
N. J.	48.9	36.7	39.3
Idaho	48.7	61.2	61.3
Vt.	44.1	47.4	57.2
Utah	43.9	49.7	62.8
Ak.	43.4	80.1	101.1
Wyo.	42.6	70.6	79.4
Maine	41.5	36.8	65.1
Neb.	39.1	48.9	60.9
Ks.	35.5	37.6	57.8
S. D.	35.1	43.4	66.6
Iowa	31.4	25.4	43.9
N. H.	30.7	31.5	66.0
N. D.	24.8	38.8	74.0

Source: Compiled by the author.

The states in which one party or the other has a much higher primary turnout (as shown in Table 6.9) are generally ones that have been traditionally dominated by one party. This includes traditional Democratic states in the Border, the Southwest, and southern New England, and a smaller number of traditionally Republican states in the Great Plains and northern New England. In a number of Democratic states the Democratic primary averaged almost as much or even more than the Democratic vote in general elections.

Variables Affecting Turnout

There are a number of political-institutional variables that might be expected to affect the turnout of voters in a state gubernatorial primary election. In order to assess the effects of these, individually and collectively, I will use multiple regression. The potential importance of each of these variables should be discussed briefly.

Open/Closed Primaries. State laws differ regarding whether a person must be registered with a party in order to vote in the primary. Closed primaries may discourage those who are independent from registering with a party and thus voting in a primary; they may also lower turnout by preventing voters from shifting to the most interesting and competitive primary in a particular election. State requirements for voting are coded in three categories: (1) closed primaries, (2) open primaries where voters must indicate a party preference, and (3) completely open, including blanket primaries.

Competitive Primaries. We would expect turnout to be heavier in closely competitive primary elections, as it is when general elections are more competitive. There are several reasons for this: When the race is close, voters presumably get more interested and think their votes make more difference, and there is also likely to be more campaigning and media coverage of the race — leading to more information and interest. If a primary is more competitive, the voter may be more likely to find a candidate whom he or she wants to support. It should be remembered, however, that there may be a spillover of voters from more competitive to less competitive races in a primary. Competition in the primary is measured by calculating the percentage of primary votes won by the winning candidate.

Patterns of Competition. There are substantial differences in the level of primary competition among the state parties. It is reasonable to expect that voters would be more likely to get into the habit of voting in primaries in those states where the primaries were usually closely contested. In other words, turnout should be affected by closeness of competition not only in the current primary but in other recent ones. The pattern of primary competition is measured by the average percentage of the winning candidate for several elections preceding the one for which the dependent variable is being measured; the winning percentage is calculated as 100 in uncontested races.*

Incumbency. There are several variables that might be expected to have a direct effect on competition in the primary (and thus an indirect effect on turnout) but might also have a direct effect on turnout. The first is the question of whether or not an incumbent is running for reelection. The presence of an incumbent is expected to discourage competition in the incumbent's own party, and possibly also in the other party. It is also possible the voters expect an incumbent to be renominated and thus take less interest in the primary, particularly in the governor's party. Incumbency is coded 1 when present and 0 when absent.

Endorsement. In earlier chapters I described the endorsement practice and the effect it has in some states in discouraging challenges to the endorsed candidate. We would expect the existence of the endorsement practice to have a measurable effect on competition and on the pattern of competition. In addition to its indirect effect through competition, endorsements might have a direct effect on turnout by persuading voters that the endorsees had the nomination

---

*The pattern of primary competition in recent elections and the recent two-party balance were both calculated using the SPSS LAG program, under which it is possible to create a new variable for any given case by taking information (such as primary competition) from one or more previous cases. Where possible, both primary competition and the two-party balance were averaged for the five or six preceding elections (depending on the frequency of gubernatorial elections). This procedure has the disadvantage of creating missing data for cases prior to the beginning of the data set. Two steps were taken to avoid this problem. Although the regression procedure includes dependent variables beginning in 1952 (or 1951 in a few states), the data set actually begins in 1950, 1948, or 1946 in all states, providing at least one previous election for each state. Moreover, the lag procedure was modified so that in the early years being covered (roughly the 1950s), the average for previous elections was based on fewer than five or six elections, the number depending on how many were available in the data set.

locked up. It is true that several states using party endorsements have a low proportion of contested primaries and also rank near the bottom of the states in primary turnout, including Connecticut, Rhode Island, and Massachusetts. Endorsement is coded 1 when the practice is followed in a state and 0 when it is not. Eight states in which the endorsement process is most strongly entrenched are coded as having endorsements in both parties: Connecticut, Massachusetts, Illinois, Minnesota, Colorado, North Dakota, Rhode Island, and Utah.*

Two-Party Balance. A number of studies have demonstrated that primary competition is greater when the party has a greater chance of winning the general election, and we would expect this to be true of gubernatorial elections. The majority party is likely to have closer competition (although this may be reduced when the incumbent is running), and this should lead to higher primary turnout. The question is whether turnout in the majority party is higher than can be explained by the greater competition; does party status have a direct effect on primary turnout? It seems likely to be true, in part because voters might register with a majority party (in a closed primary state) or get in the habit of voting in the majority-party primary (in an open-primary state) and might be slow to change if primary competition began to develop in the minority party primary. Note, however, that two-party balance may be expected to have indirect effects on turnout through three intervening variables: incumbency, primary competition, and the pattern of competitive primaries; this may reduce the direct effects on primary turnout. Two-party balance is calculated in the same way that primary competition is; the party's percentage of the two-party vote for governor is averaged over the last several elections.

Control Variables. There are also several variables that have no theoretical relationship to primary turnout or to primary competition but that might nonetheless be expected to have some effect on the regression analysis. These are all related to the year in which the election is held. If the election is held in a presidential year, the party's vote for governor, senator, and congressmen (the denominator used in calculating the dependent variable) is likely to be *higher* than it would be in nonpresidential years. Consequently,

---

*New York was excluded because it has held too few primaries for inclusion in the data set, and New Mexico was omitted because endorsements have been used only intermittently.

we would expect primary turnout, using our measure, to be *lower* in presidential years. Some states electing a governor in presidential years also have held a presidential primary. Where this is the case, and where it is held on the same date as the gubernatorial primary, we would expect primary turnout to be higher than in other states electing governors in presidential years. Finally, it is possible that there are some long-term trends in primary turnout that are not explained by other variables. Each election is coded as to whether it occurred in a presidential year and whether it coincided with a presidential primary (coded 1 when each of these occurred and 0 when it did not); and each election is coded by year.

Multiple Regression Analysis

The data for this analysis include all contested primaries in 36 northern states from 1952 to 1982 (1951 to 1981 in states with elections in odd-numbered years): a total of 265 Democratic and 258 Republican primaries. Primary elections for one or more of the years 1950, 1948, and 1946 were included in calculating the lagged variables in order to minimize missing data problems. The data come from the volumes of *America Votes* (Scammon and McGillibray 1958-82) and where necessary from official state documents. Delaware, Indiana, and New York are omitted because primaries have only recently been adopted for gubernatorial nominations and therefore the number of cases is too small for this analysis.

Figure 6.2 describes a model of the variables that should have some effect on primary turnout. (The + or − shows the predicted effect, taking into account how the variables are coded.)

Table 6.10 shows the results of a multiple regression analysis in which turnout in northern Democratic and Republican primaries (measured as a percentage of the average general election vote for the party in several races) is separately regressed on the institutional variables that have been outlined.* In order to detect any important

---

*Multiple regression analysis is a statistical technique for predicting a dependent variable from a group of independent variables. In a multiple regression table, R^2 shows the proportion of variance in the dependent variable that is explained by the combination of independent variables, while standardized regression coefficients, or beta weights, show the relationship between the

Figure 6.2
Model of Institutional Variables Affecting Primary Turnout

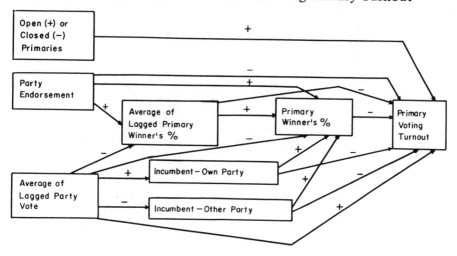

Source: Compiled by the author.

changes over time, regressions have also been carried out for the 1951-64 and 1965-82 periods. The regression analysis is somewhat more successful in predicting primary turnout for the Democrats (R^2 is .45, .49, and .49 for each of three time periods) than for the Republicans (R^2 is .34, .41, .35 for each period). In each of the cases most of the variance is explained by the top three or four variables.

The variables that are most consistently important in explaining primary turnout are the primary winner's percentage, the pattern of winning percentages in past years, the party's vote in past years, and the type of primary used (open or closed). These relationships are in the expected direction for both parties in all time periods, and in most cases the relationships are statistically significant, although there are some exceptions that must be noted.

As would be expected, the current level of primary winning percentages is consistently one of the best predictors of turnout (with beta weights ranging from .218 to .267 in the six regression equations). In Democratic primaries, the past pattern of primary winning

---

dependent variable and each independent variable, while holding all other independent variables constant.

Table 6.10
Regressions of Voting Turnout in Northern Democratic and Republican Primaries on Institutional Variables (based on party vote in general elections)

Independent Variables	1951-82	1951-64	1965-82
Democratic Primary			
Primary winner's %	-.263(-.468)*	-.266(-.493)*	-.267(-.458)*
Average of lagged primary winner's %	-.428(-.755)*	-.348(-.563)*	-.539(-1.05)*
Open/closed primaries	.112(.038)*	.187(.067)*	.098(.032)*
Average of lagged party % of general election vote	.268(1.57)*	.365(1.81)*	.177(1.42)*
Incumbent – own party	.011(.008)	-.101(-.080)	.073(.044)
Incumbent – other party	-.111(-.067)*	-.014(-.009)	-.196(-.111)*
Party endorsement	.000(.000)	-.058(-.044)	.081(.064)
Control variables:			
Presidential/off year	-.237(-.149)*	-.217(-.170)*	-.138(-.093)
Presidential primary	.040(.032)	.054(.042)	.025(.021)
Year of Election	-.071(-.002)	.050(.004)	-.179(-.009)*
	$(R^2 = .45)$	$(R^2 = .49)$	$(R^2 = .49)$

Republican Primary

Primary winner's %	−.255(−.323)*	−.242(−.311)*	−.218(−.273)*
Average of lagged primary winner's %	−.113(−.162)*	.001(.001)	−.282(−.488)*
Open/closed primaries	.285(.067)*	.277(.062)*	.306(.074)*
Average of lagged party % of general election vote	.406(1.32)*	.518(1.25)*	.284(1.72)*
Incumbent — own party	.050(.024)	.104(.048)	−.049(−.025)
Incumbent — other party	.014(.006)	.047(.021)	−.054(−.024)
Party endorsement	−.177(−.102)*	−.083(−.044)	−.197(−.120)*
Control variables:			
Presidential/off year	−.092(−.040)	−.200(−.080)*	−.043(−.021)
Presidential primary	−.018(−.010)	.037(.018)	−.073(−.047)
Year of election	.055(.001)	.124(.006)	.021(.001)
	$(R^2 = .34)$	$(R^2 = .41)$	$(R^2 = .35)$

Note: Entries are beta weights; parenthesized entries are unstandardized regression coefficients.
*Significant at .001 level.

Source: Compiled by the author.

percentages turns out to be even more important (with a beta weight of .348 in the 1951-64 period and .539 in the later period). Democratic primary voters seem to vote when they perceive that the primary has usually been competitive. In the Republican primary during the early period the past level of primary winning percentages had absolutely no impact on turnout, but during the later period it had an impact that was substantial and significant, but less than in Democratic primaries.

We might wonder whether it is the *frequency* of contests or the *closeness* of primary competition in the past that is more important. Originally two lagged variables were created to measure the pattern of competition in previous elections: the proportion of contested primaries and the average percentage of the winning candidate. Each was added separately to the regression equation, and it became evident that it was a pattern of close competition, and not just a pattern of contested primaries, that helps to explain turnout.

How long are the voters' memories; how far back can we go to find an impact of past competition on current voting turnout? This analysis averages primary competition over the last six races for states electing a governor every two years in the 1950s (back to 12 years before the current election); it includes five elections for the other states (back to 20 years). Competition in primaries was originally lagged for only three previous elections, but the predictive power of this variable increased considerably when five or six elections were included, suggesting that the effect of traditional patterns of competition persists over a long period. (The lagging procedure includes fewer years in the first few elections to avoid problems of missing data.)

In both parties the pattern of two-party competition in past elections affects turnout significantly; voting is substantially higher in the primary of a party that has won a larger percentage of the gubernatorial general election vote in recent years. As the unstandardized regression coefficient indicates, over the whole period, the percentage of turnout in the Democratic primary increases by 1.57 points for every percentage point increase in the past average Democratic percentage of the two-party vote; the comparable Republican gain is 1.32 points. Because we would expect much of the effect of party dominance on primary turnout to be mediated by immediate and long-term patterns of primary competition and by incumbency, it is important to emphasize how much direct impact party dominance has on primary turnout.

We would expect turnout to be higher in open primary states, and this proves to be true for both parties, but this variable is more important in the Republican party; on the Democratic side its effect declines to a nonsignificant level in the later period. There is no obvious reason for these differences between the parties.

We would expect the major effects of incumbency and endorsement on turnout to be indirect, through their impact on primary competition, but both might have a modest direct effect on turnout that would be negative. Table 6.10 shows that the only significant effect of incumbency is found in the Democratic party, in the later period; there is less turnout when there is a Republican incumbent in the race. In the Republican primary, party endorsement has a modest but significant direct effect in lowering turnout in the later period.

Table 6.10 shows that, among the control variables, only the presidential year has a significant impact on turnout; it is modest but stronger among Democrats, and stronger in the earlier period. This means that the higher turnout in presidential years inflates the denominator used in calculating the rate of primary turnout. There is no significant trend toward higher or lower primary turnout (compared to that in general elections) over the whole period.

Figure 6.2 suggests that the impact of many of these variables on turnout may be indirect as well as direct. The use of endorsements and the presence of an incumbent in a race may decrease competition and thus decrease turnout. If a party's electoral strength is greater, competition should be higher in its primary. Endorsements and electoral strength also affect past primary competition. Where a party is stronger, it is more likely to have an incumbent running.

In order to assess both the direct and indirect effects of these variables on turnout, a path analysis was conducted. When both types of effects are measured, the impact of long-term party strength on turnout in the Democratic primary is substantially increased; in the Republican party that variable has a large direct, but very little indirect, effect. The pattern of previous primary competition has very little indirect effect, because the correlation between this variable and current primary competition is surprisingly low in most cases.

The presence of an incumbent in a party's primary generally has a strong effect in decreasing primary competition and as a consequence it has an indirect effect on primary turnout that is greater and more consistent in direction (negative) than the direct effect of incumbency. The existence of endorsements has a modest effect in decreasing competition. As a consequence, endorsements have a substantial indirect impact on Democratic turnout and on recent Republican turnout.

When the total effects of variables are assessed through path analysis, the most important variables continue to be current primary competition and the pattern of two-party strength for both parties; the pattern of past primary competition for the Democrats; and the type of primary and endorsement practices for the Republicans.

PRIMARY VOTING IN SOUTHERN STATES

Southern primaries differ from those in other states in several respects. Until very recently most state Republican parties did not use primaries, but made nominations through the party organization. For many years the Democratic primary was the decisive election in all southern states because of the weakness and sometimes the nonexistence of Republican opposition. Even though Republican opposition has been growing throughout the South, and some Republican governors have been elected, the average number of votes cast in Democratic primaries continues to approximate and sometimes exceed the number cast for Democrats in general elections for governor. The use of the runoff if no candidate wins a majority in the primary is another characteristic of southern primaries (except for Tennessee).

It is necessary to use different measures of primary turnout in southern states than were used in northern states. The weakness and inconsistency of Republican competition in general elections makes it impractical to calculate Democratic primary turnout as a percentage of the party's vote in general elections. Instead Democratic turnout is compared to voting-age population. Until the mid-1960s turnout in the Democratic primary was deflated in most southern states by restrictions on voting by blacks. In order to control for that factor — to measure turnout of those who were able to vote — voting-age population has been adjusted in southern states to take into account the proportion of blacks not registered, the proportion of the population that was black, and normal registration rates among whites; the adjustment has not been necessary in recent years.

There have been substantial differences among the southern states in the proportion of persons voting in the Democratic primary. Over the whole 1951-82 period turnout as a proportion of adjusted voting age has averaged about 52 percent in Louisiana and Mississippi; only about 25 percent in South Carolina, Florida, Texas, and North Carolina; and only 13 percent in Virginia (Table 6.11). The most obvious reason for the large variations is that Democratic turnout is lower in those states having substantial numbers of Republicans who do not participate in Democratic primaries. The table shows that Democratic primary turnout has been consistently low in Virginia and North Carolina; in recent years it has declined sharply in Tennessee, South Carolina, and Florida; and it has declined more gradually in Georgia and Texas. Democratic primary turnout is generally dropping most in states where the Republican party is becoming more competitive in general elections. Most of this decline cannot be accounted for by a growth in Republican primary turnout (as will be shown in Chapter 7).

Table 6.11
Vote in Democratic Primaries in Southern States as Percentage of Adjusted Voting-Age Population

State	1951-82		1951-64	1965-82
Louisiana	52.6	(48.2)	53.5	50.6
Mississippi	52.1	(44.5)	50.1	54.1
Alabama	39.1	(36.4)	40.7	38.2
Arkansas	35.8	(34.9)	36.2	35.5
Tennessee	30.2	(24.5)	37.3	24.6
Georgia	28.4	(26.8)	33.7	25.2
South Carolina	26.8	(23.6)	32.4	18.4
Florida	26.3	(25.2)	35.0	17.6
Texas	25.1	(24.5)	28.3	21.3
North Carolina	24.0	(22.7)	26.8	21.3
Virginia	13.3	(12.5)	12.5	14.5

Note: The voting age is adjusted to control for restrictions on the black vote in some southern states, particularly during the earlier period. The figures in parentheses for the 1951-82 period are on unadjusted voting age. The non-partisan primaries in Louisiana are omitted.

Source: Compiled by the author.

A multiple regression analysis of Democratic primary turnout in southern states — using voting-age population for the calculations — shows (Table 6.12) that the same variables that were most successful in explaining primary voting in the North are in most cases even more successful in southern states, although there are some differences between the 1951-64 and the 1965-82 time periods. The level of primary competition (measured by both present and past margins of primary winners), the strength of the Democratic party in recent general elections, and the presence of an incumbent are significant variables for the period as a whole. In more recent years the pattern of past primary competition has become more important than the current levels, incumbency has become less important, and the type of primary has become more important. The effect of Democratic electoral strength on primary turnout has also declined in recent years. In the past, Democratic primary turnout was highest in overwhelmingly Democratic states because there were few Republicans who stayed home on primary election day. As the general election has grown closer in many of those states, primary turnout has declined and the relationship between the two variables has declined. The existence of a contest in the Republican primary has only a weak effect on Democratic turnout, perhaps an indication that there are not large numbers of voters who shift back and forth from one primary to the other. In most southern states the growth of the Republican party has led occasionally to contested primaries in that party. The choices between party primaries being made by southern voters is discussed in the next chapter.

IMPLICATIONS FOR THE PARTY SYSTEM

The strongest and most consistent findings about variations in primary turnout among the states are that turnout is higher when the party's vote in general elections is greater, when primaries are currently and traditionally competitive, and — particularly for Republicans — when there is no endorsement procedure and when state law provides for open primaries.

None of these findings is surprising. Voters naturally are more interested in helping to nominate candidates in the party that usually wins elections. Primaries that are more competitive attract more voters because there is more active campaigning and because

Table 6.12
Regression of Voting Turnout in Southern Democratic Primaries on Institutional Variables
(based on voting-age population)

Independent Variables	1951-82	1951-64	1965-82
Primary winner's %	-.403(-.294)**	-.456(-.288)**	-.302(-.234)
Average of lagged primary winner's %	-.407(-.389)**	-.321(-.241)**	-.548(-.622)**
Average of lagged party % of general election vote	.387(.333)**	.519(.484)**	.236(.229)*
Incumbent-Democratic	.228(.058)**	.462(.101)**	.083(.023)
Open/closed primaries	.140(.039)	-.229(-.052)	.336(.103)**
Contest in Republican primary	-.186(-.044)*	-.020(-.005)	-.235(-.059)
Control variables:			
Presidential/off year	.263(.066)**	.023(.005)	.358(.106)**
Presidential primary	-.051(-.017)	-.058(-.015)	-.026(-.011)
Year of election	.018(.000)	.138(.004)	-.101(-.002)
	(R² = .58)	(R² = .65)	(R² = .66)

Note: Entries are beta weights; parenthesized entries are unstandardized regression coefficients.
*Significant at .01 level.
**Significant at .001 level.

Source: Compiled by the author.

voters have a broader choice among candidates. Because voting in primaries is a matter of habit, traditional patterns of primary competition affect turnout. Republican voters, at least, are less interested in voting when they perceive the party leaders to be selecting candidates through endorsements. Voters are more likely to vote in open primary states because (in some of them) they do not have to disclose a partisan preference and presumably because they are free to vote for candidates in either party.

In states that have been dominated by one party, particularly in the South, disproportionate levels of turnout can have important implications for both parties. Lower turnout in the minority party can hurt that party's chances of picking strong nominees, particularly if the turnout is unrepresentative of the party's potential support in general elections. On the other hand, a low turnout gives party leaders a better chance of controlling the choice. If most voters in such states enter the majority party primary, this may contribute to disunity in the party because the voters represent such a wide spectrum of opinions and interests. These problems are discussed more fully in the next chapter.

The closer the competition between two parties in a state, the more incentive each party has to pick the strongest possible candidates, and it may use some form of endorsement machinery in an effort to accomplish this. Anything that reduces the level of primary competition will lead to a lower turnout of voters, and this in turn enhances the ability of the party leadership to influence the choice of nominees. Low turnout in the primary might appear to help a party, at least one that holds a competitive position in the state. Party leaders have a better chance of choosing the strongest possible candidates while avoiding a highly divisive primary that could endanger the party's chances in the general election.

There may be some disadvantages to a party, however, in discouraging party turnout. It is not necessarily true that party leaders always know better than the voters and choose the strongest candidate. The ability to win a competitive primary is one test of a candidate's political skill. Moreover, the candidate who wins a competitive primary is able to attract media attention during the campaign, to develop an organization, and to attract the interest and loyalty of voters.

There is modest evidence that open primary laws attract more voters to the polls, and this remains true when other variables are controlled. Open primaries create risks for parties because of the possibility that candidates will be chosen by voters who have little loyalty to the party and its principles. How much voting behavior is actually affected by the laws regulating participation in primaries is a more difficult question — one that is addressed in the next chapter.

7

Choosing a Party Primary

The goal of the previous chapter was to find out who votes in primary elections, and why. In this chapter the purpose is to determine how voters choose between Democratic and Republican primaries and how that choice is affected by laws that establish closed and open primaries.

In the 26 states with closed primaries a person must be registered with a party in order to vote in that party's primary. Usually party registration must occur in advance of the primary, and there is usually a deadline several months before the primary for shifting party registration. In a few closed primary states it is possible to shift party registration at the last moment, but voters may not be aware of that opportunity. Open-primary states are defined as ones where there is no party record of party registration and no restriction on shifting party primaries. In 12 open-primary states, mostly in the South, a voter must openly choose a party primary at the polls, while in nine others, mostly in the West, a voter may secretly choose which primary to vote in. In the two blanket-primary states a voter may vote in one party primary for some offices and in the other for the rest. The states are divided into closed and open states for our analysis of the consequences of legal requirements, but we should keep in mind that there are some variations within each category.

It is important to understand how the laws establishing closed or open primaries affect the political party system. Does the closed-primary system protect the dominant position of a majority party?

Does the open-primary system help the minority party by making it easier to attract voters to its primary, thereby broadening the party's base and enhancing its ability to nominate electable candidates? Does the open-primary system weaken both parties by undermining voter loyalties to parties? The frequent ambivalence of party leaders about laws regulating primaries suggests that they do not understand the effects of these laws.

Little is known about how legal requirements for primary voting affect parties because almost nothing is known about how voters choose party registration in closed states or choose a primary in open states. We do not know whether voters are more likely to shift from one party primary to another in open than in closed-primary states.

The structure of the primary determines the specific questions that must be asked about the choice of a primary. In a closed-primary state the voter makes a choice between parties at the time of registration. Is that choice dictated largely by party identification — and if so, how do independents register? Is there a tendency for voters to register with the party more likely to have competitive primaries, and/or more likely to win the general election? It is possible to shift party registration from one primary to the next if the deadline is met. To what extent do voters shift their party registration over time?

In an open-primary state, where voters are free to shift back and forth between parties from one primary to the next, how common are such shifts? Do most voters stick to one party primary? What kinds of voters are most likely to shift primaries from one year to the next? What types of primary elections are most likely to produce such shifts? Do voters shift primaries to vote for particular candidates or to vote in the closest races? How much difference does it make in practice whether a state has a closed or open primary system?

These are questions that have seldom been raised in studies of primary elections, and they are not easily answered.* In search for answers, I will rely on the same data sources used in the previous chapter: surveys of registered voters in California, Massachusetts,

---

*For studies of crossover voting in presidential primaries, see Ranney and Epstein (1966); Adamany (1976); Hedlund, Watts, and Hedge (1982); and Jewell and Olson (1982).

and Michigan, and data from national election surveys; and aggregate data on primary voting for all state primaries and (in greater detail) for a few individual states.

SURVEYS OF PRIMARY VOTERS

The three states where surveys of primary voting were conducted in 1982 have different requirements for voting in a primary. California requires that voters be registered with a party, while Michigan has no such requirement. Massachusetts permits registered voters not enrolled with either party to enroll temporarily with a party in order to vote in a primary; only those registered with the opposite party are excluded from the primary. In Michigan the "rational voter" seeking to maximize the value of the vote would shift back and forth between primaries. The "rational voter" in Massachusetts would be enrolled with neither party, to accomplish the same purpose.

Ideally the study of voters' registration and their choices of a party primary should be based on a panel study. Since the only survey data available are recall questions, we must interpret the results cautiously. The surveys demonstrate one major difference between the two states with registration requirements (Tables 7.1 and 7.2): 90 percent of registered voters in California are registered with a party, while over one-third of those in Massachusetts are not — presumably because the laws in the latter state permit voters without party registration to vote in either primary. In both states about four-fifths of those registered with a party claim they have always been registered with that party.

In California more than half of those registered as independent say they have registered with a party at some time in the past. In Massachusetts over half of those not enrolled in a party say that in the past they have enrolled temporarily in order to vote in a primary; over three-fourths of these have voted in the Democratic primary, while the rest have entered the Republican primary or in some cases have voted in both. Those voters who enroll temporarily with a party are usually either supporters of that party or of neither party; half of those who have never enrolled temporarily with a party are supporters of neither party, while most of the rest are Democratic supporters.

Table 7.1
Registration and Party Support among California Respondents
(in percentages)

Registration Record	All Persons	Party Support					N
		Strong Dem.	Weak Dem.	No Party	Weak Rep.	Strong Rep.	
Registered							
Democratic	53	39	23	30	3	5	(308)
Republican	37	1	2	22	21	54	(217)
Independent	8	18	20	35	12	14	(49)
Other	2	–	–	–	–	–	(10)
All Persons	100	23	15	28	10	24	(584)
If registered with a party, always same one?							
Yes	80	26	15	27	9	23	(409)
No	20	12	14	25	16	34	(104)

Source: Compiled by the author from 1982 telephone surveys.

199

Table 7.2
Registration and Party Support among Massachusetts Respondents
(in percentages)

Registration Record	All Persons	Party Support					N
		Strong Dem.	Weak Dem.	No Party	Weak Rep.	Strong Rep.	
Registered							
Democratic	46	49	20	29	2	1	(294)
Republican	17	6	5	28	24	38	(108)
Independent	38	28	16	39	10	7	(240)
All Persons	100	34	15	32	9	10	(642)
If registered with a party, always same one?							
Yes	81	38	15	30	7	11	(323)
No	19	33	20	23	13	11	(75)

If independent, ever temporarily registered with a party?							
Yes – Democratic	38	43	21	27	7	2	(89)
Yes – Republican	9	14	5	38	19	24	(21)
Yes – Both	6	19	13	19	38	13	(16)
No	47	21	14	50	7	7	(108)
If registered independent, voted in which primary in 1982?							
Democratic	88	44	19	24	7	6	(115)
Republican	12	0	20	27	27	27	(15)

Source: Compiled by the author from 1982 telephone surveys.

When respondents were asked why they were registered as Democratic or Republican, close to 45 percent in both states said that they had always been – or their families were – Democrats or Republicans. Over one-third in California and over one-fourth in Massachusetts said that they agreed with the party on issues; much fewer numbers gave candidate- or group-related answers. Only 4 percent in California and 7 percent in Massachusetts gave as their reason the desire to vote in that party's primary – what might be considered a "rational" answer.

On the other hand, one-third of the large number of those in Massachusetts enrolled with neither party said that they chose that course in order to be able to vote in either party's primary. Those registered as independent in California were much more likely to claim that they disliked both parties. Over 40 percent of the independents in both states said they registered that way because they wanted to remain independent or because they generally voted for candidates in both parties. Two-thirds of all respondents in California said that they would prefer to be able to vote in a primary without being registered with either party.

A study by the secretary of state's office of aggregate voting in Massachusetts primary elections in a sample of communities in 1978 and 1980 sheds some light on the behavior of enrolled independents (Connolly 1982). Generally independents were less likely to vote than were party enrollees. When there were contested primaries in both parties at the state or local level, the proportion of independents voting in each party primary approximated the party enrollment in that community. In 1980, when there were no statewide primaries, the enrolled independents voted overwhelmingly in the local primary where there were more serious contests, which was usually the Democratic one.

Table 7.3 shows that in Michigan, where the primary is open, almost half (45 percent) of those respondents who have voted at least occasionally in the past say that they have shifted back and forth between party primaries, more than one-fourth usually vote in one party's primary, and only one-fourth always vote in one primary. Table 7.3 shows that those who always or usually vote in one party's primary are composed almost entirely of persons who support that party or who support neither party; very few support the other party. Among those who say that they shift back and forth, almost half say that they support neither party.

Table 7.3
Vote in Primary and Party Support among Michigan Respondents
(in percentages)

Registration Record	All Persons	Party Support					N
		Strong Dem.	Weak Dem.	No Party	Weak Rep.	Strong Rep.	
Voted in which primary?							
Democratic	59	61	15	18	3	3	(196)
Republican	41	4	4	19	21	52	(135)
All Persons	100	38	11	19	10	23	(331)
Previous votes in primary							
Always Democratic	17	79	12	8	0	1	(100)
Usually Democratic	18	63	24	12	0	1	(107)
Always Republican	9	2	4	13	15	66	(53)
Usually Republican	11	0	0	12	31	57	(68)
Shifting	45	16	13	45	11	15	(263)
All Persons	100	32	13	26	10	19	(592)

Source: Compiled by the author from 1982 telephone surveys.

It is impossible to judge the accuracy of this recall question, or know how often such shifts occurred, but this does suggest that voter mobility between primaries is much greater in open than in closed primary states. Those Michigan voters who did not always vote in the same party primary were asked how they decided which primary to enter; more than half said they made the choice in order to vote for a specific candidate; most of the rest emphasized issues; less than 4 percent said they chose the primary contest that was closer or more interesting.

Michigan respondents who voted in 1982 were asked which primary they entered and why; the results are similar to the recall question about previous voting. About 30 percent simply identified themselves as Democrats or Republicans or said they always voted in that party; one-third said they wanted to vote for a specific candidate or candidates; over one-fourth mentioned issues or groups or said it was time for a change. Only 7 percent described one contest as closer or more interesting. About 80 percent of those voters who said that they shifted back and forth between primaries explained their primary choice in 1982 by referring to candidates or issues or saying it was time for a change.

One of the most consistent and important findings from the three states is the strong relationship between party support and the choice of a party primary in which to vote. Almost all voters in California and Massachusetts who express some degree of support for a party are registered with that party rather than the other one (Tables 7.1 and 7.2). In Massachusetts even the large number of persons enrolled as independents usually vote in the primary of the party they support, if they vote at all. The percentage of those registered with one party who say that they support the other is only 5 or 6 percent in each state. An analysis of the party support of those voting in each primary in 1982 in Michigan shows the same results (Table 7.3), with less than 7 percent of the vote cast by those supporting the other party. This is a surprising result in an open-primary state where voters can shift easily between primaries, but it may result from the fact that in 1982 both parties had closely contested gubernatorial primaries and thus there was little incentive to shift to the other party. The survey shows that one-fourth of Michigan respondents who say they vote at least occasionally are persons who support a party but say that they shift back and forth between party primaries; but there is no evidence of how frequently they make such shifts.

This pattern of registering and voting in the party one identifies with or supports is shown in national survey data as well.* As part of the 1978 national election study, the actual party registration (if any) of each respondent was recorded from registration lists. The proportion of those registered with a party who were strongly or weakly identified with the other party was only 4 percent (only 8 percent if independents leaning to the other party are included).

Data from the 1958, 1964, 1966, and 1968 national election studies show that the percentage of party identifiers (including independents leaning to a party) who voted in the primary of the other party rather than their own was consistently only 6 or 7 percent (Scheele 1972 ch. 2). These data are based on reported primary vote rather than actual registration, and include open- as well as closed-primary states.

Voters should be most likely to vote in the opposite party primary if their party is in the minority and/or if it seldom has competitive primaries. Southern Republicans, if they vote in any primary at all until recently have had to vote in the Democratic primary. A breakdown of the 1958 and 1964 national election data by region and party shows that in southern states about half of the small number of Republican identifiers who voted did so in Democratic primaries and almost no Democrats shifted to one of the infrequent Republican primaries (Wolfe 1966, p. 104).

National surveys are of little use in understanding particular circumstances in a state, or in a specific state primary election, that may cause voters to vote in the opposite party's primary. Relatively few state surveys are available to shed light on this question. Kentucky may be typical of border states where the primary is closed, the Democratic party wins most state elections, and Democratic primaries are more competitive than those in the Republican party. Slightly more than half identify as Democrats (in a three-way classification), about one-fourth are Republican, the rest independent.

---

*For the purposes of this analysis, there seems to be little difference between the traditional measure of party identification used in national election surveys and the measure of party support used experimentally in the 1980 and 1982 national election surveys and used in our surveys of three state primaries.

The Democratic registration lead is about 70-30, with very few registered independent. This does not mean, however, that many Kentucky Republicans register Democratic. In fact only about 3 percent of those identifying with each party register in the other party. About 60 percent of those identifying as independents, however, register Democratic.

Surveys from states with open primaries would be particularly useful in clarifying the relationship between party identification and primary voting. Indiana is a state where voting patterns in the general elections show a strong sense of party loyalty and straight ticket voting. Does this loyalty carry over into primaries, despite the existence of an open primary? In 1980, both political parties had statewide primary competition for one major race, but the Democratic race was closer. A survey showed that only 4 percent of party identifiers who voted chose the opposite primary along with 24 percent of independents who lean to a party. There was no significantly greater shift to the Democratic side where competition was greater (Cranor, Crawley, Perry, Sargent, and Scheele 1980, p. 41). In 1966 in Minnesota, an open-primary state, the Democratic-Farmer-Labor party had a bitterly contested primary for governor while the Republican party had a lopsided contest. It would appear to be a perfect opportunity for Republican identifiers to shift to the Democratic primary, but a Minnesota poll showed that only 4 percent of them planned to do so.

The most important conclusion to be drawn from survey data is that most voters who perceive themselves as identifying with or supporting a party vote consistently in the primary of that party rather than the other. Whatever shifting of party primaries occurs seems to be done largely by independents. Obviously it is eaiser to shift primaries in an open-primary state, but the limited amount of survey data available leaves unanswered questions about how many voters shift how frequently. The survey data do suggest that voters usually choose a particular primary because of candidates or issues rather than because of the closeness or importance of a primary — despite the evidence from aggregate data about which primaries have the heaviest turnout.

PARTY REGISTRATION IN CLOSED-PRIMARY STATES

Those who register to vote in closed-primary states must choose whether to register with a party, and if so, which one. Those choices may be influenced both by the individual's own party loyalty and by the partisan environment in the state. Because survey data on these choices are lacking in most states, we turn to aggregate data in order to describe and try to explain variations among the states. One of the most striking differences among those states with closed primaries is the proportion of those who register without designating a party. Table 7.4 shows that the proportion registered as independent is one-third or more in 8 states and under 10 percent in 13 states. Voters appear to be much more interested in the chance to vote in primaries in some states than in others. Where the data are available, figures are included for an earlier year, usually 1970. There is a slight trend in a majority of states toward more independent registrants.

Table 7.4
Proportion of Registered Voters Who Are Independent
in Closed-Primary States
(in percentages)

State	Percent 1982	Independent 1970 (or date shown)	State	Percent 1982	Independent 1970 (or date shown)
N. J.	46		S. D.	8	14
Ohio	46		Nev.	7	7
Mass.	41	35	Neb.	7	3
Colo.	38	35	N. M.	7	5
Maine	36	25	Md.	7	2
Iowa	35		Fla.	6	3
Conn.	34	36	Penn.	5	2
Ks.	33	45 (1974)	N. C.	4	2
N. H.	30	32	Ore.	3	1
N. Y.	17	12	Ky.	3	2 (1971)
Wyo.	12	16	W. Va.	2	1 (1968)
Calif.	10	5	Okla.	2	1
Ariz.	8	4			

Source: Compiled by the author.

There are unique explanations for the high proportions of independents in some states. Massachusetts, as we have seen, permits those registered independent to vote in either primary by temporarily registering with a party. Ohio has a peculiar registration requirement on the borderline between a closed and open system.* New Jersey has shifted from closed to open and back to a closed primary, changes probably confusing to voters. New Hampshire makes it relatively easy for independents to join a party on short notice.

If large proportions of voters pass up the opportunity to vote in either party primary, the most plausible explanation is that neither party has a very competitive primary. In fact, Colorado and Connecticut are among the states that least often have competitive primaries, because of the effectiveness of party endorsements. It is more difficult to understand the high proportion of registered independents in such states as Iowa, Maine, and Kansas.

At the other end of the scale are the states with remarkably low proportions of independent registrants. This includes several southern and border states where the Democratic primary is almost always contested and where that contest is often more important than the general election. Among the other states with the lowest proportions of registered independents that have a high proportion of competitive gubernatorial primaries are West Virginia, Oregon, Pennsylvania, Nebraska, and Nevada.

There is also the possibility that states with a higher proportion of persons who register independent also have a high proportion who identify as independents. It is impossible to test this thesis precisely because we lack comparable survey data on party identification from all of the states and because national samples do not provide samples in each state that are either large enough or representative. A number of single-state surveys conducted between 1976 and 1980 are available that shed some light on this question.† The proportion of

---

*In Ohio, when a voter participates in a primary election, a record is kept of his party preference; if at the next election he or she wants to vote in the other party primary, the vote will be challenged and he or she must sign an affidavit indicating support for candidates in the other party.

†These surveys come from Cambridge Research Associates, Peter D. Hart Research Associates, and Market Opinion Research (made available by Ruth S. Jones and Warren E. Miller), and from the *New York Times* and surveys by several university survey research centers.

persons identifying as independent (in a three-way scale) has been reported to be in the 48-50-percent range in a number of the states ranking high on independent registration: New Jersey, Massachusetts, Maine, Connecticut, and New Hampshire, and in the 30-40-percent range in Ohio and Iowa. The proportion of independent identifiers is lower in some of the states with fewer registered independents: 26 percent in Oklahoma, 20 in Kentucky, 30 in North Carolina and Maryland.

It is obvious that the states differ much more in the proportion of registered independents than in the proportion of those identifying as independents. But there are some modest differences in the proportions of independent party identifiers that may help to explain differences in registration patterns. It is also possible that the causal effect works in reverse. In states where voters are less likely to register with a party and thus to vote in the primary (because of low competition or other reasons) they may be less likely to identify with a party. This possibility is intriguing, but not susceptible to proof or disproof with available data.

A closely related question is whether voters are more likely to identify with a party in states where they must be registered with a party to vote in the primary than in open-primary states. Does the act of party registration reinforce party identification? Although national surveys cannot be used to measure party identification in a single state, they can be used to make comparisons among voters in several categories of states, particularly if several national surveys are combined to increase the sample size. I have combined the data on party identification in the national election surveys for the years 1972, 1976, and 1978, producing a sample size of nearly 6,300 respondents. Voters are divided into two basic categories: those who identify with a party (strongly or weakly) and those who are independent (whether or not they lean to a party). The proportion of voters identifying with a party is 66.4 percent in closed-primary states, 66.3 percent in southern open-primary states, and only 59.2 percent in northern open-primary states.

These findings suggest that in northern states voters are slightly more likely to identify with a party if a system of party registration exists. (It is implausible that slight variations in party identification cause states to adopt particular primary systems.) There are several reasons why the proportion of party identifiers is higher in southern than in northern open-primary states. Most southern open-primary states, and few in the North, require a voter to specify publicly in which primary he or she wants to vote. Moreover, the Democratic primary has played such a dominant role in southern politics that those who vote in it may be less likely to consider themselves as independents. We know relatively little about the reasons why persons choose to identify with a party, but most previous research has emphasized personal reasons rather than the influence of institutions such as legal requirements for voting in primaries.

To what extent do voters choose their party registration on the basis of political circumstances in the state? Our survey data suggest that voters who identify with a party register the same way; therefore state variables probably have more influence on voters who have little if any identification with a party. This group of voters may be expected to choose the primary where their vote will make the most difference, either the majority party or the primary that has the most competition.

The analysis of aggregate voting and registration data is limited to those election years in the 1952-82 period for which party registration figures are available; this includes 57 percent of the election years, but in a few states only a very few elections are included. There is a very high correlation (.97) between the Democratic proportion of the vote in both primaries (with both contested) and the Democratic proportion of total party registration in those years. There is a correlation of only .51, however, between the Democratic proportion of total party registration and the Democratic candidates' percentage of the vote in gubernatorial, senatorial, and total congressional races. One reason why this correlation is not higher is because the party's share of registration is quite stable over short periods of time, while the voting returns vary with the strength of candidates and national political trends. Another reason for this low correlation is that in some states one party consistently has a larger share of the registration total than its voting percentage. In most cases if one party normally is in the majority, it will attract a larger share of registrants than of voters, presumably because its primaries are more competitive and important.

VOTING PATTERNS IN NORTHERN OPEN-PRIMARY STATES

In any open-primary state, where no records are kept of party registration, it is possible for voters to shift back and forth between party primaries from one election to the next. It would theoretically be possible for all primary voters to move from the Democratic primary one year to the Republican primary the next. In the two states with blanket primaries, Washington and Alaska, it is possible in one election to vote in the Democratic primary for some offices and in the Republican primary for the others. Although the survey data from Michigan indicate that almost half of the voters have shifted back and forth, other surveys suggest that in any single election relatively few voters enter a primary contrary to their own identification. None of the survey data tells us explicitly how many voters shift party primaries in any pair of elections.

Voters might be expected to shift primaries in order to vote for a particular candidate or because of dislike of the candidates in their own primary. They might also shift because one primary appears to have closer races in one year. Despite the ease of shifting in an open-primary state, there are several reasons for doubting that many voters shift frequently:

1. Those voters who identify with a party may be reluctant to enter the other primary, particularly in those open-primary states where they must openly ask for the ballot of one or the other party in the primary.

2. Voters may not actually know which primary has closer races, unless they follow politics closely.

3. Because there are usually several races on the primary ballot, an interest in one race in the other party primary may not be enough to make a voter shift.

If we use aggregate data, it is impossible to measure precisely how many voters shift from one primary to the other, and it is even difficult to make reliable estimates. If we could assume that the same persons voted in primaries at two time periods, and that most of the shifting occurred in one direction, as illustrated in Figure Model 7.1a, it would be relatively easy to estimate primary shifting. Unfortunately, some shifting may occur in both directions, and, more importantly, there may be large increases or decreases in the total number voting. The actual pattern can be complex, as shown in Figure Model 7.1b, making reliable estimates of the number who shift primaries impossible.

Changes in the relative size of Democratic and Republican primary electorates are likely to result more from persons dropping

Figure 7.1
Models of Voting in Two Elections

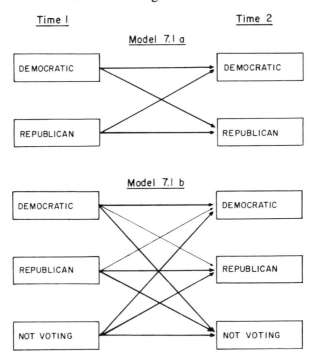

Source: Compiled by the author.

in or out of the electorate than from those shifting primaries, as indicated by the darker lines in Figure Model 7.1b. Persons who vote only occasionally in the primary but do not shift parties might be motivated to vote for the same reasons as those who shift: closer contests or more attractive candidates in one of the primaries. For this reason the relative size of the Democratic and Republican primary electorates may vary just as much in closed- as in open-primary states.

As the first step in comparing closed and open northern primary states, I calculated for each contested gubernatorial primary the total vote in each party primary as a percent of the voting-age population, and as a percent of the vote cast for both parties in the gubernatorial general election. I then calculated the mean and standard deviation for each party on each measure. (I omitted cases where there were fewer than five contested primaries over the

1951-82 period and several states that had shifted between open and closed primaries.) The assumption is that there should be less variation, and thus a lower standard deviation, in closed-primary states.

On the Democratic side, the standard deviations for the primary as a percent of voting-age population are almost identical in the two kinds of states, while the standard deviation for the primary as a percent of the total general election vote is slightly higher (.066 to .061) in closed-primary states. The Republican data show differences that are greater and in the expected direction. The standard deviation for the primary as a percent of population was .044 in open and .026 in closed primaries; for the primary as a percent of the total general election vote, it was .075 in open and .043 in closed primaries. Republican primary turnout varies more in open-primary states (a finding compatible with the regression analysis in the preceding chapter). Obviously if these differences result from shifting between primaries, we would expect greater turnout variation for both parties in open-primary states.

The data for the two states with blanket primaries are treated separately from other open-primary states because the standard deviations are much higher (.052 and .068 for Democratic and Republican primaries as percent of population and .120 and .188 for Democratic and Republican percent of total general election vote). It appears that the blanket primary system encourages many voters to shift primaries, particularly in Alaska.

One plausible theory about the effects of open and closed primary systems is that a minority party that is becoming more competitive should be able to attract voters to its primary more rapidly in an open-primary state. One reason why it is difficult to test this theory is that minority parties usually have relatively few contested primaries, and even fewer with close contests, in the years before their revival. A comparison of states that have enough data on minority-party primaries fails to show any consistent differences between open- and closed-primary states. Minnesota is an example of an open-primary state in which turnout in the DFL party primary grew as the party was becoming more competitive. In New Hampshire, a closed-primary state, Democratic primary turnout remained very low despite the party's competitive position beginning in the 1960s. But Nebraska is an example of a closed-primary state where the growth in the Democratic party primary turnout has matched the growth in the party's electoral strength.

This comparison of closed- and open-primary states, based largely on aggregate data, leads to the general conclusion that the legal requirements for primary voting have a quite limited effect on voting behavior and on the fortunes of the parties. Obviously any conclusions must be tentative because of the difficulty of measuring shifts between primaries with aggregate data. But these data support the conclusion drawn from survey data that in open-primary states large numbers of voters do not frequently take advantage of the opportunity to shift primaries. If we are going to find evidence of any significant effect of the closed or open primary on the party system, it might be better to explore how they affect the long-term growth of a party and participation in its primary. The best recent examples are found in southern states.

VOTING IN SOUTHERN PRIMARIES

Since the early 1950s the Republican party has developed gradually into a significant competitive force throughout the South. By the late 1970s the Republicans had elected a governor and/or a senator at least once in every southern state. They had succeeded in holding the governorship for more than one four-year term in Tennessee and Virginia, and had reelected senators in several other states. Despite these gains, there has been a very modest increase in the proportion of southerners identifying as Republicans (while the proportion of independents has grown rapidly). The questions that concern us are to what extent have voters chosen to enter the Republican primary, and how often has there been competition in that primary?

During the 1950s and early 1960s the voters in most southern states had no choice about which primary to enter. Southern politics was dominated by the Democratic primary, and in every state except North Carolina turnout in that primary was almost always higher than turnout in the general election. Georgia, South Carolina, and Mississippi rarely if ever had any Republican gubernatorial candidates. In other states most Republican candidates were nominated in conventions or in uncontested primaries. Only the Florida Republicans held contested primaries with any frequency (Table 7.5). Since the mid-1960s, as Table 7.5 shows, there have been Republican candidates in almost every gubernatorial race, and in most states

Table 7.5
Levels of Competition in Southern Republican Primaries and Turnout in Contested Primaries

State	Total	None	One	Several	Average	High	Average	High
	Number of Elections Having Various Numbers of Candidates				*Republican Primary-Vote as Percent of:*			
					Total Primary Vote		*Republican Vote in General Election*	
				1951-64				
La.	4	2	2	0	—	—	—	—
Ala.	3	1	2	0	—	—	—	—
Miss.	4	3	1	0	—	—	—	—
S. C.	3	3	0	0	—	—	—	—
Ga.	3	3	0	0	—	—	—	—
Ark.	7	0	6	1	1.1	—	8.8	—
Texas	7	0	6	1	7.4	—	16.1	—
N. C.	4	0	3	1	7.5	—	10.2	—
Fla.	5	0	1	4	6.9	10.3	24.7	51.4
Tenn.	4	1	2	1	4.3	—	86.8	—
				1965-82				
La.	2	1	0	1	0.9	—	2.2	—
Ala.	5	1	3	1	2.8	—	13.1	—
Miss.	4	1	2	1	4.0	—	11.5	—
S. C.	5	0	2	3	8.8	11.3	11.2	13.1
Ga.	5	0	1	4	6.9	10.3	19.2	25.2
Ark.	9	0	2	7	4.6	12.2	10.4	30.5
Texas	7	0	1	6	8.0	16.8	11.9	18.1
N. C.	4	0	0	4	16.7	18.2	21.3	22.2
Fla.	5	0	1	4	24.4	32.0	34.3	48.1
Tenn.	5	1	1	3	27.2	29.3	44.5	50.1

Source: Compiled by the author.

contested Republican primaries have become common. (Virginia is excluded from the table because the Republican party in that state has consistently nominated by convention. The data for Louisiana exclude the elections since 1972 because of the use of the non-partisan primary in recent years.)

As the Republican party in most southern states has begun to hold contested primaries more frequently, have these attracted large numbers of voters? How does turnout in Republican primaries compare to the vote cast for Republican candidates in general elections? The table measures the vote in the contested Republican primaries as a percentage of the vote cast in both primaries and as a percentage of the Republican vote for governor in general elections; it includes an average for the period and the highest percentage reached.

In three states where primary contests have been rare — Louisiana, Alabama, and Mississippi — and also in South Carolina, turnout has been low, consistently less than 15 percent of the party's vote in the general election. Turnout has been slightly higher in Georgia, averaging just under 20 percent of the vote in November. In both Arkansas and Texas, turnout has usually been low, averaging 10 to 12 percent, even though most primaries have been contested. The highest primary turnout in Arkansas occurred in 1970, when the Republican governor was seeking a third term with insignificant opposition in the primary. Similarly, the highest Republican primary turnout in Texas occurred in 1982 when the party's incumbent governor had little primary opposition.

North Carolina, Florida, and Tennessee are the only states in which large numbers of voters have entered the Republican primary. All three are states where the Republican gubernatorial primary has sometimes been closely contested. North Carolina and Tennessee are states with large pockets of traditional party strength in the mountain areas. Voters in traditionally Republican counties may choose that party's primary in order to vote in local primaries. The Republican party in Florida is the only southern party to have frequently held contested primaries in the 1952-64 period, and turnout was substantial in these (although only once over 20 percent of the general election vote). It is particularly interesting to note that North Carolina and Florida are the only southern states to have closed primaries (except for Louisiana prior to 1972). In other words in those two states, substantial numbers of Republicans entered the party's primary despite the fact that they had to register as Republicans to do so. Of course, the same registration requirement that might make it difficult to enter the Republican primary also would make it difficult to return to the Democratic primary in subsequent elections.

Several types of voters might enter Republican primaries in any southern state: (1) Republican loyalists who have never voted in Democratic primaries and who regularly vote Republican in state general elections; (2) Republicans who have voted in the past in the Democratic primary but who have usually supported Republicans in the November election; (3) conservative Democrats or independents who used to vote in the Democratic primary and may have voted for either party in the fall; (4) new voters, including those who have just come of voting age and older voters who have not participated in state elections, perhaps because they were totally controlled by Democrats.

Some voters from each group are presumably included in the Republican primary electorate. The first group is likely to be concentrated in traditional Republican counties of states like North Carolina and Tennessee, and they may vote for candidates who can appeal only to the narrow group of traditional Republican voters. If the Republican primary attracts voters from the second and third categories, they may support candidates who can appeal to a broader range of voters in November. There are obvious limits on our ability to identify the sources of Republican primary votes with aggregate data. If there is a decline in Democratic primary turnout as voting in the Republican primary increases, however, this would suggest that voters are being drawn from the second and third categories. (At the same time, the entrance of black voters into the Democratic primary might conceal such shifts.)

One way of estimating to what extent voters are shifting from the Democratic to the Republican primary is to calculate the total primary vote as a proportion of the voting-age population, and break down that total into its Democratic and Republican components. Figure 7.2 shows the trends in Democratic and Republican primaries for Florida, Tennessee, North Carolina, and Texas. In each state it is obvious that there has been a decline since the early 1960s in the Democratic primary turnout, at the same time that turnout in the Republican primary has been growing. But in each state it is also true that total primary turnout has been declining steadily; the

Figure 7.2
Total Primary Vote and Democratic Primary Vote as Percentage
of Adjusted Voting-Age Population in Selected Southern States

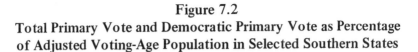

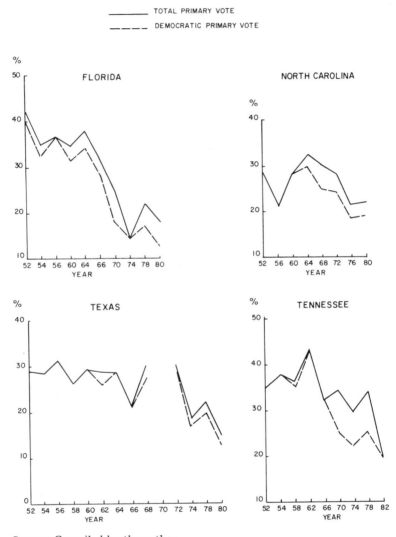

Source: Compiled by the author.

Democratic decline is much larger than can be explained by a shift to the Republican primary. These trends are strongest in Florida and Tennessee, somewhat less consistent in North Carolina and Texas; a similar trend is evident in Georgia.

One explanation for this trend in southern states is that the growth of Republican competition has made the general election more significant, compared to the Democratic primary. Those voters whose interest in politics is limited and who do not want to vote several times in a year may be shifting from the Democratic primary to the general election, particularly if they are more conservative and expect to vote for Republican candidates in the fall. This is only conjecture, of course; we have little hard evidence about shifting voting patterns in southern states.*

In North Carolina and Florida, however, data are available on trends in party registration. Figure 7.3 compares the Republican shares of the general election vote, the primary vote, and party registration over a number of years. In both states primary voting and registration have lagged considerably behind the Republican share of the general election vote. In North Carolina Republican registration has grown slowly since the mid-1960s, but primary turnout has never caught up with it. This registration trend helps to explain the decline in Democratic primary turnout. In Florida there has been a steady and dramatic increase in the Republican share of registration since the early 1950s, and since 1970 the share of the primary vote has approximated the party's share of registration.

CONCLUSIONS

The consequences of varied legal requirements for voting in state primaries can be analyzed at two levels: the effects on individual voting behavior and the impact on the political party system.

------

*The analysis of primary voting in southern states uses the same adjusted voting-age population data described in Chapter 6, in order to control for restrictions on voting by blacks in earlier years. If voting-age population figures are used without adjustment, the decline in total primary turnout is almost as great; most of the decline occurred after the time when the restrictions on black voting had ended, and therefore the adjustments to voting-age population data had little effect.

Figure 7.3
Republican Proportion of Votes Cast in General Election and in Primary and of Registration in North Carolina and Florida
(in percentages)

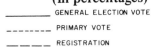

_____ GENERAL ELECTION VOTE

_ _ _ _ _ _ _ PRIMARY VOTE

_ _ _ _ _ REGISTRATION

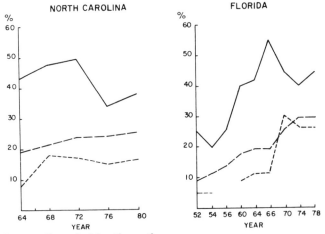

Source: Compiled by the author.

At the individual level there is evidence that voters are more likely to identify with a party if they live in a closed-primary state. This suggests that the act of registering with a party reinforces the sense of allegiance or loyalty to a party.

It is difficult to measure the impact of legal requirements on voting in the primary, partly because variations in levels of party primary turnout may be caused by voters who shift primaries but also by those who enter and leave the primary electorate. The available evidence does not support the assumption that many voters frequently shift between primaries in open-primary states, with the exception of states having blanket primaries. In open-primary states, voters who identify with or support a party are likely to stick to one party primary over a period of years, while independents may occasionally shift primaries. When such shifts occur, they appear to be motivated by interest in particular candidates or issues rather than a calculation that a particular race is close or the winners in one party primary are more likely to win the general election. In the long run, however, voters do tend to vote more often in the primary of the party that is in the majority and the party that has the most primary competition. When the two-party competitive situation is changing, voters seem quicker to vote for the minority party in the general election than to vote in the minority-party primary — whether they are in open- or closed-primary states.

Little is known about the impact of open and closed primaries on political party systems. We lack any historical record on the reasons why some states have adopted open primary laws and others have closed primaries. It is plausible to assume that open primaries were adopted in states where the Progressive movement was strong, such as Wisconsin, North Dakota, Minnesota, or Washington. The closed primary would seem to serve the interests of strong party organizations, and we would expect it to be used in states where the party organizations have such strength. That could explain closed primaries in states like New York, New Jersey, Pennsylvania, and Connecticut. The problem with these logical assumptions is that they do not explain why strong-party states such as Indiana, Michigan, and Illinois have open-primary systems. Nor do they explain the presence of closed primaries in states where the Progressive movement was strong such as South Dakota, or Nebraska (which has nonpartisan legislative elections), or California (which for a long time authorized cross-filing of candidates). It is difficult to understand why Massachusetts uses a system that clearly encourages voters to enroll with neither party to maximize their voice in the primary.

Most southern states have an open primary system in which voters must identify their party preference to enter the primary; until a few years ago voters were sometimes asked to swear allegiance to that party if they were challenged. This system can be understood in the context of a political system where the Democratic primary was the most important election and was often run by the party organization, while Republicans seldom held primaries.

If it were obvious that a closed-primary system, not open primaries, benefited the majority party at the expense of the minority, we would expect to find closed primaries used in every state except those where control of government is very closely balanced between the two parties. We would also expect to see southern legislatures, under Democratic control, adopting closed primary laws. Neither of these has happened. It is probably true on balance that a closed primary benefits the majority party, particularly in situations when the minority party is becoming more competitive. The minority party finds it difficult to identify potential supporters among voters registered with the majority. Equally important, nominations in the minority primary are made by relatively small numbers of voters, traditional supporters, who may fail to select candidates who can appear to a wider variety of voters — including independents and members of the majority party. Although this is logical, it is difficult to find examples in specific states to prove it. In recent years there are a number of cases of minority parties becoming competitive, in states with both types of primary laws. Florida is a particularly good example of a closed-primary state where the minority party has not only become competitive but attracted a large number of registrants and primary voters.

If leaders of both parties in a state clearly recognized that the primary system had partisan consequences, we might expect to see frequent attempts to change to a closed- or an open-primary system when partisan control of the legislature changed, but in fact changes in primary systems are infrequent, and there seem to be few efforts to bring about change. In 1982 the DFL convention in Minnesota adopted a platform amendment to end the open-primary system, and more than three-quarters of the delegates who were surveyed favored the closed primary. Delegates were apparently concerned because they believed that the DFL endorsee for senator in 1978 had been beaten in the primary by conservative crossover voters. There was little reason to believe that the situation would be changed.

One of the curiosities of state primary systems is that several states combine open-primary systems with endorsement practices in one or both parties: Minnesota, North Dakota, Utah, Wisconsin, and Illinois. Although this may appear to be an incongruous combination, in several of these states the party leaders believe an endorsement system is needed precisely because the open primary creates the risk of primary decisions made by outsiders.

At a time when a large number of voters profess to be independents, political leaders may believe that efforts to shift from open to closed primaries would be unpopular. They may also believe that the form of the system makes little difference — a belief that is generally supported by the evidence presented in this chapter.

Part IV
Who Wins
Primaries and Why?

8

Primary Campaigns in 1982

In 1982 there were 36 states that elected a governor. Of the 72 major-party nominees, 16 were nominated without primary opposition, and 56 won contested primaries. This chapter consists of a number of case studies of primary elections; the following chapter is an effort to assess the most important variables that affected the outcome of primary elections in 1982. Case studies are useful both to illustrate some of the more common patterns and trends in primary campaigns and to show the importance of personal and idiosyncratic factors in such elections.

In many respects primary campaigns are like general election campaigns; the most important difference is the absence of traditional party voting patterns. Primary campaigns are affected by the political strength and record of incumbents, the personal characteristics of candidates, and the issues that they succeed in making salient to voters. Primaries are also affected by the success of campaign techniques and the resources that candidates have to pay for them. Incumbency is an important ingredient in many primary campaigns not only because of the political advantages usually enjoyed by incumbents, but also because voters very often make a choice based on their perception of the incumbent's record. The first three case studies (Democratic primaries in Massachusetts and Minnesota and the Republican primary in Michigan) describe various ways in which incumbency can affect a campaign. The relative importance of issues and personalities in races where no incumbent was running are examined in the New York and Michigan

Democratic and California Republican primaries. The effects of traditional and modern campaign techniques are compared in Tennessee and Kentucky Democratic primaries. Finally, the role of amateur candidates who are well funded and who utilize modern campaign techniques is described in the New York and Minnesota Republican primaries.

THE ADVANTAGES OF OFFICEHOLDING: PRESENT AND PAST

The incumbent governor has obvious advantages in seeking renomination. In 1982, 25 of the 36 governors sought renomination, with the following results: 10 were renominated without opposition; 8 defeated challengers by at least 80 percent of the vote; 6 others won with smaller margins; only 1 incumbent was defeated. It is worth noting that 14 of the 16 persons who were nominated without opposition were either incumbent governors or were nominated to run against an incumbent governor who had little or no primary opposition. Only two incumbents faced close primary contests: Governor George Ariyoshi of Hawaii, who beat his closest challenger by a 53-45 margin, and Governor Edward King of Massachusetts who lost, 54-46, to former Governor Michael Dukakis. The victory of Dukakis illustrates another interesting aspect of the 1982 race: the primary victories of four former governors – Rudy Perpich of Minnesota, Bill Clinton of Arkansas, and George Wallace of Alabama, in addition to Dukakis. (Two of the least successful also-ran candidates in gubernatorial primaries were former governors – Harold Stassen in Minnesota and "Big Jim" Folsom of Alabama.)

It is perfectly clear that the typical pattern is for a governor to be renominated with little or no opposition, and the reasons for this pattern are obvious. The governor usually controls the political machinery of the state and, even more importantly, has the visibility and name recognition that make him difficult to beat. If the governor is challenged successfully in a primary, the resulting disunity may be so serious as to undermine the party's chances in the general election, if the opposition party mounts a serious challenge.

Although lopsided primary victories by the incumbent are common, they do not make very interesting case studies. This section includes three of the more interesting primary races of 1982 in which the advantages of holding political office were tested. The first is the classic battle in the Massachusetts Democratic primary between former Governor Dukakis and incumbent Governor King, the man who had beaten Dukakis four years earlier in the primary. The second is the Minnesota victory of former Democratic Governor Rudy Perpich (who had lost to a Republican in 1978) over Warren Spannaus, who had the party convention's endorsement. The Michigan Republican primary involved the incumbent governor indirectly. Governor William Milliken was retiring after 14 years in office, and sought unsuccessfully to win the nomination for Lieutenant Governor James Brickley; instead the voters chose Richard Headlee in a close race over three opponents.

The Massachusetts Democratic Primary

The 1982 Democratic primary in Massachusetts had all the elements of a dramatic confrontation; Michael Dukakis was seeking to defeat Edward King, the man who had ousted him from the governorship in 1978; the two men differed in personal style and on major issues; charges of corruption were commonplace in the campaign; large amounts of money were spent on the race; and the Democratic electorate was deeply divided.

This last point may be the most important. The Massachusetts Democrats have traditionally been a fragmented party, divided along ethnic, religious, racial, socioeconomic, and geographic lines. They are also deeply divided on the social issues that have become important in recent years: abortion, divorce laws, capital punishment, and law and order. These differences on issues are particularly correlated with levels of education (White 1982, 1983). In 1978 King won the primary in large part because of his support for capital punishment, an increase in the drinking age, tougher treatment of criminals, and his opposition to funding of abortions — along with his support for property tax cuts.

Much of King's efforts during his administration were devoted to gaining legislative support for these programs, and much of his

1982 campaign was focused on these issues. He emphasized his bills to raise the drinking age and impose the death penalty, and to repeal an income surtax adopted during the Dukakis administration. King believed that a majority of Democrats were closer to his position on these issues than they were to that of Dukakis. Therefore, if he could define these issues as the central ones in the campaign he could once again defeat Dukakis.

In order to present these issues and his record on them to the voters, King embarked on an expensive and skillful media campaign. He started using television early in the campaign, and never let up, outspending Dukakis in this aspect of the campaign at least two-to-one. The television campaign was evidently effective. Polls that had shown Dukakis with a huge lead early in the campaign indicated on the eve of the election that his margin was much narrower. King devoted fewer of his efforts and resources to building a strong organization at the local level. He did, however, succeed in generating support from a number of organized groups, including some unions and police organizations. He also won substantial support from political leaders such as mayors and state legislators.

King's greatest liability was the series of scandals that plagued his administration. From the start of his administration, many of his appointments were criticized. A member of his cabinet went to the penitentiary. During the primary campaign, the newspapers reported a developing scandal in the revenue department, and the suicide of an employee in that department who was a friend of the governor and had allegedly been under investigation. Massachusetts voters are accustomed to newspaper headlines about scandals, but the Dukakis administration had been able to maintain a clean image, and the contrast in administrative styles, which was a constant theme of the Dukakis campaign, seriously hurt King's prospects.

In his previous administration, Governor Dukakis had alienated many liberal supporters because of his cutbacks in a variety of expensive social programs, and he had irritated many people by a personal style that appeared to be characterized by arrogance and inflexibility. King's victory in the 1978 primary was a surprise to most people and the conventional wisdom was that Dukakis had "blown it." The former governor began his campaign early in 1981 with an extensive effort to build a powerful grass-roots organization of contributors and workers. The success of these efforts became clear in February 1982, when Dukakis won two-thirds of the convention delegates at local caucuses. That organization remained an important part of the Dukakis strategy throughout the campaign.

As Dukakis toured the state for a year and a half, he tried to change his personal image and also to rebuild his ties to liberal groups, some of whom had supported a third candidate in the 1978 primary. Dukakis found most liberals receptive because Governor King had proved to be so conservative on both social issues and on taxing and spending policies. Public employee organizations, and particularly the teachers, who had split with Dukakis during his administration, joined his campaign. Dukakis was still not prepared to make bold new spending promises, but in the new political and economic environment his record and his policies seemed far more attractive to liberals than did those of King.

The primary offered the voters of Massachusetts an unusually clear choice. Both candidates had very high name recognition, and the policies and governing styles of the two successive administrations had been distinctly different. The winner of an election is often the one who succeeds in persuading the voters which issues are most important. Most analysts of the primary election believed that Dukakis won because voters gave higher priority to his issues of integrity and competence than to the social and tax issues emphasized by King.

Our survey showed that one-fourth of those who voted in the Democratic primary thought that corruption was the most important issue in the campaign, and another one-fourth mentioned taxes. About one out of six mentioned jobs and the economy. Surprisingly these were the three issues emphasized most frequently by supporters of both candidates, although more Dukakis voters mentioned corruption and taxes, and King supporters frequently stressed law-and-order questions. Respondents who mentioned an issue as being most important were asked if they preferred one of the candidates because of this issue. Nearly all who mentioned corruption and two-thirds of those who stressed taxes or the economy preferred Dukakis; most of those who emphasized law and order preferred King.

A somewhat different pattern emerged when respondents were asked what they liked or disliked about each candidate. Supporters of both candidates often commented favorably on their experience and record in office. Opponents of Dukakis criticized his record generally or his record on taxes. One-third of those opposing King and one-fifth of his supporters criticized corruption in his administration. Voters reacted much more favorably to personal characteristics and style of Dukakis than of King. Half of the Dukakis supporters mentioned things they liked about him personally, and only one-sixth mentioned personal dislikes. Very few King supporters had anything personal to say about King, and it was a little more likely to be negative than positive.

On the other hand, King drew more favorable comments on issues than his opponent and, unlike Dukakis, got some of this response from those who voted against him. Specific issues mentioned most often were law and order and the lowering of taxes. King was sometimes criticized by opponents as being too conservative, while Dukakis was criticized often by opponents and sometimes by his own voters as being too liberal.

Our survey shows that in 1982 Dukakis did better among college graduates than among those with less education, but the difference was smaller than in 1978, perhaps because social issues played a smaller role in the 1982 primary. Dukakis won a slightly larger share of the votes among enrolled independents than among enrolled Democrats; on the other hand he had 74 percent of the vote among those who support the Democratic party, half the vote of those supporting no party, and one-third of the vote among the small number of Republican supporters.

On balance, the survey data support the conclusion of local observers that Dukakis's victory was due less to his stand on issues than his ability to emphasize the contrast between his personal record of integrity and the corrupt image of the King administration. The voters in Massachusetts were able to make a choice based on their perceptions of the last two administrations. In a situation where the candidates and their records are so well known, it seems likely that media advertising, and disparities in spending on such advertising, are less crucial to the outcome.

The Minnesota Democratic Primary

The victory of Rudy Perpich over Warren Spannaus in the DFL primary was one of the most surprising results of the 1982 primary season. Spannaus brought to the race the overwhelming endorsement of the DFL convention, a three-term record of experience as attorney general, a well-organized campaign operation, and a four-to-one advantage in campaign financing. If he was not a highly charismatic figure, he was a well-known and respected leader of the DFL. His moderately liberal stance seemed to be as close as possible to the mainstream of a party suffering from divisions on social issues. As attorney general he had given priority to legislation tightening controls on hand guns, a stand that had aroused some opposition from supporters of the National Rifle Association.

Rudy Perpich entered the race with both significant liabilities and assets. He had been elected lieutenant governor in 1974, inherited the governorship two years later when Governor Anderson moved to the Senate, and had only two years in office before losing in the 1978 Republican landslide. He took a job in Europe, losing direct contact with state politics, and returned to the state so late in 1982 that he did not consider it practical to seek endorsement at the DFL convention in June. Perpich was not a skillful fund raiser and had a campaign fund of less than $130,000 in the primary. His campaign organization reflected his own casual, even disorganized style, rather than that of modern professional campaign managers.

Perpich's major asset was that during his brief term as governor he had been able to capture the attention and the imagination of Minnesota voters. It is an understatement to describe Rudy Perpich as an unorthodox political leader. As governor he was informal and very accessible to the people. Impatient with formal meetings and the routines of government, he preferred impromptu trips around the state to deal directly with problems. His style of governing sometimes played havoc with administrative routine, but it was good publicity and struck a responsive chord from citizens who often perceive government to be distant and unresponsive.

In order to understand Perpich's popularity, one must understand his political base. Rudy Perpich is a product of the Iron Range in northern Minnesota. It is an area where politics is often a matter of family and ethnic loyalties. The Iron Range was very proud of the miner's son who became governor, and it was prepared to support him for another term. The Iron Range is an area economically devastated by the prolonged depression in the American steel industry, and Perpich was perceived as a candidate deeply concerned about the area's problems.

Perpich was fortunate to have served as governor during a period of prosperity, and he left office with a surplus in the state budget.

His successor, Republican Governor Albert Quie proved so ineffective in coping with the state's budgetary problems in the face of recession that he did not seek another term in office. Perpich often reminded voters of the "golden years" of prosperity and fiscal stability during his administration. But he also developed an elaborate and imaginative plan to provide energy independence for the state and to develop the resources of northern Minnesota. He talked knowledgeably about the deveopment of resources such as peat and aspen, reforestation, and new industries for the area. Perpich also apparently gained some political mileage by criticizing Spannaus's emphasis on gun control and by taking an anti-abortion position.

After the primary election, when Perpich was asked to explain his victory, he criticized the narrow base of the DFL-endorsed slate. While Spannaus had rejected proposals that he pick a woman as a running mate, Perpich had done so. Moreover, the DFL slate included no one from the entire northern half of the state. Perpich carried not only the Iron Range but most of the counties of northern Minnesota, many of them by large margins. While many of these are relatively sparsely populated areas, Perpich won a stunning 39,900 to 8,600 margin in St. Louis County, the site of Duluth. Rudy Perpich's strong political base in northern Minnesota was absolutely essential to overcome Spannaus's advantage in the Twin Cities and surrounding suburbs.

The Perpich campaign cost only 48 cents for every vote he received in the primary — less than was spent by any other gubernatorial primary winner in the country who had serious opposition, and less than spent by most losers. The Perpich victory illustrates the great advantage of holding office. It is possible, even in a two-year term, for a political figure to capture the public imagination and to establish a reputation that is positive. With these advantages, it is possible to run a successful campaign without large funds, extensive media advertising, or a sophisticated campaign organization, at least if you have a strong political base.

The Michigan Republican Primary

William Milliken had been governor of Michigan for 14 years when he announced that he would not seek reelection in 1982.

He had succeeded to the governorship in 1969 when George Romney joined the Nixon cabinet, and had been elected to three full terms. Although some of his general election victories had been narrow, he had had little trouble winning Republican nominations. Milliken had been a moderate who was generally noncontroversial and had a wide base of popular support, but his popularity began to wane in his last term as the state's economic problems grew more serious. One source of unpopularity was a temporary increase in the income tax that he pushed through the legislature to deal with the state's deficit. Although Governor Milliken decided not to run again, he endorsed his lieutenant governor, James Brickley, who was also recognized as a moderate. The primary election became a test of the governor's popularity and the strength of the moderate wing of the Republican party.

Brickley was expected to win the primary, largely because of the longterm domination of the party by Milliken and the moderate wing, but also because his three opponents were expected to divide the conservative vote. Instead, Richard Headlee emerged as the winner with 34 percent of the vote, a margin of 4 percent ahead of Brickley. Headlee was an insurance company executive, with strong support among business groups, who had gained popular attention as originator of an initiative measure to cut taxes that was adopted by the voters in 1978.

Some clues for explaining this outcome can be found in two opinion polls: one conducted as part of my research project and an exit poll conducted by the *Free Press* with a much larger sample of respondents.* The most significant difference between voters supporting Lieutenant Governor Brickley and those supporting other candidates concerned their evaluation of Governor Milliken's performance as governor, as shown in the newspaper poll. While two-thirds of Brickley's voters rated Milliken as either excellent or good, more than half of the supporters of each of the other candidates rated him as not very good or poor. Taken as a whole, Republican voters were almost evenly divided on Milliken.

Brickley was a little more likely than other candidates to draw his votes from persons who identified as Republicans rather than independents (or occasionally Democrats). The newspaper poll

---

*I am indebted to Tim Kiska of the *Detroit Free Press* for making a copy of this survey available to me.

showed that supporters of Brickley were more likely to call themselves moderates; Headlee voters were almost evenly divided between conservatives and moderates. Brickley voters were a little less enthusiastic in rating Reagan than the others. The press poll does not show large differences among the various groups of supporters on specific issues. Answers to questions in my survey on the voters' likes and dislikes about the candidates suggest that supporters of Headlee were more issue oriented. They most often mentioned issues in favorable comments about their candidate and often criticized Brickley's stand on issues, while Brickley supporters had relatively little to say about issues. Brickley's supporters most often stressed his experience, while those who voted for his opponents criticized his record in the Milliken administration and often used the phrase "It's time for a change." Both surveys show a general consensus that the most important problem facing Michigan at the time concerned the economic situation, including specifically the unemployment problem and high interest rates.

Press coverage of the Michigan Republican primary often described it as a battle between conservative and moderate wings for control of the Republican party. The survey data suggest that there were ideological differences among supporters of the various candidates, but they do not show a clear split between moderates in Brickley's camp and conservatives divided among the others. The *consequence* of Headlee's nomination might have been a victory for the conservative wing of the party if he had been elected governor, but he lost in the November election. Media analysis also suggested that the outcome of the primary was a vote of no confidence in the Milliken administration, and the survey data lend some support to that thesis — illustrating the risks of incumbency and of being allied with an incumbent governor in difficult times.

ISSUES AND PERSONAL CHARACTERISTICS

In the absence of an incumbent who is running or sponsoring a candidate, primary campaigns usually focus on the record and personal characteristics of candidates and the issues that they raise. The fact that candidates emphasize particular issues does not, of course, mean that these are salient to the voters. Some of the closest and most interesting primary races in 1982 did not involve incumbents but were contests between well-known political figures who had held major offices and, in some cases, had run for governor before. These were campaigns where the leading candidates, at least, usually had name recognition, campaign skills, and substantial financial resources. The New York Democratic primary, the first case study in this section, was a test of the record and the personal style of New York City Mayor Edward Koch. Lieutenant Governor Mario Cuomo's defeat of Koch demonstrated the importance of organizing traditional interests within the Democratic party, and the importance of issues that can be used to mobilize those interests. The Democratic primary in Michigan is one of the best examples of the important role that issues can play in a primary election. The California Republican primary is one in which each of the candidates gave a great deal of attention to issues, or at least to developing an issue-oriented image, but in which the outcome largely depended on voter perceptions of the personality and experience of the candidates.

The New York Democratic Primary

In January 1982, when Governor Hugh Carey made the surprising announcement that he would not seek another term, a crowd of candidates rushed in to fill the void. Within days came the even more surprising rumors that New York City Mayor Edward Koch might enter the race. A few weeks later, when Koch officially announced his candidacy, only Lieutenant Governor Mario Cuomo stayed in the race to challenge him. From start to finish, Koch seemed to dominate the primary. Everyone speculated about why Koch, who seemed to enjoy equally the power and the public attention of being mayor, would want to move to Albany and the governorship. He had frequently promised not to run for governor, explaining to *Playboy* magazine that to do so "requires living in Albany, which is small-town life at its worst." The press quoted from that interview a number of Koch's disdainful remarks about the quality of living in upstate New York, and then reported on his somewhat frantic efforts to mend his political fences outside New York City. There were stories suggesting that Koch had presidential ambitions and saw the governorship as a necessary step toward being taken seriously in national politics.

While he captured the lion's share of the press, Koch was hard at work to ensure the primary victory that the media seemed to be taking for granted. He raised $3.5 million and hired David Garth, widely recognized as a campaign manager par excellence, to develop his media campaign. He toured upstate New York, working very diligently to win commitments from county leaders, while he solidified his base of support in the party borough organizations of New York City. He demonstrated his organizational skills and his breadth of support from county leaders by dominating the state central committee meeting that endorsed him for governor, and conducted the necessary negotiations to put together a slate of running mates.

Mario Cuomo entered the primary with an electoral record that was less than spectacular. He had served one term as lieutenant governor, but because that official runs as a team with the governor under New York law, his election was not a demonstration of vote-getting ability. More significant was that in 1977 he had lost the Democratic primary for mayor of New York to Edward Koch, and then (as the Liberal Party candidate) lost again to him in the mayor's race in November. During that campaign he developed a reputation for poor campaign organization. As lieutenant governor he was given little opportunity to play any significant role in the Carey administration or gain any great visibility. He did have plenty of opportunities to develop and nourish contacts with political leaders in all parts of the state, and he took full advantage of these opportunities.

Cuomo had a campaign fund that was less than half of Koch's but that made possible a modest media campaign. He had experience, professional campaign advisers, and apparently was willing to follow their advice. Perhaps most significantly, Cuomo had a strong grass-roots organization of some 10,000 volunteers, stuffing envelopes, running phone banks, and ringing doorbells across the state. Many of these volunteers were provided by labor unions, which mounted one of their strongest campaigns in many years on Cuomo's behalf. He also had a well-organized campaign to get out the Italian vote, and to mobilize black and Hispanic voters.

While Mayor Koch seemed to speak for the middle-class white voter, Mario Cuomo put together a traditional New Deal coalition of union members, lower-income voters, blacks, and Hispanics. Many of these groups in New York City had felt neglected by the Koch administration, and they rallied behind Cuomo's candidacy. Turnout in many black and Hispanic districts was as high as in the 1977 mayoral race, which had both a black and a Hispanic candidate. Because of Cuomo's strength among unions and minorities, he was able to get 48.5 percent of the vote in New York City. Mayor Koch's greatest strength was not in his own city but in suburban counties such as Westchester, Nassau, Rockland, and Suffolk, where his total percentage was almost 58 percent. In the remainder of upstate New York, however, Mario Cuomo won two-thirds of the vote and carried every large county and all but a couple of small ones.

The outcome of the New York Democratic primary was a stunning political upset, almost certainly the biggest surprise of the 1982 primary season. In its aftermath New York pundits realized that they had underestimated Mario Cuomo, a man who proved to be effective as a coalition builder, political speaker, and campaigner. One lesson of the New York primary is that incumbency can be both an asset and a liability. Edward Koch's record and style as mayor made both friends and enemies. As lieutenant governor, Cuomo had no need to become involved in controversy but was able to build political contacts and alliances. Many political observers claimed that the primary demonstrated the importance of traditional organizational techniques (though not the power of old-fashioned organizations) in the face of high-priced and high-powered media campaigns. The primary also demonstrated the importance of the liberal-labor-minorities coalition at least for winning primaries within the Democratic party of New York.

The Michigan Democratic Primary

The retirement of Republican Governor Milliken and the economic problems of Michigan led Democrats to believe (correctly) that they could win the governorship for the first time since 1962. This inspired seven candidates to enter the race, most of whom could be described as serious. The two leading candidates appeared to be U.S. Representative James Blanchard and former state Senator William Fitzgerald. Blanchard took an early lead in the race on the basis of endorsements by the state AFL-CIO and several other unions, notably the United Auto Workers, which was making its first endorsement in a gubernatorial primary since 1970. Blanchard was given credit for his leading role in winning congressional approval for the Chrysler loan guarantee. Fitzgerald, the party's gubernatorial nominee four years earlier, enjoyed high name recognition. Lacking the union support that he enjoyed in the earlier campaign, Fitzgerald ran a campaign that was highly critical of unions, charging that they bore some responsibility for the state's economic plight. Among the other candidates, the two who eventually got at least ten percent of the vote were Zolton Ferency, who was seeking liberal support in his fifth gubernatorial bid, and state Senator David Plawecki, who had strong ties to unions and to the Polish community.

On the eve of the election, the race between Blanchard and Fitzgerald was thought by some observers to be very close, but Blanchard won half of the vote, to 17 percent for Fitzgerald. Blanchard outspent Fitzgerald by almost two-to-one, but his total of almost $1.2 million was relatively modest for a large state, and was less than one-third of that spent in the Democratic primary. On the surface, Blanchard's victory would appear to be a manifestation of labor's influence within the Democratic party and a sign that Democratic voters continued to believe in traditional Democratic solutions to economic problems.

My survey and that conducted by the *Free Press* generally support these assumptions, but they also illustrate the difficulty of generalizing about the attitudes and behavior of voters. I will concentrate on those voting for the four leading candidates: Blanchard, Fitzgerald, Ferency, and Plawecki. The press survey showed that 59 percent of the Blanchard voters and 53 percent of the Plawecki voters came from families with a union member, but Fitzgerald (43 percent) and Ferency (40 percent) were not far behind. About 55 percent of the Blanchard and Plawecki voters in the newspaper poll described themselves as Democrats, with most of the rest being independents. Ferency and Fitzgerald each drew about half their voters from independents and about 40 percent from Democrats; Fitzgerald in particular had been seeking independent support and his voters even included some independents who leaned Republican. (My survey suggests that the proportion of Blanchard voters who supported the Democratic party was even higher.) A majority of those supporting each of the leading candidates described themselves as moderates; of the remaining voters, three-fourths of Ferency voters and two-thirds of Blanchard voters were liberal rather than conservative, while the remaining Plawecki and Fitzgerald voters were evenly split between liberal and conservative. Fitzgerald voters were considerably more critical of President Reagan's performance than were the others.

It is not surprising to find that in Michigan voters for each of the candidates overwhelmingly agreed that the most important issue in the campaign was the state of the economy and the level of unemployment. The supporters of Fitzgerald were the only ones who often described strong unions as the most important issue or problem in the state (in 17 percent of the cases). My survey showed that Democratic voters who were asked to express their likes and dislikes about candidates most often talked about issues; such comments about Blanchard were usually favorable, while Fitzgerald's views on issues were criticized nearly as much as they were supported. In a sample that was disproportionately pro-Blanchard, he also drew many favorable comments about his experience and personal qualities. Very few persons explicitly mentioned the union endorsements.

The importance of the labor vote in the Michigan primary is very clear; half of the voters surveyed came from families containing a union member. James Blanchard's victory in the Democratic primary was obviously a victory for the labor union leadership because they had endorsed and worked for him and because he emphasized issues important to organized labor. Presumably the unions organized effectively to get out the vote for Blanchard. It is clear from the polls that he drew more of his votes from union members and Democrats than most of his opponents. But it would be a mistake to assume that all union members followed the lead of their organizations. Blanchard, who won half of the total vote, won about 56 percent of the voters in the press survey who came from union families. There were some differences in partisanship, liberalism, and views on specific issues between voters for Blanchard, Fitzgerald, and Ferency, but they were not drastic differences. There are many voters who apparently do not perceive the candidates exactly as they are portrayed in the media or do not make choices on the basis of issues that are emphasized in the campaign.

California Republican Primary

The Republican gubernatorial primary in California was one of the closest and least predictable, and one of the most bitter, primaries of the year. As in any close race, it was difficult to tell what factors were most significant in determining the outcome, and whether voters were more influenced by substantive issues or by their assessments of the candidates. It was also difficult to estimate the impact of the many charges and counter-charges in the campaign.

This was essentially a two-man race between Attorney General George Deukmejian and Lieutenant Governor Mike Curb, two very different personalities. Deukmejian is an experienced politician who served for 16 years in the legislature before his election as attorney general in 1978. In the legislature he developed a reputation as a moderate conservative; as attorney general he developed a strong law-and-order reputation; and as a gubernatorial candidate he emphasized his authorship of laws to establish the death penalty and require mandatory sentencing for criminals who use handguns. Deukmejian's dull style as a campaigner was a liability, but his image as a stable, solid leader may have been a significant asset in his campaign against the more flamboyant Mike Curb.

During the years that Deukmejian was toiling in the legislature, the much younger Curb was in the music business, producing records and developing a reputation as "the man who cleaned up rock and roll." Oddly enough, it was Curb's promotion of squeaky clean music and performers that gave him an entry into Republican politics because during the early 1970s his groups were often invited to perform at Republican functions. He developed close ties to the highly conservative "king-makers" closely associated with Ronald Reagan, and they promoted and helped finance his first venture into elective politics – the 1978 campaign for lieutenant governor. Once elected to that office, Mike Curb frequently made the headlines, not always to his benefit. During Jerry Brown's frequent trips out of the state, particularly as a presidential candidate, Curb often sought to use his authority as acting governor to take actions and make appointments that were embarrassing to the governor. The voters' reactions to these tactics are hard to judge. Clearly damaging to Curb was a prolonged investigation in 1978 by Attorney General Deukmejian's office of alleged contacts between Curb's record company and the underworld, though the case was eventually dropped for lack of evidence.

One of the unusual aspects of the Deukmejian-Curb race was the shifting fortunes of the two candidates in the polls over the extensive campaign. Curb took an early lead in the race, raising much more money and gaining more endorsements from many Republican leaders. Late in 1981 the momentum shifted, apparently as a result of Curb's widely reported attacks on members of the press. As the campaign started down the home stretch, Curb launched an aggressive advertising campaign, he regained his lead in the polls, and the media marveled at the skill of his campaign managers in carrying out "one of the best comebacks in California political history." In the closing days of the campaign Deukmejian took the offensive with personal criticisms of Curb, and won a 51-45 percent margin in the primary. Deukmejian won by large margins in major southern counties where Curb was believed to have a lead, including Los Angeles, San Diego, and Orange counties.

Both candidates spent enough to get their messages before the public: $5.5 million for Curb and $4.1 million for Deukmejian. But the amount spent tells us nothing about the impact of the two media campaigns. In a race where political preferences appear to have been so vacillating, it is difficult to sort out the variety of factors that may have influenced voters, particularly with brief surveys taken at the end of the campaign. Mike Curb based his credentials as a conservative heavily on his identification as a Reagan ally and follower. One of the central themes of Curb's campaign was that Deukmejian was a moderate Republican. In some states that might not appear to be an damning indictment, but the California Republican party is haunted by the spirit of Reagan, and it seems to be important for primary candidates to demonstrate that they are sufficiently conservative. Deukmejian's best defense against the charge was his carefully developed image as the law-and-order candidate, an image easily cultivated as attorney general.

Exit interviews published in the press suggest that Curb benefited from his image as a Reagan supporter and Deukmejian benefited from his law-and-order image. Both candidates seem to have met the "conservatism" test required of those who run in the Republican primary, and Deukmejian does not seem to have been hurt significantly by the "moderate" label. My survey indicates, instead, that Deukmejian's stand on issues, particularly those related to law-and-order, were mentioned more often as assets by his supporters than were the issues emphasized by Curb's supporters.

Late in the campaign Curb announced his opposition to the peripheral canal, an issue hotly debated, particularly in the northern part of the state. Deukmejian remained a supporter. The canal was defeated at the polls by almost a two-to-one margin, and the polls suggest that Curb gained considerably more than he lost by supporting it. Had Curb won the primary, there would have been good reason to point to his stand on that issue, one oddly enough outside the mainstream of the debate over who is the most conservative.

It is hard to escape the conclusion the outcome of the primary hinged on voter assessment of personal characteristics of Deukmejian and Curb. Deukmejian was not a charismatic figure, but he was stable and predictable, with a long record of public office. Curb was more colorful and lively, but he was also impulsive, relatively inexperienced, and immature, as evidenced by his outbursts at the press. My survey suggests that, while Deukmejian was rarely criticized on personal grounds, Curb's positive qualities were praised by his supporters less often than they were criticized by other voters.

When Deukmejian launched his counterattack late in the campaign, he disclosed that the 37-year-old Curb had never bothered to register as a voter until he was 29, and thus had failed to vote for Reagan in either of his gubernatorial campaigns. It was a damaging attack because it reminded voters of Curb's inexperience and at the same time undermined Curb's image as a valued and loyal supporter of Reagan. In my survey this point was mentioned by a number of respondents, including some who supported Curb. Published exit polls indicated that this issue was of crucial importance in the last-minute shift of opinion that elected Deukmejian.

Exit polls suggested that Deukmejian would be a much stronger candidate in the fall election than Curb would have been, and he proved capable of winning a very close victory over Democrat Tom Bradley.

TRADITIONAL AND MODERN CAMPAIGN STRATEGIES

One of the most obvious trends in American politics is the growing use of sophisticated campaign techniques, such as television advertising, mass mailings, public opinion surveys, and professional campaign managers. It is a trend that has affected primary as well as general election campaigns to some extent in most states. The traditional campaign strategy for primary candidates, particularly in southern and border states, has been to build alliances with courthouse politicians and other political activists at the county level, and to count on them to deliver the vote. In some states these alliances have had an enduring quality, producing factional alignments that have persisted over a period of years. This strategy has not entirely disappeared, but modern campaign tactics are used more frequently in the South and border states. The 1982 Democratic primary in Tennessee provided a contrast between these two styles, while the winner in the 1983 Kentucky Democratic primary proved that it was possible to combine the two strategies successfully.

Tennessee Democratic Primary

For many years Tennessee Democratic primaries have been characterized by various kinds of factional alignments. Some of these alignments have had ideological bases, as in several earlier primaries involving liberal senators Estes Kefauver and Albert Gore. Often the alignments have had a geographic base. To a considerable extent, however, the factions have been based on personalities and family ties. For many years one of the dominant political figures in Tennessee politics was Frank Clement, elected governor in 1952, 1954, and 1962, and holding the office for ten years. He formed an uneasy alliance with Buford Ellington; between them the two Democrats controlled the governorship from 1953 through 1970.

In recent years, two of Clement's relatives have become active in politics. His son, Robert, had been elected at age 28 to the Public Service Commission, had been often mentioned as a gubernatorial candidate, and in 1982 was running for Congress – winning the primary and narrowly losing the general election. Anna Belle Clement O'Brien is former Governor Clement's sister and had played an active role in his administrations. When she entered the 1982 gubernatorial primary, she was supported by many Democratic leaders and perceived to be a strong candidate. She was a state senator with strong ties to local party leaders across the state. She campaigned in traditional Tennessee style, from courthouse to courthouse. But she was less effective in the urban areas, and she was handicapped in public forums and television appearances by her weakness in articulating the issues.

Her opponent was Knoxville Mayor Randy Tyree, who was closely allied with Knoxville banker Jake Butcher. Butcher had built a banking empire in Tennessee, in association with his brother.

He had run a well-financed race for the gubernatorial nomination in 1974, narrowly losing in a crowded field. Four years later, a second well-financed media campaign brought him the nomination but not the election. In 1982 he raised substantial funds for Tyree, who was able to spend $1 million on his primary campaign, almost three times as much as O'Brien. Tyree and Butcher had worked closely together in promoting the controversial Knoxville World's Fair. Tyree used his resources for an extensive and effective media campaign.

Tyree won the primary by a 50-40 margin over Anna O'Brien, carrying the major metropolitan areas except for Knoxville, where ironically his taxing and annexation policies made him unpopular. The lesson of the primary seemed to be that modern media campaign techniques were more effective than traditional strategies based on alliances among courthouse politicians. The campaign was both less expensive and less bitter than the recent gubernatorial primaries involving Jake Butcher, and O'Brien fully supported Tyree in the fall campaign. The success of the Tyree-Butcher alliance was short-lived, however. Tyree lost the fall election to Republican governor Lamar Alexander in November, and early in 1983 Jake Butcher's banking empire came crashing to the ground.

Kentucky Democratic Primary

For many years the Kentucky Democratic party had one of the strongest factional alignments of any southern or border state. It was not based on geographic or economic interests, but simply on personal loyalties. Candidates for governor formed alliances with local courthouse leaders and, if they were nominated and elected, often sought to pick their successors. Some Democratic voters developed loyalties to these factional leaders, though the extent of voter commitment to factions is impossible to measure. The most important of these leaders for an extended period were A. B. "Happy" Chandler and Earl Clements. Chandler was elected as governor in 1935, later entered the Senate, served as baseball commissioner, and returned to Kentucky to win another term as governor in 1955. Clements was elected governor in 1947 and as senator in 1950. The two men never ran against each other, but direct clashes between Chandler or his candidate and one of Clement's candidates occurred in 1955, 1959, 1963, and 1967. A divisive Democratic primary in 1967 led directly to a Republican gubernatorial victory and marked the end of the factional strife between the two camps. The 1971 primary contest was between Wendell Ford and Bert Combs, both of whom had been allied with Clements.

In Kentucky politics today there are no persistent or pervasive factions, but rather the shifting alliances and allegiances among political leaders and workers. Most recent Democratic governors have tried to influence the choice of their successors, but without notable success. Another significant trend — like that in Tennessee — has been the shift in campaign tactics from building alliances among courthouse politicians and other political activists to using modern media techniques and professional campaign management firms. Ned Breathitt used television effectively to defeat "Happy" Chandler in the 1963 primary, and every candidate since has made some use of the media, but the importance of television has been most obvious in the last two campaigns. In 1979 the Democratic candidates for governor included one candidate supported by Governor Carroll; a woman with a long record of election to lower statewide offices now serving as lieutenant governor; the auditor, who had been highly critical of the Carroll administration; the mayor of Louisville; and a congressman from western Kentucky. John Y. Brown, Jr. dropped into this crowded field at the last moment, invested his own resources in the campaign, and used most of his $1.5 million fund in a television campaign that was skillfully managed and made the most of his talents. He also barnstormed the state in a helicopter. Brown was a highly successful businessman (Kentucky Fried Chicken), the son of a well-known party leader; he had recently gained greater celebrity status by marrying television personality Phyllis George. Brown became the perfect example of the successful amateur in politics when he won the primary by a narrow margin and went on to win the election.

In 1983 three major candidates sought the Democratic nomination. Harvey Sloane had run for governor four years earlier, finishing a close second in the primary. He was a medical doctor, who had been elected mayor of Louisville in 1973, and after a four-year interval won another term in 1981. He had attracted primarily liberal and urban support in his first gubernatorial race; in 1983 he had more support from businessmen and from party leaders (including many aligned once with Combs). A second candidate was the lieutenant governor, Martha Layne Collins. She was a schoolteacher who had become an active and skillful party worker, developed ties to Wendell Ford, and won a statewide office, clerk of the Court of Appeals, in 1975. In 1979 she won a surprising victory in a crowded race for lieutenant governor, and had followed the Kentucky tradition of trying to use that office to gain visibility for a gubernatorial race. The third candidate, generally perceived to be trailing during the campaign, was Brady Stumbo, a doctor from the eastern Kentucky mountains, who had served as Commissioner of Human Services during most of the Brown administration and who succeeded in drawing labor support away from Sloane. Although Governor Brown had appeared willing to stay out of the race, barely a week before the primary he launched an intensive television and personal campaign for Grady Stumbo.

The winner of the primary, by less than 5,000 votes over Sloane, was Martha Layne Collins, who won the general election. Brown had failed in his effort to pick a successor, although Stumbo ran better than had been expected. The Collins strategy was a skillful combination of old and new politics. During her years as a campaign organizer and officeholder she had developed a strong network of political contacts across the state. During her campaign she repeatedly cited her record of having visited all 120 counties as lieutenant governor. She succeeded in raising a campaign fund of over $2.6 million (about 45 percent of that raised by all candidates) and used it skillfully to develop an effective television advertising campaign. Although she was less effective in public debates, she appeared to be forceful and articulate in televised commercials. The candidates did not appear to differ sharply on issues; each claimed that his or her experience was most pertinent to the governorship. In the last analysis, the voters seemed to be making judgments about the candidates as individuals, without much regard to specific accomplishments or issues.

AMATEUR CANDIDATES IN PRIMARIES

One trend in American politics that has been noted by commentators, usually with dismay, is the election to high office of amateur candidates, that is, persons with no political base or record of office holding. These amateurs have won because of their ability to buy skillful campaign managers and ample television time to gain name recognition and develop a favorable image. The well-financed amateur has greater success against better-known politicians in primaries than in general elections because partisan loyalties are not involved.

One recent example of an amateur winning his first political campaign is John Y. Brown, Jr. in the 1979 Kentucky Democratic primary. Another example is Bill Clements, a Texas millionaire in the oil-drilling business, who won the 1978 Republican gubernatorial primary in his first bid for political office by outspending the state party chairman by almost twenty-to-one.

Obviously not every well-funded amateur wins the first gubernatorial primary he enters. One reason is that those professionals with strong credentials for the gubernatorial nomination are usually able to raise adequate funds for television advertising and other campaign costs. An amateur's expensive media campaign may be a failure if he turns out to be inarticulate or inept. An example is John Lakian, whose victory in the Massachusetts Republican endorsing convention was described in Chapter 4. His primary campaign was undermined by charges in the press that there were major discrepancies between his campaign literature and public statements about his accomplishments and his actual biographical record. If issues play an important role in a primary election, the amateur may have more flexibility in choosing positions but usually lacks an established record to demonstrate credibility on the issue.

The two examples of amateurs in the 1982 primaries to be described here were both discussed in Chapters 4 and 5 because each was running in a state with an endorsing convention. Despite his lack of political experience, Lew Lehrman won the New York Republican party endorsement and went on to win a lopsided victory in the primary election. Wheelock Whitney defeated the party endorsee in winning the Minnesota Republican primary. Both of these amateurs had tremendous financial advantages. Lew Lehrman spent roughly $7 million in the primary, which was about $15 per vote and about twenty times what his opponent was able to spend. Wheelock Whitney spent only a little more than $900,000 ($5 per vote), but still outspent his opponent by four-to-one.

New York Republican Primary

In early April 1982, *New York* magazine ran a lengthy profile with the title, "Who Is This Guy Lew Lehrman?" It was a question that many residents of New York must have been asking during that spring. Lehrman is a millionaire businessman who helped to build a chain of nearly 1,000 discount drug stores and who did not take up full-time residence in New York state until 1977. He is a leading exponent of supply-side economics, articulate, intelligent, and hardworking; and he has served on several state Republican committees. But he was totally unknown to the average voter until he launched a television campaign early in 1982. Night after night his ads appeared on television. *The New Yorker* ran a cartoon showing a parrot perched beside a television set saying. "I'm Lew Lehrman, I'm Lew Lehrman . . ." (It must have puzzled readers outside the state.)

By the time the endorsing session of the state Republican committee met in mid-June, Lehrman had already spent $2.9 million, mostly on the media. Members assembling in New York City for the meeting were greeted by a poll in the New York *Post* showing that Lehrman led his three opponents by a margin of 43-6-5-5, with the rest undecided. Lehrman was endorsed by the convention, and spent another $4 million during the summer on the primary campaign, continuing to flood the television screens with ads. In the September primary he defeated Paul Curran, his only opponent, by a margin of four-to-one. In the November election, he narrowly lost to Mario Cuomo.

Lew Lehrman provides the best example in 1982, and one of the best examples in recent years, of the power of money in primary elections. Seven million dollars can buy a great deal of name recognition, even in the expensive media markets of New York. As described in earlier chapters, Lehrman won the party committee's endorsement largely because of his financial resources and his willingness and ability to use them skillfully. It is difficult to believe that Lehrman could have captured either the party's endorsement or the attention of the voters if he had been only an articulate, hardworking conservative without his own bankroll.

At the same time, it is important to recognize that several other ingredients went into Lehrman's success. His television commercials made an impact not only because they were numerous but also because of Lehrman's skill in using the media. Throughout the campaign he chose issues that would appeal to the primary electorate, particularly taxes and crime, and he was an articulate spokesman for his views. Moreover, he was not campaigning against political giants. There was no Rockefeller or Javits in the race. Potentially his strongest opponent, State Comptroller Edward Regan, dropped out of the race early. The three persons whom Lehrman defeated at the state committee meeting were experienced political leaders, but were not charismatic figures with widespread public support. In short, the conclusion must be that a large bankroll was a necessary but not a sufficient condition for Lehrman's success in the primary election.

Minnesota Republican Primary

It seems unlikely that anyone would have chosen Wheelock Whitney as the political amateur most likely to succeed in the 1982 primaries. He had built a successful career as an investment banker, and then in 1972 at age 45 had abandoned that career to pursue his interests in teaching, social activism, philanthropy, the promotion of health and chemical dependency treatment, and raising race horses. He had a record of Republican activity highlighted by nomination as the party's candidate for the Senate in 1964 against Eugene McCarthy. In the late 1960s he served a term as nonpartisan mayor of a small city. But in recent years his involvement in party politics had been minimal. When he decided to run for governor in 1982, he made no effort to get the party convention's endorsement because he lacked many contacts in the party and because he perceived that his views on issues – particularly abortion – would be too liberal for the tastes of convention delegates.

Before the convention met in June Whitney had already spent more than $100,000 of his own funds in television commercials designed particularly to show that as an experienced businessman he could manage the state's escalating financial problems. After the convention, Whitney stepped up the television advertising and began his active campaign across the state emphasizing his management skills and proposals for economic development. As his campaign gained momentum he seemed to have little difficulty in raising funds from business interests to supplement his own resources;

he spent over $900,000 in the campaign ($700,000 of his own funds), much of it on television. Whitney not only won the primary, but defeated the party endorsee, Lieutenant Governor Lou Wangberg, by a margin of 60 to 34 percent (with Harold Stassen finishing third).

To understand Whitney's victory, one must know something about his opponent. Lou Wangberg served as lieutenant governor during the administration of Governor Albert Quie. When Quie decided not to seek a second term, Wangberg was quickly endorsed by the governor and most of the Republican congressional delegation, but he still had to struggle to win the party convention's endorsement after seven ballots. A survey conducted by the Minnesota Poll in late March and early April (before the convention) showed that only half of the respondents were aware of Wangberg, only 20 percent had some impression of him, and only 10 percent had a favorable impression. Wheelock Whitney did almost as well. After the convention, Wangberg had great difficulty getting his campaign organized and raising funds. Seven weeks before the primary Wangberg had raised only $165,000, had yet to start an advertising campaign, had held few press conferences, and showed few signs of gaining momentum. Wangberg's campaign eventually spent $213,000, which averages out to about $2 a vote – one of the lowest amounts spent by any serious gubernatorial candidate in the country in a competitive race.

It is tempting to explain the outcome of the primary entirely in terms of finances, television advertising, and the use of the media. It is much more difficult to assess the importance of ideology. Wangberg was a very conservative candidate endorsed by very conservative delegates to the state convention. Although Whitney said little about his more liberal positions on social issues, his image of a moderate may have helped him to attract voters in the primary. While Whitney might have been vulnerable to attack on issues such as abortion, Wangberg never succeeded in putting him on the defensive. It does seem clear that Wangberg's record of association with the Quie administration was as much of a liability as an asset because of the governor's ineptitude in dealing with the economic crisis. This was an election in which the normal advantages enjoyed by the incumbent and the professional were missing, which made the task of the well-financed amateur much less difficult.

9

Primary Election
Outcomes in 1982

The case studies of primary elections in the preceding chapter illustrate the diversity of candidates and campaigns and demonstrate how many different things may affect the outcome of primary elections. The purpose of this chapter is to provide a more systematic analysis of primary outcomes.

PATTERNS OF COMPETITION

A starting point is to examine variations in the level of competition in primaries held in 1982. The first seven columns in Table 9.1 measure the frequency and closeness of contested primaries by region, incumbency, and party in 1982. There were contested primaries in 87 percent of races with no incumbent running in the party primary. When an incumbent was running, there were contests in only 60 percent of the primaries, and most of these were won easily by the incumbent. (Only one incumbent, King of Massachusetts, lost a primary.) In northern states the Democrats were a little more likely than the Republicans to have contested primaries and close primaries. The contrast is most obvious in races with no incumbent running. There were no absolute differences between North and South in the levels of competition. However, the southern Republican parties had no close primaries, while most southern Democratic primaries without an incumbent were closely contested.

Table 9.1
Levels of Primary Competition as Measured by Percent of Contests and Margin of Winner

	1982 Primaries							1951-64 Primaries			1965-82 Primaries		
	Total (N)	Contests %	Contests (N)	\[Number of Contested Primaries Won by Percentages of:\] 80+	60-79	50-69	Under 50	Total (N)	% Contests	Average Win %	Total (N)	% Contests	Average Win %
Total	72	78	56	14	14	16	12	441	63	60	500	76	59
North	58	78	45	9	13	15	8	350	64	62	394	75	60
Incumb.	20	60	12	5	4	3	0	109	45	69	136	59	67
No Inc.	38	87	33	4	9	12	8	241	73	59	258	84	57
Dem.	29	79	23	4	6	9	4	175	65	61	197	77	57
Rep.	29	76	22	5	7	6	4	175	64	62	197	74	62
Dem. Inc.	13	62	8	3	3	2	0	51	43	71	74	61	68
D. No Inc.	16	94	15	1	3	7	4	124	73	58	123	86	53
Rep. Inc.	7	57	4	2	1	1	0	58	47	67	62	56	66
R. No Inc.	22	82	18	3	6	5	4	117	73	61	135	82	60

South	14	79	11	5	1	1	4	91	61	51	106	78	56
Incumb.	5	60	3	3	0	0	0	15	100	58	21	86	71
No Inc.	9	89	8	2	1	1	4	76	53	49	85	76	52
Dem.	7	86	6	1	0	1	4	47	100	48	55	89	46
Rep.	7	71	5	4	1	0	0	44	18	67	51	67	70
Dem. Inc.	2	50	1	1	0	0	0	15	100	58	15	87	67
D. No Inc.	5	100	5	0	0	1	4	32	100	44	40	90	39
Rep. Inc.	3	67	2	2	0	0	0	0	–	–	6	83	83
R. No Inc.	4	75	3	2	1	0	0	44	18	67	45	64	68

Source: Compiled by the author.

255

The last six columns of Table 9.1 summarize similar data for two time periods: 1951-64 and 1965-82. In the North in both periods there were substantially more contested primaries and closer contests when there was no incumbent running; there were few differences in levels of competition between parties. A comparison of the two time periods in northern states shows that contested primaries have become more frequent for both races with and without incumbents and for races in both parties. There has been a very slight decline in winning margins.

In the South the pattern of competition is quite different in the two parties. The Democrats continue to have contests in most races, and these are much closer when there is no incumbent running. Races with incumbents have become a little more one-sided, and those without them a little closer. There has been a dramatic increase in the proportion of contested southern Republican primaries, but the average winning margin in such races remains high (about two-thirds of the vote), in sharp contrast to Democratic races without incumbents. We might expect to find that the presence of an incumbent would discourage primary competition not only in the incumbent's party but in the other party. The best place to test that is in northern states where there is a larger number of cases in both parties both with and without incumbents. (Comparisons are made within one party in races where it has no incumbent running; the two time periods are combined to increase the number of cases.) The data (not shown in the table) indicate that the Democratic party has slightly closer primary races when there is no Republican incumbent running. The Republican party has considerably more contested primaries (83 compared to 73 percent) and slightly closer races when there is no Democratic incumbent running.

Generally the pattern of competition existing in 1982 was typical of that found during the 1965-82 period, although in the southern states the number of cases in a single election was too small to expect close comparisons. Half of the contested primaries were won by less than 60 percent, and most of these were in races without incumbents.

EXPLAINING ELECTORAL OUTCOMES

The outcome of primary elections is obviously affected by many political forces and circumstances, some of which are idiosyncratic, but two variables that we would expect to have the broadest impact are the experience of candidates and the amount of campaign funds they spend. The ease with which gubernatorial incumbents usually win renomination leads us to expect that the previous office-holding experience of candidates will be important in explaining the results of primaries. The large variations in campaign spending suggest that this variable should also be important.

In 1982 the candidates in the 56 contested gubernatorial primaries spent a total of about $92 million.* In absolute terms, the most expensive races were in the Republican primary in California ($9.5 million), the Democratic primary in Georgia ($9.1 million), and the New York Republican primary (almost $7.5 million). Because of variations in state population it may be more meaningful to measure campaign costs in relation to votes cast in the primary. By that standard, the most expensive campaigns were in Alaska ($33 and $16 per vote for the Democratic and Republican primaries) and in Republican primaries in Arkansas ($26 per vote) and Georgia ($23 per vote). In several primaries where there was serious competition the total cost of primaries was less than $1 per vote, including Democratic primaries in Oregon, South Dakota, and Wisconsin.

Campaign spending data are available for 50 of the 56 contested primaries (and in most of the other 6 the races were lopsided). In 37 of these 50 races the winning candidate was the one who spent the most money, and in 30 of these 37 cases the winner's proportion of total spending was greater than his proportion of the vote. All of the incumbents who won in the primary also were the top spenders in their races (in states where data are available). One incumbent who was defeated in a primary, Democrat Edward King of Massachusetts, was the leading spender in that race.

In most races won by large margins the winner spent an even larger percentage of the funds, more than appeared necessary to win comfortably. In several southern Republican primaries the winning

---

*Information on campaign spending in the 1982 primaries was obtained from official sources wherever possible and in a few cases was obtained from the press. I am indebted to political scientists who tracked down the information for me in several states. Most states require primary candidates to file a financial statement just before a primary and again shortly after it. In most cases the latter statement is used here, except where the post-primary report came so late that it appeared to include significant amounts of spending by the winners for the general election. Because reporting requirements differ among the states, the totals reported for the various states may not be strictly comparable.

candidates outspent their opponents by huge margins in lopsided races, presumably in order to lay the groundwork for general election campaigns. The New York Republican primary is one example of a race in which spending had a major impact on the outcome. Lew Lehrman spent about $7 million in his campaign, roughly twenty times as much as his opponent, whom he beat overwhelmingly.

There are some interesting examples of races in which the top spender did not win. Governor King of Massachusetts outspent Michael Dukakis by about $3.2 to $2.4 million, but lost, while in the Republican primary John Lakian lost despite spending about twice as much as his two opponents combined. Mayor Koch of New York outspent Lieutenant Governor Cuomo by a margin of $3.6 to $1.6 million, but lost in a close race. In the California Republican race, Attorney General George Deukmejian defeated Lieutenant Governor Mike Curb despite being outspent by a margin of $5.5 to $4.1 million.

The two primaries in Minnesota illustrate the difficulty of generalizing about the impact of campaign spending on outcomes. In each primary one candidate outspent the other by a four to one margin, but in only one case did the top spender win. In the Republican primary Wheelock Whitney spent over $900,000 in a skillful media campaign and easily defeated the party endorsee, Lou Wangberg, who was seriously handicapped by the inability to raise funds. But in the DFL primary former Governor Rudy Perpich spent only 48 cents per vote (less than any other winning candidate in the country with serious opposition) and defeated the incumbent attorney general.

In order to make sense out of these apparently contradictory findings, we need to understand the relationship between campaign funds and the characteristics of candidates. The candidate who starts the campaign without any previous office-holding or political experience needs the most funding in order to gain visibility and develop a public image. Candidates who are incumbents or have held other offices are already well known and have less need for large-scale funding. In most cases those candidates who are most experienced and have the least need for funds are also most able to raise funds because they are perceived as having the best chance to be elected.

Consequently candidates who are well known and well financed almost always beat those who are little known and poorly financed. If both candidates are well known and have substantial funding, differences in spending may not be crucial, as shown by the King-Dukakis, Curb-Deukmejian, and Koch-Cuomo races. A very well-known candidate, such as Rudy Perpich, may be able to overcome a large gap in spending. A very well-financed amateur, such as Lehrman in New York or Whitney in Minnesota, may be able to defeat more experienced politicians, particularly if the latter have other political liabilities.

The fact that the best-known candidates are usually the best financed makes it difficult to weigh the relative importance of these two variables. The best analytical tool for accomplishing this is multiple regression. I have conducted a multiple regression analysis for the 50 contested primaries in 1982 for which spending data are available. The dependent variable is the percentage of the vote won by each candidate. (In southern states with runoff elections, the first primary and not the runoff is used.) The independent variables are measures of candidate experience and campaign funding.

The simplest way to measure experience is a dichotomous variable indicating whether or not the candidate is the incumbent. While this proves to have some effect on the percentage of the vote received, a broader measure of experience has a greater effect. Candidates were coded for experience on a scale from 4 to 0, as follows:

4 includes incumbent governors;
3 includes former governors;
2 includes elected state officeholders, congressmen, the House speaker and Senate president, and mayors of major cities (such as Los Angeles or New York);
1 includes persons who formerly held the offices listed in (2), current state legislators or mayors of smaller cities, and persons who have run before for governor or U.S. senator;
0 includes all other candidates.

Obviously these offices might be weighted differently, and the results might be different; this scale is an estimation of the relative visibility of various levels of office holding and previous campaigns.

We would expect each candidate's share of votes in the primary election to be affected by the amount of money spent by the candidate and also the amount spent by all others in the race. The first step in measuring the effects of campaign spending is to calculate for each candidate his or her spending and that of all opponents combined. There are large variations among the states in the size of the primary electorate. In 1982 the total primary vote cast ranged from almost 2.8 million in the California Democratic primary to 13,000 in the Arkansas Republican primary. Obviously it is more expensive to reach voters in states with a large voting population. Therefore the simple correlation between spending and the share of the vote should not be very high (it is .38). It is possible to control for the size of the electorate by dividing the amount spent by each candidate (and by opponents) by the total vote cast in the party primary. There is reason to believe that it costs more per vote to campaign in sparsely populated states. In order to take this into account, and moderate the effect of the control for size of the electorate, I divided candidate spending by the square root of the total primary vote. This measure of spending was used in the regression equation because it proved to have more explanatory effect than the other measures of spending.

Table 9.2 shows the result of a regression analysis in which each candidate's percentage of the vote was regressed on three measures: the measure of candidate spending, the measure of spending by all opponents, and the measure of the candidate's experience. The multiple R is .78, and these three variables explain 61 percent of

Table 9.2
Regression of Gubernatorial Candidates' Percentage of Primary Vote in 1982 on Spending by Candidate and Opponents and on Experience

Independent Variables	
Spending by candidate (divided by square root of total vote)	.350(.002)*
Spending by all opponents (divided by square root of total vote)	−.340(.001)*
Experience of candidate	.421(.081)*
	(R = .61)

Note: Entries are beta weights; parenthesized entries are unstandardized regression coefficients.

*Significant at .001 level.

Source: Compiled by the author.

the variance in the vote share. If only spending by the candidate and by opponents is included in the equation, the multiple R is .68. The beta weights indicate that the candidate's experience is slightly more important than either candidate or opponent spending in explaining the outcome. The simple correlation between experience and candidate spending is only .32.*

We can conclude from this analysis that both the experience of candidates and the level of campaign spending (by them and by their opponents) affect the outcome of primaries. Each of these variables has a strong, statistically significant effect on outcomes when the others are controlled.

MEASURES OF VOTING BEHAVIOR

The multiple regression analysis indicates that more than 60 percent of the election result can be explained by the political experience of the candidates and the amount they spend on campaigns. That leaves almost 40 percent to be explained by such variables as the candidates' campaign techniques and skills, their mobilization of interest group support, their use of issues, and a variety of idiosyncratic factors. It is not feasible to quantify these variables and add them to the regression equation, but it is possible to provide a few more data and to make some generalizations about the conditions under which particular variables become important. Most of the data come from my survey of primary voters in three states; the brevity of these interviews and the modest numbers of voters in the sample suggest that we must be cautious in interpreting the results.

The state surveys in California, Massachusetts, and Michigan provide evidence about voter contact with the major gubernatorial candidates. This is a measure of the effectiveness of campaigns and of the advantages enjoyed by incumbents and other officeholders. Voters were asked the following about each of the major candidates:

---

*It is possible that the impact of a candidate's spending on his electoral success declines at higher rates of spending — that the relationship is curvilinear as some other research has suggested (Patterson 1982). An examination of scattergrams, however, fails to show any clear evidence of a curvilinear relationship in this case.

- Have you ever met him personally?
- Have you ever attended a meeting where he spoke?
- Have you received mail from him?
- Have you read about him in the newspaper?
- Have you seen him on TV or heard him on the radio?

The results are summarized in Table 9.3, where the data for individual candidates are clustered. For each party primary the table shows the various kinds of contact reported by those voting for a candidate and by other voters. (In the Michigan Republican primary only data on contact with supporters are available.) For example, in the Massachusetts Democratic primary, 28 percent of those voting for either Dukakis or King said they had met their candidate, while 18 percent of the voters said they had met the candidate they had not voted for.

Several findings stand out in the table. Voters report relatively low levels of first-hand contact, but it is highest in the Massachusetts Democratic primary that involved two governors. The sharpest contrasts between supporters and opponents occur in personal contacts (meeting a candidate or attending a meeting where he spoke). This suggests that candidates are more likely to meet or speak to persons supporting them; it may also mean that such first-hand contact is most effective in winning supporters. In most states there are also substantial differences between supporters and opponents in receiving mail from candidates. In most of the races the major candidates were well known through the media, and similar proportions of supporters and opponents had read about them or heard or seen them. In the California and Michigan Democratic races voters had less media contact with candidates they opposed because most respondents had voted for the leading candidate and had heard little about some less well-known candidates.

Similar questions were asked of voters in the 1978 general elections for the U.S. Senate and House. Voters in the 1978 elections had about as much personal and indirect contact with senatorial candidates as the 1982 voters had with gubernatorial candidates. They had as much personal contact but less media contact with incumbent representatives, and much less contact of any kind with challengers in House races than voters had with gubernatorial candidates. In other words, both gubernatorial primaries and senatorial elections frequently attract candidates (incumbents and

Table 9.3
Frequency of Voters' Contact with Candidates They Support and with Other Major Candidates
(in percentages)

Type of Contact	California				Massachusetts				Michigan			Total	
	Dem.		Rep.		Dem.		Rep.		Dem.		Rep.		
	Sup.	Oth.	Sup.	Oth.	Sup.	Oth.	Sup.	Oth.	Sup.	Oth.	Sup.	Sup.	Oth.
Met	18	7	9	6	28	18	16	3	10	4	19	19	19
Attended meeting	22	7	15	13	28	19	16	2	11	4	19	21	11
Received mail	38	24	75	65	58	48	43	27	63	42	47	56	43
Read about	91	63	92	89	96	94	86	78	85	65	94	92	80
Radio or TV	91	64	88	86	97	96	92	78	90	69	95	93	81
(N)	171	183	150	150	326	326	51	102	131	205	121	950	966

Source: Compiled by the author.

others) who are able to get the attention of the voting public, in contrast to challengers in House races. In statewide races, however, the contact with voters is largely indirect, through the media and the mail.

Voting behavior is normally explained in terms of party identification, candidates, and issues. Obviously party identification can play no role in choosing candidates within a primary, and therefore we would expect voters to make their decisions largely on the basis of their familiarity with and impression of the candidates and their perceptions of the positions taken by candidates on those issues that they believe are salient. Descriptions of a campaign in the media can tell us what the candidates are saying about themselves and each other and what issues they are emphasizing, but surveys of voters are needed to find out what impact candidate images and issues have on the voter. Very few academic surveys have been made of voters in primaries, and most of these have concerned the very special case of presidential primaries.

The voting surveys that I conducted in three states were too brief to probe voter motivations for their vote in any detail, and did not include any questions about the opinions of voters on issues. Two sets of questions, however, shed some light on voters' attitudes toward the candidates and issues. Each person who voted in a party primary was asked, with regard to his or her candidate and other major gubernatorial candidates: "Was there anything in particular that you liked about _____? Was there anything in particular that you disliked about _____?" Respondents had a chance to give more than one answer, and the answers were coded into broad categories. The voters were then asked: "In the primary campaign for governor, what was the most important single issue? How important was this issue to you? Did you tend to prefer one of the candidates because of this issue; which one?"

Table 9.4 summarizes the answers to the question about likes and dislikes. The answers for all candidates in a race are combined except in those cases where the responses for individual candidates were distinctly different. The answers in the first three columns are the percentages of persons voting for each candidate who mentioned one or more things they liked falling into that category. The last three columns show the percentages of all those not voting for a specific candidate who expressed a dislike for that candidate in one of these categories.

Table 9.4
Proportion of Voters Stressing Various Reasons for Liking or Disliking Candidates
(in percentages)

Candidate	Likes Expressed by Those Voting for Candidate				Dislikes Expressed by Those Voting Against Candidate			
	Experience or Record	Personal Char.	Issues	(N)	Experience or Record	Personal Char.	Issues	(N)
California								
Bradley	62	43	17	(143)	0	15	6	(34)
Garamendi	21	32	39	(28)	0	5	1	(149)
Curb	34	39	33	(67)	0	47	1	(83)
Deukmejian	27	42	46	(83)	0	3	9	(67)
Massachusetts								
Dukakis	42	51	35	(216)	30	31	39	(110)
King	46	14	44	(110)	34	26	19	(216)
Republicans	25	59	12	(51)	11	25	0	(102)
Michigan								
Democrats	21	29	61	(168)	2	4	9	(336)
Republicans	28	29	60	(123)	*	*	*	

Note: The N for those expressing likes includes all those voting for a candidate. The N for those expressing dislikes includes all those voting for other candidates; in the Michigan Democratic race, with more than two major candidates the N is higher because voters may express dislikes of more than one candidate not voted for.

*Missing data.

Source: Compiled by the author.

The table distinguishes between two types of references to candidates: those referring to his experience or his record in office (or occasionally his lack of experience) and those that refer to other personal qualities. All references to issues, either in general or specific terms, are listed under issues. The walls separating these categories are not very high. If a candidate is praised for having lowered taxes in a previous term, it is classified as part of his record, while a favorable reference to a promise to cut taxes is listed as an issue reference.

The first, and perhaps most important, conclusion to be drawn from the table is that we cannot generalize about voting behavior in primaries. Each of the six primaries is different, and if we conducted surveys in three more states, we might find other patterns. The Massachusetts Democratic race, a classic confrontation between a governor and an ex-governor, produced large numbers of both positive and negative references to both candidates in all three categories. Almost half of the supporters mentioned their records positively and almost one-third of their opponents criticized their records. This is a reminder that an incumbency or recent incumbency may be both an asset and a liability. The record in office was a major asset to Mayor Bradley in his noncontroversial race in California and was an asset to the Republican candidates in that state. In most races from one-third to one-half of the supporters made favorable comments about their candidate's personal qualities; less frequently these were attacked by other voters. It is obvious that personal criticisms were a major handicap to Mike Curb in California and hurt both Democratic candidates in Massachusetts. Most of the personal criticisms in the Massachusetts Republican race were focused on Lakian, who was accused by the press of misrepresenting his background.

Another significant finding reported in Table 9.4 is the variation in the importance of issues. They were mentioned more frequently in Michigan than in other states, and more frequently than anything else in Michigan. This was partly because of the serious economic problems facing the state and partly because of substantial differences between candidates in both party primaries there. Issues were important in the Massachusetts Democratic race, where there were sharp differences between the candidates, and where both were often attacked on issues. Moreover, in that race many of the references to the records of the two candidates had an issue orientation. It is less obvious why issues should have been important in the

California Republican race, where there was little difference between the candidates, but both candidates were trying to prove how strongly conservative they were. Issues had little to do with Mayor Bradley's low-keyed race or the Massachusetts Republican contest. In general it is true that candidates were seldom criticized on issues unless they were recent incumbents.

Voters in the three states were asked to name the most important issue of the campaign and asked how important it was. In Michigan 91 percent of Republicans and 85 percent of Democrats named an issue and described it as important; the comparable figure was 77 percent in the Massachusetts Democratic primary and about 70 percent in the other three primaries. Michigan Democrats overwhelmingly named the problem of the economy and jobs; Michigan Republicans mentioned this and the need to cut taxes and manage the state budget. Massachusetts Democrats named a variety of problems.

When asked if they would choose a candidate on the basis of the issue that they considered most important, nearly two-thirds of all voters answered positively in both parties in Michigan and in the Massachusetts Democratic party; in the other parties the percentage of positive answers ranged from 35 to 40 percent of all voters. These figures reinforce our conclusions about the importance of issues in Michigan and in the Massachusetts Democratic primary. It appears that in the California primary, where there were few differences between the candidates, issues were less important a criterion for voter choice even though supporters of candidates often mentioned their issue positions favorably.

When voters were asked why they liked or disliked candidates, almost all of them referred to the personal characteristics of candidates, their record or experience, or issues. Very few of them mentioned the endorsement of groups. The only exception was in Michigan, where labor unions had endorsed Blachard in the Democratic primary and where one of his opponents had blamed the unions for many of the state's economic problems. In that race 6 percent of the voters mentioned Blanchard's labor support as a reason for endorsing him. The influence of interest groups is undoubtedly greater than can be measured by a question on candidate likes and dislikes, but it may be indirect and difficult to measure. In an earlier chapter I noted that no voters mentioned party endorsement of candidates as reasons for their vote, either in Massachusetts or in a separate poll in New Mexico.

CONCLUSIONS

Because gubernatorial primaries differ in so many respects, we must be cautious about drawing conclusions from aggregate data and from surveys in only a few states in one year. In recent years the proportion of contested elections has increased slightly, to about three-fourths; the increase has occurred in both parties in northern states, and most notably in southern Republican parties. Nevertheless, many contested primaries are one-sided; the average margin for the winning candidate in recent years has been about 60 percent. Incumbents are unlikely to be seriously challenged, and when they have opposition the winning margin averages two-thirds of the vote. It is unusual for an incumbent to be beaten in a primary. Data from the 1982 primary show that incumbents are usually able to spend more in their campaigns than other candidates do. They obviously start the campaign being better known than most of their opponents. Both the fact of incumbency and the higher levels of spending contribute to the outcome. It should not be forgotten, however, that incumbency can be a liability, if the incumbent has had to raise taxes or deal with economic crises, or if his administration has been hit with scandals. This can hurt not only the incumbent governor (as in the Massachusetts Democratic primary) but others in the administration, as demonstrated by the Michigan and Minnesota Republican primaries.

Usually, even if there are no incumbents in the race, there will be some candidates who have run for governor (or senator) before and/or who have served in other statewide office, or served in Congress, or held other visible public offices. Candidates with such experience are likely to defeat less well-known candidates. Experience, along with campaign spending, is of major importance in explaining outcomes. A well-known and well-financed candidate will almost always defeat those who are less well known and who have limited financing. Data from state surveys in 1982 indicate that, when experienced candidates and/or well-financed candidates are running, a very high proportion of the voters will read about them and see or hear them on television or radio.

When the experienced candidate meets the amateur who had more funding, the outcome is likely to be in doubt. The 1982 Minnesota primaries offered contradictory answers to the question of whether high spending is enough to overcome the advantages of name recognition and experience in office. In races with closely matched candidates, issues may assume greater importance.

My surveys of six primaries in 1982 show how much variation there is in the specific events and issues that may affect the outcome. When voters are asked what they like about candidates or why they voted as they did, the answers given most consistently from one race to another describe the personal characteristics of candidates. (This was also the case in both primaries in New Mexico in 1982.)* Some of these answers are very general: "He's a good man; the best qualified." Some are a little more specific: "He is honest." Candidates who are not very well known to the voters, but come under attack during the campaign, may be more vulnerable to personal criticism, as in the case of Curb in California and Lakian in Massachusetts.

When candidates are well known their record in office is likely to be mentioned frequently by voters. As mentioned earlier, such a record may be an asset or a liability, or both, depending on the perceptions of voters. The voter may judge a candidate's record in terms of competence or honesty, but often the judgment has issue connotations.

The difficulties of generalizing from a few cases are most obvious when we try to assess the importance of issues. They are very important in the Michigan primaries, and important in the Massachusetts primary; they were much less often mentioned by voters in the California Democratic primary or the two New Mexico primaries. We would expect that levels of taxation and government services would be an underlying issue in most of the 1982 races — but in some states such issues seemed to be of limited importance to the voters. There is no certainty that the issues emphasized by candidates will appear salient to the voters. In the California primary, for example, there is little evidence that most voters were interested in the question of which Republican candidate was more conservative.

In some recent elections social issues, such as abortion, the equal rights amendment, gun control, and the death penalty, have assumed great importance in statewide gubernatorial or senatorial campaigns. These do not appear to have been major issues in the 1982 campaigns

---

*The data on New Mexico came from the following source: F. Chris Garcia, Zia Research Associates, Survey Conducted for KOAT-TV, Albuquerque, New Mexico.

examined in these two chapters. They were discussed in the press in both Minnesota primaries (and attracted much attention at both party conventions). In the absence of survey data, it is difficult to estimate their salience to the voter.

More comprehensive conclusions about the voter motivations and the reasons for the outcome of gubernatorial primaries must await more surveys of voters in such primaries. We need to know more about how voters evaluate incumbent governors and also more about how organized groups influence voters in primary elections. Generally our efforts to understand how voters make decisions in primary elections will be enhanced by combining survey data with analyses of the media, group activities, and other contextual data from individual states.

Part V
Conclusions

10

Consequences for the Political Systems

The political systems of the fifty American states are characterized by diversity, and this diversity is manifest in the political parties and in the operation of state primaries. We should be cautious in generalizing about the nominating process because of that diversity and because much of our evidence is drawn from primary elections in a single year, with particular emphasis on a few states. The purpose of this chapter is not only to summarize what has been learned about state parties and primaries but also to suggest some implications of these conclusions for the future of state political systems.

THE ROLE OF PARTIES IN NOMINATIONS

Political party organizations have the most direct impact on nominations in those states where the party makes endorsements either informally or legally. The record of the past 20 years or so demonstrates that endorsements have a major impact on the nominating process. When endorsements are made, there are fewer contested gubernatorial nominations and, if there is a contest, the endorsee wins about three-fourths of the time. There are several explanations for the effectiveness of endorsements. In some states, particularly where the law gives the endorsee easier access to the ballot, nonendorsed candidates may be discouraged from running. The endorsee may find it easier to mobilize volunteer workers and financial contributors. There is no evidence to indicate that endorsements have a direct impact on the voters.

A closer examination of primaries in 1982 shows that a wide variety of factors affects the operation of the endorsement process and its success. Endorsements are most effective in state parties where norms or traditions support the principle. Connecticut is the best example of a state where the endorsing system appears to have broad support among leaders and activists in both parties and where nonendorsed candidates are reluctant to challenge the system. Massachusetts is a good example of a state where in the past the norms of the Republican party virtually eliminated challenges to the endorsee, while the Democratic endorsements carried very little weight.

In those states where the endorsement process has a long history and has broad normative support within the parties it appears to be effective. Despite this record of success, in a number of states the partisan norms that support the endorsement process appear to be fragile. Evidence of this fragility can be found in the Republican party in Massachusetts and in both parties in Minnesota, where endorsees in recent elections have been defeated by other candidates, some of whom did not even seek party endorsement. There is evidence from the responses of delegates to the 1982 conventions to questions about endorsements that in most state parties there is not a broad consensus in support of endorsements. Rather there are divisions of opinion and some ambivalence on the part of individual delegates about the conditions under which endorsements should be used and its advantages and disadvantages.

Further evidence that endorsements rest on shaky foundations can be found in those states and state parties that in recent years have considered abandoning or weakening the system. The Wisconsin Republican party recently voted to make the process of endorsement optional rather than a standard procedure at the state convention. In New Mexico there is a continuing debate among political leaders about whether to abandon the legal endorsement process. On the other hand, in recent years the Massachusetts Democrats have revived endorsements; the Michigan Democrats have authorized such a process in the party rules, and it has been seriously discussed by Maryland Republicans and some California Democrats.

One of the most interesting questions about endorsements remains unanswered: Are convention delegates more successful than primary voters in picking candidates who can win the general election? It is difficult to answer because in most states either both parties or neither party uses endorsements. Examples can be found in 1982 of both wise and unwise choices by the conventions. There are cases where the strong ideological commitments of delegates led them to pick candidates lacking political strength, and also cases where they chose candidates in large part because of their ability to finance campaigns personally.

Party endorsements work in those states where candidates, political leaders, and party activists want them to work. The endorsement process provides a means of unifying the party and selecting the strongest candidate, although there are many examples of endorsements that have failed to achieve one or both of these goals. The process provides the party leadership with a device for meeting the challenge of well-financed amateurs seeking nominations, although there are recent examples of failure in this respect. The endorsement process is vulnerable to attack, however, because many party activists are ambivalent about it and because there is a growing likelihood that candidates who are not endorsed – or who do not seek endorsement – will have enough resources to mount a serious challenge to the endorsee. Each time an endorsee is defeated the myth of endorsement invulnerability is damaged.

THE CONVENTION AS A DEVICE FOR PARTY BUILDING

State political parties may hold conventions for a number of purposes – choosing delegates to national conventions, adopting platforms, selecting state executive committees – whether or not they make endorsements in primary elections. Such conventions may serve a number of latent functions for the party: socializing party activists who serve as delegates, providing a forum for leaders and future candidates, enhancing party unity. A comprehensive analysis of state conventions is beyond the scope of this study, but it is important to consider whether endorsing conventions have latent functions that are useful for developing the party. A convention that makes endorsements in statewide primaries can be distinguished from other state party conventions because the power to influence state nominations is more important and more central to the state party than other functions (including presidential nominations). (Obviously a party convention that nominated statewide candidates, rather than just making endorsements would be even more important.)

One valuable finding from questionnaires sent to delegates was the widely expressed belief that endorsing conventions are valuable because they offer party activists an opportunity to play an important role in the party. One of the major tasks faced by political parties, particularly in states where little patronage is available, is to provide incentives to activists to work within the party and not merely to enlist in candidate organizations. Some party workers, at least, enjoy not only the excitement and socializing of conventions but the opportunity to share in a meaningful decision-making process of endorsements.

In some state parties those activists who want to attend a state convention have little difficulty in doing so. In other parties, if there are contests for major races, the candidates mobilize their supporters to battle for delegate positions in precinct or county caucuses, and loyal party workers may be defeated by newcomers. This was the case in the Dukakis-King battle in Massachusetts, and also in the Minnesota Independent Republican party when church groups mobilized on behalf of one of the candidates and defeated some long-time party activists. Where such contests occur, the role of party activists may be eroded. On the other hand, it can be argued that this is a device for attracting new workers to the party. It is frequently the case that those who enter party politics on behalf of a particular candidate develop a long-term interest in party affairs.

When the Progressive reformers were campaigning for adoption of primary laws, they described party conventions (with considerable accuracy) as the tool of party bosses and machines. Today, there are relatively few examples of state or local organizations that are able to handpick delegates and exercise discipline over them at the convention. The New York conventions were the only ones I attended where some county leaders appeared to control delegations. Obviously in some other local organizations there are leaders who have some influence over other delegates, but generally party conventions appear to be wide-open affairs where individual delegates are free to bargain and vote; if some county delegations vote as a bloc, it appears to be the result of collaboration and bargaining rather than intimidation.

There are several state parties in which the endorsing conventions were established, and have been maintained, not merely to serve the interests of one faction, and not just to select more electable candidates, but to strengthen the party itself. That seems to have been one of the major purposes of the endorsing conventions adopted by both parties in Minnesota. Party activists in that state are committed to parties that are well organized, issue oriented, and wide open to rank-and-file participation. Members of the Democratic-Farmer-Labor (DFL) party in particular have a strong sense of pride in the heritage of the party of Hubert Humphrey, Orville Freeman, Eugene McCarthy, and Walter Mondale. It is, of course, difficult to measure these attitudes and the atmosphere that pervades the DFL convention, just as it is difficult to provide quantitative measures of political culture. I believe that these attitudes are important and widely shared among active Democrats and Republicans in Minnesota, and that most of these members perceive that endorsing convention to be an important ingredient in the kind of political party that they want.

The Massachusetts Democratic party has a very different heritage, one of deep factional divisions among ethnic groups, sections of the state, and personalities. The Massachusetts Democrats have had their own heroes, from James Michael Curley to the Kennedy family, but each hero has led his own faction into frequent battles with others. I have described in earlier chapters the failure of the endorsing convention in the past to solve or even ameliorate this factionalism. I have also described the party charter movement designed to revitalize the party and to give active workers an important role to play in the state party. As important ingredients in that plan for revitalization, those who wrote the charter, and those who ratified it, established both an issues convention in odd-numbered years and an endorsing convention in even-numbered years. It is clear that the endorsing convention is intended not merely to affect the nominating process but also to contribute to party building.

The Connecticut parties are different from both the Minnesota parties and the Massachusetts Democrats because they have had stronger traditional organizations, in which patronage has played a role. In the Democratic party in particular, the legacy of John Bailey — one of the last of the real state party bosses — has not disappeared. Connecticut party leaders are very interested in maintaining their control over the nominating process. But in addition, I believe they perceive the endorsing convention to be an important ingredient in maintaining a strong party.

There are some inherent, though not inevitable, conflicts between party activists and members of the party who hold public office. (This is a phenomenon familiar to those who have studied the British Labour party). High-ranking incumbents, and particularly governors, may expect to be renominated without opposition and without being held responsible to a party convention. They may want to use their own political influence to pick running mates or a successor.

The Massachusetts Democratic charter movement developed without much support from the governor's office, and Governor King criticized the entire concept of an endorsing convention. The Democratic-dominated legislature refused to enact into law the endorsing system that was written into the charter with the expectation that it would be legalized. In 1983 the New Mexico legislature tried to repeal the endorsement law — an action vetoed by the governor who had been aided in his nomination by winning the endorsement. One reason why the endorsements of the California Democratic Club began to lose their effectiveness was because a number of Democrats elected to public office rejected the idea that they owed any responsibility to the CDC and that it had any right to make policy demands on such officeholders. In recent years the legislature has resisted some pressure to repeal laws that prohibit the official state party organizations from making endorsements in primary elections.

There is always the possibility that those holding public office will avoid such conflicts by gaining a powerful influence in the endorsing conventions. In New York state many of the political leaders hold public office, in the legislature or at the city or county level, and also lead county political organizations. They are in a position to select the members of the state executive committee, which serves as the endorsing body. In Rhode Island, where the state committee also serves as the endorsing body, the members of the committee are selected from state House of Representatives districts. In recent years, in the absence of strong party leadership by the governor, Democratic members of the legislature have been able to control selection of most members of the central committee, and thus gain a large voice in primary endorsements.

A familiar theme of party reformers is that political parties should be more responsible — that is, they should take stands on issues and require their candidates to support such stands. Delegates who are voting on endorsements may, if they wish, choose candidates on the basis of their stands on issues. In addition the convention may be an arena in which major issues are debated and the party adopts a platform.

In 1982 the best examples of conventions being used to debate and establish policy were those held by the Minnesota parties. Delegates to the DFL and Independent Republican (IR) conventions took issues very seriously, and devoted much of their time to debating and voting on them. The county and district caucuses also adopt proposals for consideration in the platform. Delegates are elected in subcaucuses that often bear ideological and issue labels. In Massachusetts the party holds an issues convention every second year (although in the 1983 convention issues were overshadowed by a presidential straw poll). The operation of those conventions is beyond the scope of this study. In New Mexico and Connecticut the adoption of a platform is a relatively routine matter that draws little attention or dispute. The New York party committees adopt platforms, with little apparent controversy, at a time different from the endorsing convention.

As the Minnesota conventions illustrate, it is possible to use the endorsement process and the convention as devices for emphasizing issues. Where this is done, there is a serious question about how candidates can be held accountable to the platform. There is the possibility that delegates who have strong commitments to a candidate will follow the preferences of the candidate in voting on controversial issues. Except for votes on moral issues in the Minnesota IR convention, I did not find examples of this practice, which is a familiar one in national conventions. There is, of course, the possibility that the endorsee will be defeated in the primary by a candidate who holds different views on issues and who feels no obligation to support the platform. This was certainly the case in the Minnesota IR party in 1982; Wheelock Whitney took a stand on social and moral issues that was considerably more liberal than the platform of the convention.

One final question is whether there is a risk that an issue-oriented convention will become an arena for interest groups, and particularly single-issue groups, to make demands on the party. If that occurs, is there a risk that votes on controversial issues will fragment the party, making electoral victory more difficult to achieve? This was a problem faced by the Minnesota DFL on the abortion question, although it was able to surmount that problem in the election. If the convention becomes an arena for single-issue groups, the result may be adoption of positions on issues that are more extreme than those taken by rank-and-file voters, a problem faced by the Minnesota IR party.

There is so much diversity among the states that we would not expect to find consistent trends among all of them in the roles played by parties. On the other hand, there are some national trends that may have similar impacts in various states. There is a trend toward greater two-party competition in the states. During the 1950s and 1960s Democratic parties began to compete effectively in a number of northern Republican states. Since that time Republican parties have grown more competitive in a number of southern states. The increased competition might be expected to make one or both parties in some of these states give serious consideration to strengthening the party organization, and specifically to seeking an influence over nominations. As yet, however, there are few signs of such developments.

The rules imposed on state parties by the national Democratic party has forced them to permit broad participation in the caucus and convention process. When endorsing conventions are held, this means that there is less chance of control by organizational leaders at the state or county level and more opportunity for wide-open battles.

Recent research (Gibson, Cotter, Bibby, and Huckshorn 1981) has shown that the state party organizations have more resources at their command than in the past. Many of them have the skills and equipment enabling them to provide candidates with assistance in campaign management, polling, mass mailing, and fund raising. If a party organization was willing to use such resources in a primary on behalf of an endorsee, the endorsement might be worth more than in the past when parties lacked such resources. There are only limited examples, however, of state party headquarters providing such resources for endorsees, notably in Minnesota. At the same time the importance of modern campaign techniques such as these has given the well-financed amateur a better opportunity than in the past to challenge a party endorsee in the primary.

IMPLICATIONS OF PRIMARY VOTING PATTERNS

The analysis of voting in primaries is based on a wealth of aggregate data and a very limited amount of data from press sources and from voter surveys. Consequently some of the conclusions must be stated cautiously.

It is clear that age and education levels affect whether persons will vote in primaries, as well as in general elections, and that party identification or support is even more important in explaining decisions to vote in primaries than in general elections. Even though voters have been growing more independent, the level of turnout in primaries has not declined any more than turnout in general elections.

We know that the level of primary voting varies substantially by state and by state party, and that the variations by state are not the same as those that apply to turnout in general elections. It is possible to identify quite clearly those characteristics of states and of state parties that contribute to higher turnout in primaries. When turnout in primaries is measured as a percentage of each party's vote in the general election, turnout is higher in parties that have been most successful in general elections. In other words, the stronger the majority party, the more primary voting is concentrated in that party. Primary turnout is higher also in primaries that are most competitive; in the case of Democrats, a previous pattern of competitive primaries leads to higher turnout — voters get in the habit of voting because primaries are often close.

Survey data help to demonstrate clearly that nearly all primary voters who express some degree of party support or identification register (if necessary) and vote in their party rather than the opposite party. This is true in both closed and open primary states.

What impact do laws that set requirements for primary voting have on patterns of voting? An analysis of aggregate data shows that open primaries do lead to higher levels of turnout, but the data do not make it clear whether this results from higher turnout among independents in open primary states. Among closed-primary states there is much variation in the proportion of persons who register as independents, and there seem to be more registered independents in states where the primaries are less competitive. There is some evidence to suggest that the requirements for party registration lead more voters to profess identification with a party in closed-primary states than would be found in open-primary states.

Do voters in open-primary states shift back and forth frequently from one party primary to the other? Survey data from Michigan suggest that in the long run as many as half of the voters may cross over at least once to the other primary. But there is little evidence from aggregate data to suggest that large numbers of voters make such shifts frequently. It is difficult to distinguish between voters who shift primaries and those who drop in and out of the primary electorate. This is one question that deserves more research.

An analysis of aggregate voting patterns in the 1982 gubernatorial primaries shows that a large proportion of the outcome of these races can be explained by the office-holding experience (including incumbency) of the candidates and by the amount of money spent by the candidate and by the opponents in each race. Analysis of aggregate data over a prolonged period shows how well incumbents do in gubernatorial primaries. Many incumbents are not even challenged when they seek renominations, and most of those who have an opponent win by comfortable margins. There are more exceptions to these generalizations in southern states.

The voter surveys in three states in 1982 show that a high proportion of voters read about or hear or see the major candidates for governor, although first-hand contact with candidates is infrequent. Voters are more likely to judge candidates on the basis of their personal characteristics and their experience than on the basis of issues. There are enough examples of issues having an impact on voters to make us recognize how much variation is possible from one primary to another. Although incumbents usually are renominated with relatively little trouble, incumbency can be a liability as well as an asset, particularly at a time when governors are confronted with increasing demands for services, cuts in federal grants, limited resources, and growing public resistance to tax increases. A survey of the media coverage of a number of primary elections in 1982 shows how many variables can affect the outcome of primaries.

Generally, we can conclude that experienced, well-financed candidates will almost always defeat inexperienced, poorly financed ones. Incumbents and other experienced candidates have a big advantage in raising funds. When political amateurs are able to spend as much or more than those with more experience, they can sometimes make very effective challenges. When two or more candidates are well known and reasonably well financed, the outcome may be affected by a variety of personal characteristics and issues that are idiosyncratic for particular elections.

These findings about voting in primaries have certain implications for the political party system in the states. Although party organization endorsements in primaries do not appear to have any significant direct impact on voters, there is a lower turnout of voters at the polls in states where strong party organizations have been able to discourage serious opposition to endorsed candidates. It may be possible for party organizations to influence a larger proportion of voters in primaries when turnout is light, although there is no direct evidence to show whether there are many remaining states and localities where party organization is strong enough to control significant numbers of voters.

In theory, political parties are handicapped by open primary laws that permit persons loyal to the other party to enter a primary and vote for a candidate who may not share the party's stand on issues or who will be a weak candidate in the general election. In practice, such crossover voting apparently does not occur frequently enough or on a large enough scale to be a serious problem for the political parties. Variations in relative turnout in the two parties appear to result largely from shifts by those who identify as independents and by persons entering and leaving the primary electorate. Open primaries may have a more serious impact on the parties if they erode party loyalties, if the absence of registration requirements leads a larger proportion of voters to think of themselves as independents. Closed and open primary laws also have implications for emerging minority parties, a question to be discussed below.

The finding that the outcome of primary elections depends very much on the experience of candidates and the levels of campaign spending has important implications for the parties. Generally the party benefits from the voters' preference for experienced candidates. The importance of campaign funding threatens the party's influence over nominations because candidates who are not accountable to the party can sometimes raise more funds than the party endorsee and perhaps win the primary. One implication for those political party organizations that make endorsements is that they may need to pay more attention to helping endorsees raise funds, or provide other tangible services to the endorsee, in order to overcome the advantages enjoyed by the well-financed outsider.

The operation of the primary system has major implications for a minority party that is struggling to become competitive — the situation faced by Republican parties in most southern states. Although the Republican party has won statewide elections in every southern state, the number of voters who enter Republican primaries is usually very small, in both open and closed primary states. Most southern states have open primaries, which should make it easier for voters who sometimes vote Republican in the November elections to enter Republican primaries when they are contested. One reason why so few voters have made the shift is that primary voting appears to be a matter of habit, and the Democratic primary has been recognized as the most important election in southern states for a long time. Another reason is that in most southern states there have been only a few contested Republican primaries in recent years, and an even smaller number have been close contests between well-known, viable candidates. The ease with which voters can shift to the other primary in an open primary state may be a disadvantage to the minority party because it is just as easy to shift back to the Democratic primary on the frequent occasions when that race is more interesting or appears to be more important. Moreover, the act of registering with a party in a closed primary state may represent a commitment to a party that can help to solidify the voter's new allegiance.

What harm does it do to a minority party if relatively few voters participate in its primaries? The greatest risk may be that a small and unrepresentative group of minority party voters will choose a candidate who lacks an appeal to a broader group of voters. In addition, if large numbers of voters participate in a primary, they may have a greater incentive to support that party in the general election, particularly if they have supported the winning candidate. There is the risk of course that a closely contested primary will cause deep divisions within the minority party, and this may be more damaging if the turnout in the primary has been high and therefore a large number of voters have supported the candidate who loses the primary.

There may be advantages to the minority party in a small primary turnout and/or a lopsided primary race. The leaders of the party may be more successful than the primary voters in putting together a strong, balanced slate of candidates. It may be easier to get the best candidates to run if they can be assured of little or no opposition in the primary. Whether this will be the result of such a slate-making operation depends largely on the skill and wisdom of the party leaders.

In the past most southern Republican parties used conventions to select nominees, but the party's main job was to find candidates rather than to choose among them. In recent years most of these parties have used primaries to settle contests, even in those southern states that make the primary optional. In Virginia, however, the Republican party has continued to use conventions at a time when there has sometimes been a vigorous contest for the nomination. The party believes that this is the best way of picking the strongest candidate and avoiding divisive battles. The Virginia Republican party has been one of the most successful in the South, but it is impossible to prove how much of this result can be attributed to the convention system. The Virginia Democratic party apparently believes that the convention system has worked for the Republicans, because it has adopted conventions on several recent occasions. The Virginia Democratic party has been plagued with deep divisions, often along ideological grounds. In 1973 the party was so deeply divided that no Democrat ran for governor in the primary, and the general election was between two former Democrats, running as an independent and as a Republican. In 1981 the Democratic party used a convention to nominate a gubernatorial candidate, and succeeded in selecting one, Charles Robb, who had enough political strength to be elected.

IN SEARCH OF A TREND

Do the findings of this study offer any clues to the future of the nominating process in the states? Clearly there is no national trend affecting state primaries comparable to the Progressive movement that led to the widespread adoption of state primaries early in this century or the rapid growth in presidential primaries during the 1970s. The expanded use of presidential primaries has had no apparent effect on state primaries. The only effect of the new national Democratic rules for the nominating process has been to encourage broader participation in caucuses leading to state conventions. The state political systems seem to operate in isolation from each other, even though they are susceptible to national trends such as the growing importance of media advertising.

There are historical reasons for the variations we find in the operation of state primary systems and party endorsements. The persistence of particular nominating methods in specific states often seems to be more a matter of inertia than because these methods serve the interests of dominant political forces.

While most state nominating systems have remained largely unchanged, the presidential nominating system is rapidly evolving. The process of change at the national level suggests certain conclusions about how change might come about in state primaries.

1. Changes in the rules and procedures for making nominations can affect the way in which candidates seek nomination and even the results. The changes in Democratic rules for presidential nomination, inaugurated by the McGovern Commission, have affected the strategies of candidates and contributed at least to the nomination of George McGovern and Jimmy Carter.

2. Changes in rules and procedures can have unintended consequences. The authors of the McGovern report were principally interested in improving procedures and representation in caucuses and conventions and did not anticipate that their recommendations would lead to greater use of primaries or a decline in the importance of the national convention (Ranney 1975).

3. Changes in the political environment may have as much or greater effect on the nominating system, sometimes supporting and sometimes undermining the effects of changes in rules. Extensive media coverage and analysis of presidential primaries have enhanced their importance (particularly the earlier ones) and contributed to diminishing the importance of the national convention.

4. Most persons who are active in politics do not seem to have well thought out, coherent ideas about how political parties should be organized, the role that citizens should play in party decisions, or the impact that parties should have on nominations. They tend to approach proposals to change the rules on party governance and the nominating process from a narrow perspective: the immediate gains or losses likely for their candidate or the group or interest that they represent. A good example is the fight between the Carter and Kennedy forces at the 1980 Democratic convention over changing the rules that bind delegates to support the candidate to whom they were committed in the primary. The issue involved basic theories about the role of the convention and its delegates, but

the outcome reflected simply the dominant position of Carter forces at the convention. At the state level, delegates to endorsing conventions who answered my questionnaires were generally more supportive of the principle of endorsements if they had supported a gubernatorial candidate who got endorsed. Delegates to the 1982 Minnesota DFL convention supported the principle of closed primaries, apparently in large part because they believed that a candidate endorsed for the senatorial nomination in a recent election had been beaten by conservative crossover voters. The continuing vacillation of political leaders and party activists in New Mexico over use of the endorsement process results partly from changing calculations about which candidate might benefit from endorsements.

5. Despite the fact that political leaders judge reform proposals from a narrow perspective of immediate interests, they do not always seem to have a clear grasp of the impact that rules and procedures — and proposed reforms — have on their interests. For example, there was considerable misunderstanding of the practical implications of the McGovern Commission reforms. At the state level, leaders of minority parties often seem to be unsure about whether their interests would be better served by closed or open primaries. When Louisiana adopted a nonpartisan primary a few years ago, leaders of two minority groups — Republicans and blacks — seemed confused about the potential consequences of the new system for their interests.

The state political systems and cultures are so diverse that there is no reason why we should expect to find any consistent trend in nominating systems. Of course one reason why it is difficult to discern a trend is that we lack earlier research and longitudinal data on state primaries. This present study should be useful in providing a factual base for subsequent comparisons.

If significant changes occur over the next few years in the nominating systems of some states, these are most likely to be found in the South. If the Republican party continues to become more consistently competitive in statewide races, the Democratic primary should decline in importance, and also in turnout. This might make primary runoff elections less necessary and could lead to proposals for repeal of the runoff because of its cost and the burden it imposes on voters. Eventually, there are likely to be more frequent examples of serious competition in Republican primaries. Such a trend should lead to a gradual increase in voter turnout in Republican primaries even though traditional voting patterns are slow to change.

The most important challenge facing southern Republican parties is to recruit and support candidates who have a serious chance of winning elections. As suggested earlier, the leaders of these parties may not rely entirely on primaries to produce such candidates. They are likely to work behind the scenes in an effort to encourage the best possible candidates to run and, perhaps, to discourage others. It is possible that some southern Republican parties will turn to endorsing conventions to accomplish this goal in a more formal, structured way. In the border state of Maryland, where the Republican party faces a problem similar to that in southern states, a 1981 study committee recommended to the party that it use an endorsing convention because of its minority status. The committee reported: "A minority party can survive only by concentrating its efforts behind a single candidate for public office at the earliest possible date." I have already noted that the thriving Republican party in Virginia has consistently used a convention instead of a primary.

There is another possible trend in southern states, more likely to be launched by Democratic parties: the use of nonpartisan primaries. In 1975 Louisiana adopted its system of nonpartisan elections under which all candidates and all voters participate in a single primary, with a runoff held if no candidate gets a majority. It was initiated by Democratic Governor Edwin Edwards and passed the legislature easily despite the opposition of many organized groups, including the Republican party. One purpose was to make it unnecessary for Democratic candidates to survive three elections: the primary, runoff, and general election. One apparent purpose was to weaken the Republican party, which would not be guaranteed any candidate in the runoff. In 1979, however, Republican leaders reached agreement to support a single candidate for governor, David Treen. Treen won enough votes in a crowded race to enter the runoff, and won the runoff when all of the Democratic losers supported him in the aftermath of a bitter primary. In 1983 each of the parties endorsed a candidate for governor, and the primary became virtually a two-person race. Although the nonpartisan primary would appear to undermine the prospects of black candidates, by eliminating independent or third-party candidates, it had the support of those black leaders who were allied with Governor Edwards and won approval from the Justice Department.

The use of nonpartisan elections in a single southern state does not constitute a trend. It is noteworthy that a similar law was passed in Mississippi but rejected by the Justice Department after opposition from black leaders in that state. The nonpartisan primary might be attractive to Democratic leaders in other states for several reasons. It would appear likely to undermine the Republican party by denying it the certainty of a spot on the final ballot and by eroding the party system itself. In states where runoff elections have frequently been necessary in the Democratic primary, it offers a means of reducing the number of steps in the electoral process from three to two, which reduces the campaign burdens on Democrats. In a section of the country where voters often identify and vote independently, nonpartisan elections might appear to be in keeping with popular wishes. Whatever the arguments that might be made on behalf of nonpartisan elections for state office, it seems inevitable that adoption of such a system in any state would have a far-reaching impact on political party organizations and on the political system as a whole. There is no reason to predict a trend toward nonpartisan primaries and elections, but it would not be surprising to see its serious consideration and perhaps its adoption in some other states particularly in the South.

PROSPECTS FOR REFORM

Political scientists are often pessimistic about both the possibility and the consequences of reform, for reasons that should be clear by now. Party activists are usually more interested in their immediate goals — promoting a candidate or an issue — and perceive proposals for change only from the perspective of helping or hurting their cause. Even more academic party reformers often appear to be unclear about their goals for the party system and about the relationship between these goals and the specific reforms they advocate. This is evident, for example in the 1950 American Political Science Association report, "Toward a More Responsible Two-Party System" (APSA 1950). Poliitical scientists are well aware that reforms often have unintended consequences, which sometimes contradict the original goals.

With these caveats in mind, we may draw some cautious conclusions about the possibility and desirability of changing the role of political parties in the nominating system. State political party organizations have shown considerable signs of vitality in recent years (Gibson, Cotter, Bibby, and Huckshorn 1981), and party activists in states such as Massachusetts have demonstrated their interest in greater institutionalization of the parties. It is not unrealistic to believe that party organizations in some states might have a greater impact on the nominating process.

Obviously not all political activists or political scientists believe that party organizations should have such a role. Perhaps the best argument for more active and powerful political parties is the need to restrain the influence of specialized interests on government and to restore the party's role as an aggregator and mediator of those interests. In doing so the party can provide a buffer between the more aggressive interests and public officials such as governors and legislators. The case for a stronger party role in the nominating process rests on the need to select candidates who are capable and experienced and who are in the mainstream of the political party rather than being the creatures of narrower interests.

Whether a particular party organization should establish the mechanism for making endorsements, it seems clear that political parties have a legitimate interest in the selection of their nominees and therefore should not be prohibited by legislation from making endorsements or otherwise expressing the judgment of the organization about candidates in a primary.

Is the endorsing convention an effective device for strengthening the party and giving it an influence over nominations? There are several reasons for answering that question positively. The endorsing convention helps to strengthen the party by providing active workers with an incentive for participation and a meaningful role in the organization. This is an important consequence of the endorsing system, and is perceived by many delegates to be the most important consequence.

The endorsing system often makes it possible for the party to weed out candidates who are incapable, politically weak, or ideologically extreme, and to support those who are most able, politically skillful, and ideologically in the mainstream — candidates also most likely to win the general election. But there is no certainty that the convention will make such a wise choice. The supporters of a candidate who represents an extreme position or has other political weaknesses may win control of the convention by packing caucuses that select the delegates. Even if the convention is controlled by party regulars, they will not necessarily choose the strongest candidate available.

The endorsement process is most effective when it helps the endorsee to mobilize organizational resources, such as campaign funds and manpower. As a minimum, candidates may have the incentive to develop strong organizations because they realize that this is essential to winning convention endorsement, as was the case in Michael Dukakis's campaign in Massachusetts. Convention endorsement of a candidate is likely to establish that person's reputation as the front runner, and this may attract campaign workers and contributors. The political party organization can aid the endorsee most directly by providing campaign resources from headquarters: funds and fund-raising assistance, computers, mailing lists, manpower, and so forth. This is possible if state law and party rules permit it. Perhaps the most significant step political parties could take to strengthen the endorsement process would be to increase these direct forms of tangible assistance to the endorsee.

In some states there are also party norms that discourage candidates from challenging the endorsee, norms that are usually effective, at least in discouraging serious opposition. Even when the endorsee has opposition, in most states the record shows that the endorsee usually wins. Those victories are the result of the organizational benefits enjoyed by the endorsee, and not because endorsements make any direct impact on most voters.

One of the advantages of the endorsement process is that the endorsee is likely to be a candidate who is in the mainstream of the party, in ideological terms. But it would be a mistake to argue that endorsements are usually an effective way to ensure that candidates will be accountable to the party on policy questions. In fact, very often the choices made by delegates have very little to do with policy differences between candidates. Those parties that put the greatest stress on issues, like the Minnesota parties in recent years, run the risk of attracting to the convention delegates who are particularly interested in promoting special interests and viewpoints that may cause divisions within the party or lead to the endorsement of a candidate who represents a more extreme position than do rank-and-file members of the party.

There are, of course, some disadvantages to the endorsement process. It is often criticized for leading to "boss control," and this is possible if delegates are dominated by local party leaders. There are relatively few states, however, where such domination appears to be a reality in the endorsing conventions, because there are relatively few remaining examples of local party organizations that are strong, well disciplined, and amply supplied with patronage resources. Endorsing conventions can escalate existing divisions within a party, as was the case in Massachusetts Democratic conventions for many years. In the few remaining states where politics is dominated by a single party, it can be argued that the voters' only effective choice is in the primary election, and it should not be restrained by endorsing procedures.

It is easier to recommend endorsements as a method of strengthening parties than to describe how an effective endorsement system can be established. Unless party organizations already have substantial vitality, it is difficult to generate support for establishing endorsement machinery, although that recently proved to be possible in the Massachusetts Democratic party. Endorsements work best where there are strong party norms undergirding them, but we have seen, particularly in Minnesota, how fragile such norms can be.

It is difficult to determine whether party endorsements are more likely to be effective if they are based on state law rather than party rules. There is some evidence to suggest that this is true, but it is nearly as easy to abolish or modify endorsement procedures by legislative act as by party rule. Legal provisions that set a minimum percentage of the convention vote to get on the ballot are really effective only if it is either difficult or impossible to qualify for the ballot by other means. Legal provisions guaranteeing the top space on the ballot to the endorsee are presumably a valuable asset to the endorsee, although research is lacking that addresses this question specifically.

Another step that political parties might take to strengthen their influence over the nominating process would be to gain enactment of closed primary laws in states where these are missing. This would reduce the risk that nominations would be decided by voters with no commitment to the party and that candidates would be nominated who are outside the mainstream of the party. It would also help the party to mobilize voters in general elections by identifying their party registration. How much difference closed primary laws would actually make is a much more difficult question to answer. The research reported in this study, based on very limited data, casts doubts on the idea that large numbers of voters in open primary states frequently shift back and forth between primaries, although substantial shifts apparently occur in the long run. Open primaries may have the effect of weakening voters' sense of identification with a party, which may be reinforced by registering with that party and voting consistently in its primary.

Political parties might increase their influence over nominations by seeking changes in legislation on campaign financing. The questions involved in campaign finance reform are complicated, and the goals of such reform may diverge from the goal of enhancing the party's role in nominations. In both cases, however, there is a concern that candidates may be nominated and elected who are heavily indebted to specialized interests. An obvious step to strengthen party influence over nominations would be to enact laws, where necessary, to permit party organizations to contribute funds to candidates in a primary, or even to use state funds supplied to the party on behalf of endorsees. One of the strongest challenges to party endorsees comes from candidates with large campaign chests who can make maximum use of media advertising. State financing of primary campaigns might serve the party's interests by ending the advantages enjoyed by well-financed challengers. A number of states are experimenting with state funding of party organizations or individual campaigns, including primary campaigns in a few cases. We need to monitor these actual operations of the various plans in order to find out how they work in practice and what impact, if any, they have on the party's role in nominations.

It is difficult to predict with any assurance what effects any changes in legislation on endorsement procedures, requirements for voting in primaries, or campaign financing might have on the role of parties in the nominating process. Justice Louis Brandeis once described the American states as laboratories in the federal system. It is not unusual for other states to copy the social and economic legislation and the administrative techniques of an innovative state. But in the field of politics, and specifically in their experiments with nominating systems, the states are unusual laboratories because state political leaders seem to pay little attention to what is done in other states. Moreover, political scientists, who ought to recognize the research potential of these laboratories of federalism, have paid little attention to understanding differences among the state nominating systems and the effect of legal changes on those systems. This volume is an effort to correct that oversight by shedding some light on state primary systems and suggesting directions for future research.

Appendix

Table A.1 shows the sample of delegates polled in each state. The number of questionnaires mailed out in the states with larger conventions was somewhat larger but was a smaller proportion of

Table A.1
Surveys of Convention Delegates

State	Party	Total Delegates	Questionnaires Mailed	Questionnaires Returned	Percentage Response	Respondents as % of Delegates
Conn.	Dem.	1300	250	90	36.0	6.9
	Rep.	933	350	180	51.4	19.3
Minn.	Dem.	1286	425	226	53.2	17.6
	Rep.	2025	430	217	50.5	10.7
N. M.	Dem.	1712	325	127	39.1	7.4
	Rep.	750	175	97	55.4	12.9
Mass.	Dem.	3359	600	250	41.7	7.4
	Rep.	1348	300	192	64.0	14.2
N. Y.	Dem.	357	265	69	26.0	19.3
	Rep.	390	250	66	26.4	16.9

Source: Compiled by the author.

total delegates than in those with smaller conventions. A larger proportion was sent in New York because of the small size of the committees and the expected difficulty in getting a good response. Except for New York, the response rates were good, ranging from 36 to 64 percent, and averaging 48.3 percent. The 26 percent response rate for both New York parties was disappointing, and may reflect the fact that these delegates were members of the state committee and in a sense more professional politicians. Except in New York, where a limited follow-up effort was made, only a single mailing was sent to delegates. A second mailing to increase the response rate was not made because the initial mailing of 3,370 was costly and time-consuming, the response rates were generally good, and the anonymity made it impractical to tell which delegates had responded; moreover, it was felt that questionnaires received several months after the convention might have answers distorted by poor memory and post-convention developments in the primary.

Bibliography

Adamany, David. 1976. "Cross-over Voting and the Party's Reform Rules." *American Political Science Review* 70: 536-41.

APSA. 1950. "Toward a More Responsible Two-Party System: A Report of the Committee on Political Parties, American Political Science Association." *American Political Science Review* 44: Supplement.

Barbrook, Alec. 1973. *God Save the Commonwealth: An Electoral History of Massachusetts*. Amherst: University of Massachusetts.

Black, Merle and Earl Black. 1982. "The Growth of Contested Republican Primaries in the American South." In *Contemporary Southern Political Attitudes and Behavior*, edited by Laurence W. Moreland, Tod A. Baker, and Robert P. Steed, pp. 121-53. New York: Praeger.

Bowman, Lewis, and Robert Boynton. 1966. "Activities and Role Definitions of Grass Roots Party Officials." *Journal of Politics* 26: 121-43.

Connolly, Michael J. 1982. *Who Votes in Primary Elections?* Boston: Office of Massachusetts Secretary of State.

Cranor, John D., Gary Crawley, R. T. Perry, Thomas A. Sargent, and Raymond H. Scheele. 1980. "A Summary Report: A 1980 Survey of Voting and Citizen Attitudes in Indiana." Muncie, Indiana: Bureau of Government Research, Ball State University.

Crotty, William. 1983. *Party Reform*. New York: Longman.

Cutright, Phillips, and Peter H. Rossi. 1958. "Grass Roots Politicians and the Vote." *American Sociological Review* 23: 171-79.

Dennis, Jack. 1981. "On Being an Independent Partisan Supporter." Paper prepared for the annual meeting of the Midwest Political Science Association.

Epstein, Leon D. 1958. *Politics in Wisconsin*. Madison: University of Wisconsin Press.

Eyre, R. John, and Victor S. Hjelm. 1969. "Party Organization and Nominations in Idaho." *Rendezvous* 4: 69-78.

Eyre, R. John, and Curtis Martin. 1967. *The Colorado Preprimary System*. Boulder: Bureau of Government Research and Service, University of Colorado.

Galderisi, Peter F. 1982. "Primary Reform as Participatory Incentive: Party Renewal in a Changing American Political Universe." Paper prepared for the annual meeting of the American Political Science Association.

Gibson, James L., Cornelius P. Cotter, John F. Bibby, and Robert J. Huckshorn. 1981. "Assessing Institutional Party Strength." Paper prepared for the annual meeting of the Midwest Political Science Association.

Gopoian, David. 1982. "Issue Preferences and Candidate Choice in Presidential Primaries." *American Journal of Political Science* 26: 523-46.

Grau, Craig H. 1981. "Competition in State Legislative Primaries." *Legislative Studies Quarterly* 6: 35-54.

Hain, Paul L., and Jose Z. Garcia. 1981. "Voting, Elections, and Parties." In *New Mexico Government*, edited by F. Chris Garcia and Paul Hain. Albuquerque: University of New Mexico Press.

Harder, Marvin, and Thomas Ungs. 1966. "Midwest County Party Chairmen." Wichita, Kansas: Wichita State University, unpublished manuscript.

Hedlund, Ronald D., Meredith W. Watts, and David M. Hedge. 1982. "Voting in an Open Primary." *American Politics Quarterly* 10: 197-218.

Holmes, Jack E. 1967. *Politics in New Mexico*. Albuquerque: University of New Mexico Press.

Jackson, John S. III, Barbara L. Brown, and David Bositis. 1982. "Herbert McCloskey and Friends Revisited: 1980 Democratic and Republican Party Elites Compared to the Mass Public." *American Politics Quarterly* 10: 158-80.

Jewell, Malcolm E., and David M. Olson. 1982. *American State Political Parties and Elections*. Rev. ed. Homewood, Ill.: Dorsey Press.

_____ . 1978. *American State Political Parties and Elections*. 1st ed. Homewood, Ill.: Dorsey Press.

Katz, Daniel, and Samuel J. Eldersveld. 1961. "The Impact of Local Party

Activity upon the Electorate." *Public Opinion Quarterly* 25: 1-24.

Key, V. O., Jr. 1964. *Politics, Parties, and Pressure Groups.* 5th ed. New York: Crowell.

_____. 1956. *American State Politics: An Introduction.* New York: Knopf.

Kirkpatrick, Jeane M. 1976. *The New Presidential Elite.* New York: Russell Sage Foundation and The Twentieth Century Fund.

Kousser, J. Morgan. 1974. *The Shaping of Southern Politics: Suffrage Restriction and the Establishment of the One-Party South, 1880-1910.* New Haven: Yale University Press.

Kritzer, Herbert M. 1980. "The Representativeness of the 1972 Presidential Primaries." In *The Party Symbol,* edited by William Crotty. San Francisco: W. H. Freeman.

Kweit, Mary Grisez, Robert W. Kweit, and Ronald E. Pynn. 1982. "The Potential for Party Change: A Cohort Analysis." Paper prepared for the annual meeting of the Midwest Political Science Association.

Lebedoff, David. 1969. *The 21st Ballot: A Political Party Struggle in Minnesota.* Minneapolis: University of Minnesota Press.

Litt, Edgar. 1965. *The Political Cultures of Massachusetts.* Cambridge, Mass.: MIT Press.

Lockard, Duane. 1959. *Connecticut's Challenge Primary: A Study in Legislative Politics.* New York: Holt.

Marshall, Thomas R. 1982. "Issues Versus Personality in Voting for Presidential Candidates." Paper prepared for the annual meeting of the Southwestern Political Science Association.

_____. 1981. "Minnesota: The Party Caucus-Convention System." In *Party Renewal in America,* edited by Gerald Pomper, pp. 139-58. New York: Praeger.

McCloskey, Herbert, Paul J. Hoffman, and Rosemary O'Hara. 1960. "Issue Conflict and Consensus Among Party Leaders and Followers." *American Political Science Review* 54: 406-29.

Merriam, Charles E. 1908. *Primary Elections*. Chicago: University of Chicago Press.

Merriam, Charles E., and Louise Overacker. 1928. *Primary Elections*. Chicago: University of Chicago Press.

Milbrath, Lester, and M. L. Goel. 1977. *Political Participation*. 2nd ed. Chicago: Rand McNally.

Mileur, Jerome. 1981. "Massachusetts: The Democratic Party Charter Movement." In *Party Renewal in America*, edited by Gerald M. Pomper, pp. 159-75. New York: Praeger.

Mitau, G. Theodore. 1960. *Politics in Minnesota*. Minneapolis: University of Minnesota Press.

Norrander, Barbara. 1983. "Candidate Qualities, Issues, and Electability: Determinants of the Vote in the 1980 Presidential Primaries." Paper prepared for the annual meeting of the Midwest Political Science Association.

_____ . 1982. "Determinants of Presidential Primary Participation: A Comparison to General Election Turnout." Paper prepared for the annual meeting of the Midwest Political Science Association.

Olson, David M. 1963. *Legislative Primary Elections in Austin, Texas, 1962*. Austin: Institute of Public Affairs, University of Texas.

Omdahl, Lloyd B. 1961. *Insurgents*. Brainerd, Minn.

Patterson, Samuel C. 1982. "Campaign Spending in Contests for Governor." *Western Political Quarterly* 35: 457-77.

Patterson, Samuel C., and G. R. Boynton. 1969. "Legislative Recruitment in a Civic Culture." *Social Science Quarterly* 50: 243-63.

Ranney, Austin. 1975. *Curing the Mischiefs of Faction: Party Reform in America*. Berkeley: University of California Press.

_____ . 1972. "Turnout and Representation in Presidential Primary Elections." *American Political Science Review* 66: 21-37.

_____ . 1968. "The Representativeness of Primary Electorates." *Midwest Journal of Political Science* 12: 224-38.

_____. 1951. "Toward a More Responsible Two-Party System: A Commentary." *American Political Science Review* 45: 488-99.

Ranney, Austin, and Leon D. Epstein. 1966. "The Two Electorates: Voters and Non-Voters in a Wisconsin Primary." *Journal of Politics* 28: 598-616.

Rowe, Leonard. 1961. *Preprimary Endorsements in California Politics*. Berkeley: Bureau of Public Administration, University of California.

Rubins, Richard L. 1980. "Presidential Primaries: Continuities, Dimensions of Change, and Political Implications." In *The Party Symbol*, edited by William Crotty. San Francisco: W. H. Freeman.

Sabato, Larry. 1977. *The Democratic Party Primary in Virginia*. Charlottesville: Institute of Government, University of Virginia.

Scammon, Richard, and A. V. McGillibray. 1958-82. *America Votes*, vols. 2-14. Washington: Elections Research Center and Congressional Quarterly.

Schattschneider, E. E. 1942. *Party Government*. New York: Farrar and Rinehart.

Scheele, Raymond H. 1972. "Voting in Primary Elections." Ph.D. dissertation, University of Missouri.

Sittig, Robert F. 1962. "Party Slatemaking and the Direct Primary in Illinois and Other States." Ph.D. dissertation, Southern Illinois University.

Sorauf, Frank J. 1954. "Extra-legal Political Parties in Wisconsin." *American Political Science Review* 48: 692-704.

Soule, John W., and J. W. Clarke. 1970. "Amateurs and Professionals: A Study of Delegates to the 1968 Democratic Convention." *American Political Science Review* 64: 888-98.

Soule, John W., and Wilma E. McGrath. 1975. "A Comparative Study of Presidential Nomination Conventions: The Democrats 1968 and 1972." *American Journal of Political Science* 19: 501-17.

Sullivan, Dennis G., Jeffrey L. Pressman, Benjamin I. Page, and John J. Lyons. 1974. *The Politics of Representation: The Democratic Convention of 1972*. New York: St. Martin's.

Tobin, Richard J., and Edward Keynes. 1974. "Institutional Differences in the Recruitment Process: A Four-State Study." *American Journal of Political Science* 19: 667-92.

Torelle, Ellen (ed.). 1920. *The Political Philosophy of Robert M. LaFollette as Revealed in His Speeches and Writings*. Madison, Wis.: Robert M. LaFollette Co.

Valentine, David C., and John R. Van Wingen. 1980. "Partisanship, Independence, and Party Identification." *American Politics Quarterly* 8: 165-86.

Weisberg, Herbert. 1980. "A Multidimensional Conceptualization of Party Identification." *Political Behavior* 2: 33-60.

White, John K. 1983. *The Fractured Electorate: Political Parties and Social Change in Southern New England*. Hanover, N.H.: University Press of New England.

_____ . 1982. "All in the Family: The 1978 Massachusetts Democratic Gubernatorial Primary." *Polity* 14: 641-56.

Wolfe, Arthur C. 1966. "The Direct Primary in American Politics." Ph.D. dissertation, University of Michigan.

Wolfinger, Raymond E., and Steven J. Rosenstone. 1980. *Who Votes?* New Haven: Yale University Press.

Index

ABOUT THE AUTHOR

MALCOLM E. JEWELL is Professor of Political Science at the University of Kentucky, where he has taught since 1958. His Ph.D. is from Pennsylvania State University. He has served as editor of the *Midwest Journal of Political Science* and the *Legislative Studies Quarterly*, and as president of both the Midwest and Southern Political Science Associations.

He is co-author of *American State Political Parties and Elections*, *The Legislative Process in the U.S.*, and *Kentucky Politics*; he is author of *Representation in State Legislatures*.